MEETING AT THE HYPHEN:

Schools-Universities-Communities-Professions
in Collaboration for
Student Achievement and Well Being

MEETING AT THE HYPHEN:
Schools-Universities-Communities-Professions in Collaboration for Student Achievement and Well Being

102nd Yearbook of the
National Society for the Study of Education

PART II

Edited by
MARY M. BRABECK, MARY E. WALSH, AND RACHEL E. LATTA

20 03

Distributed by THE UNIVERSITY OF CHICAGO PRESS • CHICAGO, ILLINOIS

#52346100

National Society for the Study of Education

The National Society for the Study of Education was founded in 1901 as successor to the National Herbart Society. It publishes a two-volume Yearbook, each volume dealing with a separate topic of concern to educators. The Society's Yearbook series, now in its one hundred-second year, presents articles by scholars and practitioners noted for their significant work in critical areas of education.

The Society welcomes as members all individuals who wish to receive its publications. Current membership includes educators in the United States, Canada, and elsewhere throughout the world—professors, researchers, administrators, and graduate students in colleges and universities and teachers, administrators, supervisors, and curriculum specialists in elementary and secondary schools, as well as policymakers at all levels.

Members of the Society elect a Board of Directors. The Board's responsibilities include reviewing proposals for Yearbooks, authorizing the preparation of Yearbooks based on accepted proposals, and appointing an editor or editors to oversee the preparation of manuscripts.

Current dues (for 2003) are a modest $35 ($30 for retired members and for students in their first year of membership). Members whose dues are paid for the current calendar year receive the Society's Yearbook, are eligible for election to the Board of Directors, and are entitled to a 33 percent discount when purchasing past Yearbooks from the Society's distributor, the University of Chicago Press.

Each year the Society arranges for meetings to be held in conjunction with the annual conferences of one or more of the national educational organizations. All members are urged to attend these meetings, at which the current Yearbook is presented and critiqued. Members are encouraged to submit proposals for future Yearbooks.

Meeting at the Hyphen: Schools-Universities-Communities-Professions in Collaboration for Student Achievement and Well Being is Part II of the 102nd Yearbook. Part I, published simultaneously, is titled *American Educational Governance on Trial: Change and Challenges.*

For further information, write to the Secretary, NSSE, College of Education m/c 147, University of Illinois at Chicago, 1040 W. Harrison St., Chicago, Illinois 60607-7133 or see www.uic.edu/educ/nsse

ISSN: 0077-5762

Published 2003 by the
NATIONAL SOCIETY FOR THE STUDY OF EDUCATION
1040 W. Harrison St., Chicago, Illinois 60607-7133
© 2003 by the National Society for the Study of Education

First Printing
Printed in the United States of America

iv

Contributors to the Yearbook

Acknowledgments

The work described in this edited collection is the result of multiple collaborations. Practitioners in diverse fields of education, health care, social work, psychology, and law have contributed substantially to the ideas of the authors represented here. All of us who contributed to this volume owe these countless unidentified collaborators a debt of thanks. We acknowledge that they struggle daily in the classrooms, clinics, hospitals, and courts to deliver integrated services to children and families. The work described here is their work, every bit as much as it is the work of the authors of these chapters.

We are also grateful for the wise and supportive assistance of Dr. Debra Miretzky, of the National Society for the Study of Education. As a social worker by training, Dr. Miretzky brought a particular interest and insight to the work, as well as editorial skills. The work is better because of her contributions to this project.

Mary M. Brabeck
Mary E. Walsh
Rachel E. Latta
Editors

Table of Contents

CHAPTER 1

Meeting at the Hyphen

MARY M. BRABECK AND RACHEL E. LATTA

Over the past decade, a considerable shift has begun to occur in the way educators, human service providers, health care professionals, and policy makers provide supports for children's learning and development. The contributors to this volume advocate the delivery of comprehensive and integrated services by professionals who work collaboratively, rather than in isolation. Instead of multiple services delivered through a range of separate and distinct programs, these comprehensive networks of services are being taken to scale and institutionalized through the development of infrastructures that integrate service delivery with evaluation, dissemination, public engagement, professional capacity building, and education and knowledge development (Weiss & Lopez, 1999). Efforts to build infrastructure typically involve most of the major institutions in the community: schools, universities, health services, and community agencies.

Square in the middle of nearly every effort to build comprehensive and integrated support systems for children is K–12 education. Since the Coleman report (1966), educators have known that learning and teaching are complex endeavors that involve much more than the classroom teacher, the child, and the school. While good teachers affect student learning (Haycock, 1998; Sanders, 1998), many factors extrinsic to the school affect readiness and ability to learn (Pittman & Cahill, 1992). The list is long. Poverty, disrupted and displaced families, and the new morbidities (violence, unsafe sex, drug and alcohol use, often with accompanying school failure and dropout) can negatively affect a student's capacity to learn. Clearly, teachers cannot address these varied and complex needs by themselves. Professionals who can work effectively with other professionals to integrate services from multiple

Mary M. Brabeck is Professor of Psychology and Dean of the Lynch School of Education at Boston College. Rachel E. Latta is a doctoral student in the Counseling Psychology program of the Lynch School of Education at Boston College.

professions are better able to address the multiple needs of children and youth in today's schools.

However, disciplines and professions have unique ethical codes, professional languages, and ways of defining and solving problems. For example, a given professional may refer to his or her "student," "child," "client," "patient," or "customer," reflecting differences in perspectives. Integrating services in ways that meet the needs of the whole child takes a great deal of effort. Barriers to learning must be removed and coordinated services must be provided so that families do not fall through the cracks that professionals create (Crowson & Boyd, 1993). This volume describes new roles for professionals working in and with schools, and new models for educating professionals in universities where interprofessional collaborations are occurring (Walsh, Brabeck, & Howard, 1999).

As professionals learn to work together to meet the needs of children and youth, they are drawn into complex partnerships with the schools and communities where these children reside. As Milbrey McLaughlin (2000), has shown the community has the potential to contribute both human and material resources and to enter into partnerships that will enhance learning. Such partnerships, however, have borders that are not easily crossed. The barriers of distrust, differing goals, and problem definition within schools, universities, and communities are only a few of the inherent challenges of the work discussed in this volume.

As universities heed Boyer's (1990) call to recognize their responsibility to address the issues and problems confronting society, they are being drawn into new partnerships with schools and communities (Chibucos & Lerner, 1999). This work is changing the nature of the discipline-based, departmentally structured university, and in so doing, changing the culture of the university (Lerner & Simon, 1998). Complex interprofessional and cross-disciplinary partnerships that involve universities can result in multidimensional and practice-oriented scholarship and professional preparation (Tourse & Mooney, 1999); this volume describes some of these partnerships.

All partners—the school, professions, community, and especially the university—are forging new research-practice systems for generating useful knowledge. Armed with new and traditional methodologies for ethnography, community research, and participatory action research, university scholars are working to generate knowledge on interprofessional collaborations and integrated service delivery that will be useful to the schools and communities in which they reside. While the challenges of this scholarly work are great, and research results sparse, the emerging empirical support for interprofessional collaborations is presented and discussed in this volume.

Few practices emerge directly from theory or research; rather, they emerge from "the doing," or through practice in dialogue with theory and research. This volume examines collaborations among schools, universities, communities, and professions—all entities that share the goals of enhancing student achievement and improving student well being—and attempts to examine the work at the "hyphen" of theory-practice, where school, university, community, and the professions all meet.

Mary Walsh and Jennie Park-Taylor (chapter 2) provide an overview of the field of interprofessional collaboration and integrated services. They note the complex needs of children and families, particularly those who are poor. They describe a theoretical foundation for integrating health, educational, psychological, legal, and social services, and the research emerging from efforts to address the full array of needs of poor children, youth, and families.

Hal Lawson (chapter 3) examines and describes the various forms of interprofessional collaboration that have been attempted. He calls attention to two overarching frameworks for understanding collaboration: *industrial-bureaucratic* and *institutional redesign*. He advocates the institutional redesign frame, which requires a shift in the culture of the institution as well as in society at large. He reviews several types of collaboration, including interprofessional, youth-centered, parent-centered, family-centered, intra-organizational, inter-organizational, community, intra-governmental, inter-governmental, and international. Lawson highlights some important factors of effective collaborations for comprehensive services (e.g., interactive and never-ending collaborative relationships; recognition of collaboration's transaction costs; collaboration's connection to competent practice, etc.) and provides a way to evaluate collaborations based on his taxonomy of factors.

Most scholars and practitioners agree that the context in which children and families live can have a profound effect on their experiences. Further, the contexts of school, family, and society profoundly shape and define children's experience (Brabeck & Brown et al., 1997; Gergen, 1991). The urban neighborhood in which many residents live in poverty stands in stark contrast to the neighborhoods of suburbia in which many residents are middle- to upper-middle class. Robert Crowson's (chapter 4) premise is that changing the context of communities through empowerment will result in improved outcomes for children and families. He offers four emerging models of community empowerment: alliances, production, regime, and choice. Each of these models emphasizes the impact of community context and reminds us of the importance of the community both as a complement to academic achievement and as "an important educator in its own right" (page 89).

Some reformers have worked to identify the factors that influence educational achievement and the well being of children and youth. They highlight not only the risks and deficits of children, schools, and communities, but also the resiliency and strengths of each (Cicchetti & Toth, 1999). Crowson advocates a model of community-based empowerment through co-production and the full-service model of schooling that realizes the full capacities, resources, and internal assets of a community. While previous conceptualizations of inner city communities and neighborhoods have emphasized needs and deficits, Crowson calls on us to reconsider these communities as producers—full of assets and strengths.

Practitioners and scholars bring many motivations to interprofessional collaborations. Practice grounded in a democratic or social justice theory works toward ensuring equal access and opportunity in all education systems. Lee Benson and Ira Harkavy (chapter 5) argue that solving current societal problems requires radical changes in the education system, from kindergarten through university. Education, they believe, is the basis of all democratic progress, and problems in education are indicative of problems in democracy (Harper, 1905). Creating a socially just and democratic university is the first step in education reform. Research universities, Benson and Harkavy assert, are "the most influential institutions in the world" (page 95). Through partnerships with the school and the community, universities will play a key role in changing schools and in achieving democracy and social justice aims within the education system.

Jacquelyn McCroskey (chapter 6) discusses the influence of the university and the community contexts on schooling. She argues that school-university-community partnerships can be successful only under two conditions. First, the most powerful partner—the university—must change its perspective to be able to fully participate in the most beneficial way. The tenure and promotion practices and the missions of universities must reflect a commitment to interprofessional collaboration and the improvement of communities through education. Second, McCroskey argues that strategies for system change must take into account the context of the community in which the school is located. By examining relative power within the partnership, interprofessional collaboration recognizes the value of context and the differing ways in which partners are affected by decisions.

The comprehensive school model advocated in chapters by Joy Dry-foos (chapter 7) and Jane Quinn (chapter 8) relies on two tenets of developmental psychology—development occurs across the life span, and development occurs on multiple levels (Werner, 1957). Many comprehensive schools provide opportunities for adult development, including language and professional development classes within the school building, as well as volunteer and even paid opportunities for parents to be involved in their children's education. Comprehensive schools also attend to early childhood development through programs such as Head Start and preschool and daycare opportunities.

Collaborative practice is complex and takes a variety of forms. Dry-foos (chapter 7) provides an overview of the various models of comprehensive schooling and suggests a continuum, from add-ons to more comprehensive models. She outlines the type of interprofessional collaboration involved in each. She also provides a case example (Quitman Street Community School) to illustrate the delivery of comprehensive services. The comprehensive school model Dryfoos presents offers a range of services to address the biological, psychological, and social needs of children and their families. These services include recreation, family activities, health and social services, and cultural enrichment opportunities. This model recognizes the impact of nonacademic barriers to learning, and illustrates that the integration of services can boost development across multiple levels.

Jane Quinn (chapter 8) argues that children and youth are not primarily in need of "fixing." What is needed is an understanding that there must be both support for areas of weakness *and* opportunities for strengths to be nurtured and utilized (Benard, 1991; McLaughlin, 2000). Quinn discusses important factors that determine the success of comprehensive schooling: an inclusive group of partners who have power to make collective decisions; knowledge of the school culture; comprehensive planning at multiple levels (e.g., school system and governmental); and joint staff development opportunities.

Specific results from complex interventions are more difficult to sort out. However, Quinn outlines some lessons learned through The Children's Aid Society (CAS) model. The CAS also supports a bio-psycho-social model of development, offering dental, medical, psychological, and social services within the school building. The underlying research base for the CAS schools highlights the importance of providing integrated services for children and their families that address biological, psychological, and social domains (Eccles, 1999; Hodgkinson, 1989; Ianni, 1990).

Jacob Murray and Richard Weissbourd (chapter 9) note that children must receive adequate instruction in the basic skills necessary for resilience. They remind us that teaching and learning are complex activities, measurable in ways that provide crucial feedback for improving instruction. Further, they underscore the need for additional evidence to support the practices of interprofessional collaboration and comprehensive services—the need for outcome-based school community partnerships. Murray and Weissbourd assert that not all collaborations are effective, noting that interprofessional collaboration is so difficult, and riddled with so many challenges, that it is not surprising that many such initiatives fail or are abandoned. They argue that partnerships should focus on a single outcome, such as reading, while acknowledging that such a single focus could shortchange other academic, social, or emotional learning. They also recognize the possibility that high-stakes testing efforts will lead to a shallow pedagogy focused on raising test scores. Interprofessional collaboration offers a corrective, and these authors advocate collaborative efforts not as ends in themselves, but rather as means to an end.

Many scholars and policymakers point to after-school programs as venues for comprehensive services. De Kanter, Adair, Chung, & Stonehill (chapter 10) provide preliminary evidence to support after-school programming as an important component of comprehensive schools and as a practice that requires multiple partners. They assert that practitioners and researchers have found that effective programs combine academic, enrichment, cultural, and recreational opportunities as a balanced approach for meeting the needs of the whole child. They also cite statistics that support the growing need for schools to provide after-school activities for children, and they argue for the development of more public-private ventures/partnerships—the foundation for the sustainability of a given project. Finally, they outline other benefits of long-term, quality after-school programs, such as safety, academic support, and youth development.

Collectively these chapters make the argument that integrated and comprehensive services provided by professionals who are able to work collaboratively will enhance learning and the well being of children and youth. Together, these chapters point the way to a hopeful future for the most vulnerable of society's children and youth.

REFERENCES

Benard, B. (1991). *Fostering resiliency in kids: Protective factors in the family, school and community*. Portland, OR: Northwest Regional Educational Laboratory, Western Regional Center for Drug-Free Schools and Communities.

Brabeck, M.M., & Brown, L. (With Christian, L., Espin, O., Hare-Mustin, R., Kaplan, A., Kaschak, E., Miller, D., Phillips, E., Ferns, T., & Van Ormer, A). (1997). Feminist theory and psychological practice. In J. Worell & N. Johnson (Eds.), *Shaping the future of feminist psychology: Education, research and practice* (pp. 15–36). Washington, DC: American Psychological Association.

Boyer, E. (1990). *Scholarship reconsidered: Priorities of the professoriate*. Princeton, NJ: The Carnegie Foundation for the Advancement of Teaching.

Chibucos, T.R., & Lerner, R.M. (1999). Serving children and families through community-university partnerships: A view of the issues. In T.R. Chibucos & R.M. Lerner (Eds.), *Serving children and families through community university partnerships: Success stories* (pp. 1–11). Norwell, MA: Kluwer Academic.

Cicchetti, D., & Toth, S.L. (1999). Transactional ecological systems in developmental psychopathology. In S.S. Luthar, J.A. Burack, D. Cicchetti, & J.R. Weisz (Eds.) *Developmental psychopathology: Perspectives on adjustment, risk, and disorder* (pp. 317–349). Cambridge, U.K.: Cambridge University Press.

Coleman, J.S., Campbell, E.Q., Hobson, C.J., McPartland, J., Mood, A.M., Weinfeld, F.D., & York, R.L. (1966). *Equality of educational opportunity*. Washington, DC: National Center for Education Statistics (DHEW).

Crowson R.L., & Boyd, W.L. (1993). Structures and strategies: Toward an understanding of alternative models for coordinated children's services. Number 93-5b. Washington, DC: Office of Educational Research and Improvement.

Eccles, J. (1999). The development of children ages 6 to 14. *The future of children: When school is out, 9*(2), 30–44.

Gergen, K. J. (1991). *The saturated self.* New York: Basic Books.

Harper, W.R. (1905). *The trend in higher education*. Chicago: University of Chicago Press.

Haycock, K. (1998). Good teaching matters ... a lot. *Organization of American Historians Magazine of History, 13*(1), 61–63.

Hodgkinson, H.L. (1989). *The same client: The demographics of education and service delivery systems*. Washington, DC: Institute for Educational Leadership.

Ianni, F.A.J. (1990). *The search for structure*. New York: The Free Press.

Lerner, R.M., & Simon, L.A.K. (1998). *University-community collaborations for the twenty-first century: Outreach scholarship for youth and families*. Michigan State University Series on Children, Youth, and Families, Vol. 4. Hamden, CT: Garland Publishing.

McLaughlin, M.W. (2000). *Community counts: How youth organizations matter for youth development*. Washington, DC: Public Education Network.

Pittman, K.J., & Cahill, M. (1992). *Pushing the boundaries of education: The implications of a youth development approach to education policies, structures and collaborations*. Washington, DC: Academy for Educational Development.

Sanders, W.L. (1998). Value-added assessment. *School Administrator, 11*(55), 24–27.

Tourse, R.W.C., & Mooney, J.F. (Eds.). (1999). *Collaborative practice: School and human service partnerships*. Westport, CT: Praeger.

Walsh, M.E., Brabeck, M.M., & Howard, K.A. (1999). Interprofessional collaboration in children's services: Toward a theoretical framework. *Children's services: Social policy, research, and practice, 2*(4), 183–208.

Weiss, H.B., & Lopez, M.E. (1999). New strategies in foundation grantmaking for children and youth. Battle Creek, MI: Kellogg Foundation.

Werner, H. (1957). The concept of development from a comparative and organismic point of view. In D. Harris (Ed.), *The concept of development: An issue in the study of human behavior* (pp. 125–148). Minneapolis: University of Minnesota Press.

CHAPTER 2

Comprehensive Schooling and Interprofessional Collaboration: Theory, Research, and Practice

MARY E. WALSH AND JENNIE PARK-TAYLOR

Closing the growing academic achievement gap is an enormous challenge confronting all professionals who work with children. Educators and policymakers have offered a plethora of recommendations on how to address the increasing disparity in educational outcomes between children from wealthy communities and those from poor communities. Darling-Hammond (2000) believes that as much as half of the achievement gap between students of lower and higher socioeconomic status can be reduced by improving classroom instruction. Indeed, over the past decade, significant progress has been made in our nation's public schools as a result of explicit national learning standards and improved instructional practices. Across the country, mean scores on high-stakes tests have risen in most communities (Haney, 2000; Koretz & Barron, 1998). But in spite of our best efforts to improve educational outcomes through better instruction, a very substantial achievement gap remains and reminds us that we still have a long way to go to meet the promise of educational excellence. Improved instructional practices are obviously necessary, but not sufficient, to close this gap.

If improvements in instruction can address one half the achievement gap, what will address the other half? According to educators and policymakers, the answer to this question lies in recognizing the substantial nonacademic challenges to achievement and development faced by many of our nation's students. In 1995, Jane Stallings, then president of the American Educational Research Association, pointed out that for educational reform to have a lasting effect, educational leaders need to incorporate "all the playing pieces," that is, the systems

Mary E. Walsh is a professor in the Department of Counseling and Developmental Psychology in the Lynch School of Education at Boston College and Director of the Boston College Center for Child, Family and Community Partnerships. Jennie Park-Taylor is a doctoral candidate in the Counseling, Developmental and Educational Psychology Program at Boston College.

that contribute to children's learning, including "health, social welfare, juvenile justice, extended day opportunities, and community participation" (p. 8).

However, discussing factors that contribute to the achievement gap in terms of "two halves" is an approach that suffers from a somewhat misguided view of human development—one that unnecessarily splits development into various "parts." This approach has long dominated the professions of education and human services, where the developmental process is divided into domains that are presumed to be separate and distinct (e.g., cognitive versus socio-emotional development or physical versus psychological development). Assuming the separateness of various domains reflects a flawed understanding of human development because it "results in the view that analytic distinctions are true cuts of nature" (Overton, 1998, p. 112) and "assert[s] the priority of individual elements over the whole" (Overton, pp. 114-115).

From a relational perspective, or similarly from an organismic orientation (Werner, 1948), individual human processes are not standalone entities, but can be understood only in relation to one another and to "the whole." This assumption emerges from the nature of development: "Whenever development occurs, it proceeds from a state of relative lack of differentiation to a state of increasing differentiation and hierarchical integration" (Werner & Kaplan, 1956, p. 866). Hence, although the various domains of development (e.g., cognitive and affective) become more differentiated and more integrated later in development, they are never completely independent or distinct processes.

Consistent with the inaccurate assumption that human development is composed of distinct domains, education and human service professionals have typically been schooled to select one "part" or process as the primary focus of their concern. Teachers, for example, focus mostly on children's cognitive development, whereas counselors generally confine their interest to affective issues. A similar view of development also characterizes the major institutions that care for children. For example, the promotion of cognitive development is considered the primary task of K-12 schools, while human service and youth development agencies focus on supporting socio-emotional development.

Unfortunately, this type of specialization may encourage a child care professional or institution to unwittingly give preference to one aspect of development over another, and to view all children solely from a professional perspective while losing sight of other related issues and concerns (Sailor & Skrtic, 1996). Without an appreciation of the relationships among the multiple aspects of human development, child-serving institutions often develop a narrow and rigid focus. Child-serving professionals may not see the necessity of working in a collaborative way to form a comprehensive understanding of the individual or family seeking services. Similarly, without a holistic perspective, schools and human service or health agencies may see little or no reason to collaborate with one another in their efforts to promote the optimal development of children. In educational settings, this limited view of development has often led to a laser-like focus on teaching and learning, with little recognition of the role of other domains of development. And, in community agencies, an exclusive focus on youth development or mental health can often exclude any consideration or support for academic achievement.

In recent years, a newly developing appreciation for a relational view of knowledge has resulted in significant shifts in the relationship between education and human services. Educators and youth development professionals are beginning to recognize that cognition and affect are interrelated processes and have a significant impact on one another. Practitioners are beginning to provide an integrated approach to program development that favors no single domain of development, but instead values all aspects of development and recognizes that the whole child is more than the sum of his or her parts. For example, the gap in academic achievement is now beginning to be viewed as a result not only of inadequate teaching and learning practices, but also of the substantial nonacademic barriers to learning confronting a significant number of our nation's youth. In one notable instance, educators and youth development specialists are beginning to co-design after-school programs with "embedded curricula" that link what happens in classrooms across a variety of learning settings, and that offer a range of activities to build both academic and life skills (Institute of Medicine, 2002; McLaughlin, 2000; Melaville, Shah, & Blank, in press).

Most educators and youth development experts now acknowledge that academic achievement and student well being are the two most important goals of public education (Quinn, this volume, chapter 8; Stallings, 1995). The major contributors to each of these outcome goals appear to be excellent instructional practices (Darling-Hammond, 2000) and positive in-school and out-of-school environments (Masten & Coatsworth, 1998; McLaughlin, 2001). While excellent instructional practices contribute substantially to academic outcomes, the school, home, and neighborhood climates in which the child is developing clearly moderate those outcomes. For example, despite a high quality school experience, a child who experiences inadequate medical care and neighborhood violence is less likely to benefit from excellent instruction, thus leading to poorer academic outcomes. The converse is also true: the well being of youth relies significantly on positive biological, psychological, and social circumstances, but is moderated, among other factors, by the quality of academic instruction. A child who experiences an optimal personal-social climate but has had poor quality teaching is less likely to be a successful student. Most children who succeed academically and develop in healthy ways have benefited from both quality instruction *and* positive family and neighborhood environments.

A growing body of literature is examining the impact of various teaching and learning practices on the academic development of children (e.g., Cochran-Smith, 2001). However, the literature on the role of out-of-school environments on learning is much more limited. Therefore, a major goal of this chapter is to examine and discuss the nonacademic factors that contribute to both academic success and healthy development. We are aware of the inextricable linkages across academic and nonacademic factors. Thus, for purposes of analysis only, we make the conventional, although artificial, distinction between these two domains. Once we have discussed the various nonacademic conditions that affect learning, and the supports and collaborations that enhance learning, we will introduce an emerging model of schooling—the community school. A community school is intentionally designed to promote not only academic achievement but also healthy development. A description of the community school will make clear that the success of this type of schooling is dependent largely on the collaborative involvement of various groups (e.g., teachers, parents, psychologists). We will therefore briefly discuss the practice of interprofessional collaboration as a linchpin in successful comprehensive schooling. Finally, we will offer a theoretical framework to ground the practice of both community schools and interprofessional collaboration and outline the empirical literature that supports the efficacy of both of these practices.

Nonacademic Factors That Affect Learning

In recent years, the significant health and social needs of today's schoolchildren and youth have become increasingly apparent to educators, health workers, and social service providers (Dryfoos, this volume, chapter 7; Lerner, 1995; Stallings, 1995). The "new morbidities" of poor nutrition, unsafe sex, drug and alcohol abuse, familial and

12 COMPREHENSIVE SCHOOLING

community violence, teenage pregnancy and parenting, inadequate job skills, inadequate access to health care, and homelessness continue to threaten the healthy development of children and youth (Dryfoos, 1990; Lerner, 1995; Murray & Weissbourd, this volume, chapter 9). These conditions are directly correlated to family poverty. Census data from the past decade indicate that more children live in poverty in the United States than in any other industrialized country in the world. In fact, approximately 20% of our nation's children under 18 are living in poverty (The Annie E. Casey Foundation, 2000). The number of poor children has increased dramatically over the last several decades, and the percentage of children and youth living in poor neighborhoods where there are large numbers of welfare recipients, unemployed individuals, and single-parent families increased from 3% in 1970 to 17% in 1990 (The Annie E. Casey Foundation, 1999).

Impoverished conditions provide a context in which an increasing number of youth become involved in risky behavior. The 2001 Youth Behavior Survey (Centers for Disease Control and Prevention, 2002) indicated that the following percentages of 14- to 17-year-olds in the United States engaged in diverse problem behaviors:

- Sexual activity: 33.4% had engaged in sexual intercourse during the prior 3 months, and 14.2% had had 4 or more sexual partners in their lifetime.

- Substance abuse: 29.9% had had 5 or more drinks on one or more occasions during the prior 30 days, 28.5% had smoked cigarettes at least once during the prior 30 days, and 42.4% had smoked marijuana at least once in their lifetime.

- Suicide: during the prior 12 months, 8.8% reported attempting suicide, and 19% had seriously considered suicide.

- Violence: during the preceding 12 months, 33.2% had been involved in a physical fight, and during the prior 30 days, 5.7% had carried a gun.

Furthermore, Dryfoos (1990, 1994, this volume, chapter 7) estimates that 25% of 10- to 17-year-olds engage in multiple high-risk behaviors and that another 25% place themselves at moderate risk by engaging in some problem behaviors. Attending schools with high rates of violence affects all students, because even those who are not engaged in aggressive behavior may fear being the victim of aggression. Thirty percent of students in grades 6-10 report being bullied (Nansel et al., 2001) and approximately 9% of all students reported that they were afraid of being attacked or harmed at school (National Center for Educational Statistics, 2002). Although the remaining 50% report no problem behavior or low-risk behavior, they require strong and consistent support to avoid becoming involved.

Poverty provides the conditions not only for risky behavior, but also for poor academic outcomes (Beaton & O'Dwyer, 2002; Coleman et al., 1966). Research has shown that children living in low-income families are exposed to approximately 25 total hours of one-on-one picture book reading before entering the first grade, while their middle-class peers have been read to 50 times as much. Hence, children of low-income families begin their educational journey with just half the potential vocabulary of children from middle-class families (Hart & Risley, 1995). The barriers to learning become even more obvious once children begin school. For example, one of the greatest challenges to learning for many children living in low-income neighborhoods is excessive unstructured free time. About 8 million children spend up to 20-25 hours each week alone or in unsupervised settings with friends or siblings (Fact Sheet on Children's Out-of-School-Time, 2001).

In light of these data, it is not surprising that socioeconomic status is highly correlated with achievement scores (Conger, Conger, & Elder, 1997; Haveman & Wolfe, 1995; Hill & Duncan, 1987; Patterson, Kupersmidt, & Vaden, 1990; White, 1982). Children from low-income urban districts fare worse on statewide tests than children from high-income districts (Berliner, 1993; Martin et al., 2001). Children who live in poverty, who fear familial or neighborhood violence, whose attachments to parents have been seriously disrupted, or who lack the social skills required for productive interactions are severely challenged both academically and socially (Eckenrode, Laird, & Doris, 1993; Furstenberg et al., 1999; Schmitz, Wagner, & Menke, 1995; Warner & Weist, 1996). In an analysis of the impact of out-of-school factors on academic achievement, Maeroff (1998) concluded that "those who desire improvements in classroom learning must realize and acknowledge that school reform, especially when it focuses on disadvantaged students, cannot easily succeed if it ignores the circumstances of their out-of-school lives" (p. 5).

In short, the conditions of poverty are associated with both an increase in risky behavior and a decrease in opportunities to learn outside of school, resulting in poor academic outcomes. As many educators and policymakers have pointed out, addressing the nonacademic barriers to learning, as well as providing enriching learning opportunities, is critical to closing the achievement gap, especially in low-income populations.

Collaborations That Enhance Learning

For educators, health providers and human service professionals, the ability to recognize barriers to learning is often a less challenging task than addressing them, particularly in the current environment of education reform. The intensive and often exclusive attention to improving academic institutional practices has precluded consideration of the nonacademic barriers to learning. Paul Barton of the Educational Testing Service eloquently describes our collective challenge:

To a considerable extent, our reluctance to address important non-academic factors that limit student achievement stems from a fear that to consider such factors may cause us to lose focus, and that recognition of these factors may provide excuses for not raising standards and achievement. ... We tend to put considerations of family, community, and economy off-limits in education reform policy discussions. However, we do so at our own peril. The seriousness of our purpose requires that we learn to rub our bellies and pat our heads at the same time. (Barton, 2001, p. 20)

As the role of nonacademic barriers to learning increasingly comes into public focus, policymakers are calling for new institutional arrangements to address these challenges. Many of the proposed arrangements feature the school as a central player. For example, the Surgeon General's Report on Children's Mental Health (U.S. Public Health Service, 2000) recommends strengthening "the resource capacity of schools to serve as a key link to a comprehensive, seamless system of schools- and community-based identification, assessment and treatment services, to meet the needs of youth and their families where they are" (p. 6), and providing "access to services in places where youth and families congregate (e.g., schools, recreation centers, churches)" (p. 8).

Former U.S. Secretary of Education Richard Riley (1998) also called for schools to respond to both the academic and nonacademic barriers to learning. Aware of the complexity of this task, Riley indicated clearly that schools cannot engage in this effort alone. It requires the engagement and collaboration of families, community agencies, and local institutions. Such school-family-community partnerships would help all children to learn successfully and to develop in healthy ways.

In response to the call for collaboration with community resources, some public schools have begun to implement novel collaborative arrangements with community agencies and resources. Emerging school-community partnerships span both in-school and out-of-school time, cross professional boundaries, focus on programmatic as well as individual interventions, and address both strengths and deficits. The collaboration of multiple institutions, and in particular, school-community-university partnerships, has fostered many innovative models of practice (Benson & Harkavy, this volume, chapter 5; Walsh, Brabeck, & Howard, 1999). New sources of funding for these partnerships allow professionals to collaborate in new models of service and resource delivery. For example, Twenty-first Century Learning Centers, a federal program that funds school-community agency partnerships, has seen a substantial increase in appropriations over the past 3 years. Foundations such as DeWitt-Wallace, Charles Hayden, Mott, Stuart, Annie Casey and others have supported a substantial number of school-community partnerships. In parallel fashion, the nation's schools have seen a significant increase in public and private funding for school-based and school-linked health centers that typically involve sustained collaboration between schools and local health care facilities (Walsh & Murphy, in press).

Community Schools

New school-community arrangements have resulted in new models of practice. One of the most widely recognized of these practices is the community school, also referred to as a comprehensive school or a full-service school. Typically, community schools operate in a public school building that is open to students, families, and the community before, during, and after school, 7 days a week, on a year-round basis. Usually, they are jointly operated through a partnership between the school system and one or more community agencies, and sometimes a university. Families, youth, principals, teachers, and neighborhood residents design and implement activities that promote high educational achievement and positive youth development. A family support unit is usually available to help families with child rearing, employment, housing, immigration, and other services. Medical, dental, and mental health services can be offered by agencies, either on site at the school or in the agency setting (Dryfoos, this volume, chapter 7; Quinn, this volume, chapter 8).

Interprofessional Collaboration

Community schools are complex systemic interventions that rely on the engagement of a range of school personnel (e.g., teachers, principal, janitorial staff) and individuals who work with the school (e.g., parents, community agency staff). However, even the deep commitment of

each individual working in or with the community school is not enough
to ensure the success of these schools. Given the inclusive goals of
comprehensive schooling (addressing the academic and nonacademic
factors that contribute to learning outcomes), all professionals working
in and with a community school must also be committed to working
together across disciplinary boundaries.

In community schools, the boundaries that have existed for decades between school-based professionals (e.g., teacher, school nurse,
and counselor) and between school-based and community-based professionals (e.g., teachers and social workers, school psychologists and
clinical psychologists, school nurses and family doctors) give way to
collaborative and integrative practices. When schools partner with
community agencies to deliver health, mental health, and social services, the various professionals in each of these settings are required to
work collaboratively so that children's developmental needs are met
holistically and in an integrated fashion.

The defining characteristics of interprofessional collaboration include engagement in an interactive process, mutual control over decisions made and actions taken, some common goals and values, and
shared ownership of responsibilities and outcomes (Brandon & Knapp,
1999; Casto & Julia, 1994; Hord, 1986; Lawson, this volume, chapter
3; McCroskey & Einbinder, 1998; Payzant, 1992; Smith & Hutchinson, 1992; Whitaker & King, 1994; Wood & Gray, 1991). Generally,
in traditional school-based practice, more traditional notions of what it
means to be a professional have prevailed. The professional has been
an expert who remains at a distance, observes the student in a school,
and defines the relevant issues. In typical interactions involving more
than one profession, each of the professionals has offered his or her
assessment of the student's school issues to a team of other professionals. These individual perspectives often stood alone and were related to
one another only in that they referred to the same student. In this type
of practice, "integration" has often meant placing these separate assessments side by side in a single report. This approach could be considered cooperative but not truly collaborative.

In sharp contrast, a collaborative approach places each professional
in the role of a "co-learner" (Gergen, 1985; Lerner & Simon, 1998).
The student's school issues and the proposed plan of action are determined when all relevant points of view—those of the student, of
teachers, and of other professionals—are taken into consideration
(Bibace, 1999; Walsh & Anderson, in press), thus modifying the individual understandings of each involved professional. In this process,

the collaborating professionals collectively form a comprehensive understanding of the student and his/her issues and then work together to provide a seamless array of services (Illback, 1994; Payzant, 1992).

Interprofessional collaboration has been most fully developed within the field of education where it has been practiced most intentionally in community or full-service schools (Dryfoos, this volume, chapter 7). However, it is recognized by a number of professions as a "best practice" (American Academy of Pediatrics, 1994; American Association for Counseling and Development, American School Counselor Association, National Association of School Psychologists, & National Association of Social Workers, 1990; American Bar Association, 1993; American Psychological Association, 1997; National Association of School Nurses, 1995). Nevertheless, despite the multiple calls for collaborative practice, few working models have been implemented.

Comprehensive models of schooling and the related practice of interprofessional collaboration have emerged, like many if not most educational practices, in the world of action rather than theory. Each has been implemented on a school by school basis in a significant number of school districts across the country. In a few districts, geographically proximate schools have begun to implement community schools on a more systemic basis, bridging a number of schools in these efforts (e.g., The Connect Five Initiative in Boston). However, it is important to note that any innovative practice must eventually be grounded in theory and research if it is to be sustained and widely implemented. We will now examine the emerging theoretical basis of community schools and the related practice of interprofessional collaboration, then review the empirical research on both.

Theoretical Rationale for Comprehensive Schooling and Interprofessional Collaboration

Whether practitioners espouse theory explicitly or only implicitly, it is widely recognized that theory and practice inform one another. Any new or changing practice is viewed not simply as a novel skill, but as a fundamental shift in the professionals' understanding of and approach to the child or family. Similarly, changes in how professionals understand child/family development lead to shifts in practice.

The purpose of comprehensive schooling as well as interprofessional collaboration is to promote the optimal development of school children and families. Therefore, grounding the practice of community schools and collaborative practice with children and families requires a

theoretical framework that explains the processes of normal development and the specific ways in which they can be supported and
enhanced. One conceptualization that meets these two requirements is
provided by "developmental systems theory," a meta-theory that describes development and the ways in which developmental outcomes can
be modified (Bronfenbrenner, 1979; Lerner, 1984, 1986, 1995; Lerner,
Walsh, & Howard, 1998). As a comprehensive framework, developmental systems theory addresses many of the limitations of the earlier developmental theories (e.g., those of Freud, Jung, and Winnicott), including
their overemphasis on the "person" side of the person-environment relationship, their examination of individual processes of development in
isolation from one another, their intensive focus on childhood, and their
overriding concern with psychopathology. By contrast, the assumptions
of developmental systems theory focus on the contextual aspects of the
person-environment relationship, examine development across the life
span, consider multiple interacting levels of development (e.g., bio-psycho-social), and recognize the role of resilience and risk in development.
We will consider each of these assumptions in turn and describe their
suitability for grounding the practices of comprehensive schooling and
interprofessional collaboration.

Development Occurs in a Context

Comprehensive schooling, and indeed contemporary best practices
in education in general, assume that knowledge is not imparted to the
child independent of context, but rather is constructed by the child
within a range of contexts. Constructivist approaches to instruction
have articulated the impact of these contexts (home, family, neighborhood, ethnic and cultural groups) on the way in which a child makes
meaning of various domains of knowledge (Airasian & Walsh, 1997;
Prawat, 1992; Steffe & Gale, 1995).

The recognition that academic achievement is significantly affected
by the conditions and circumstances of a child's life has been a primary
rationale for building more intentional connections between schools
and their communities. Consistent with this framework, community
schools seek to create opportunities for parents as well as children to
develop and flourish. Comer and his colleagues (Comer & Haynes,
1998; Comer & Woodruff, 1991) argue that parental involvement is
essential in successful schooling because the family context provides
the cultural, social, and emotional support a child needs to excel in
school. Epstein (2001) has repeatedly pointed to the importance of
family variables in the lives and development of children and youth.

The interrelationship of development and context implies not only that the individual is affected by many contexts, but also that the individual shapes his or her context. Many community schools are excellent examples of how context is shaped, enriched, and vitalized by the unique individuals who are part of the school. Today's public schools on the whole reflect the increasing cultural and ethnic diversity of a changing student landscape (Hernandez, 1999).

Professionals working in comprehensive public schools are constantly reminded of how students' ethnic/cultural identity and the multidimensional contexts of their lives (family, the neighborhood, community) affect their ability to engage in learning. The continuous interaction between the school and its community provides an understanding of a child's various contexts, which becomes essential when designing, providing, and evaluating services and supports in community schools.

Developmental theory's assumption of person-context interaction also grounds the collaborative practice of the professionals who work with or in community schools. Unfortunately, the traditional practice of professionals across educational, psychological, and human service fields has not always reflected this developmental principle. In the past, some professionals (e.g., teachers) tended to focus on the "person" side of the person-context relation, while other professionals, such as social workers and lawyers, were more likely to focus on the context, emphasizing the cultural or system variables that affect human behavior. However, in comprehensive approaches to education, professionals are increasingly recognizing that effective prevention and intervention address the fit (or lack of fit) between the person and the context. Sound practice must involve the participation of professionals who focus on the person as well as professionals who focus on the context (Walsh, Brabeck, & Howard, 1999). These two perspectives broaden the understanding of the client in a manner that enriches each separate perspective (Petrie, 1992).

Development Across the Life Span

Community schools are also grounded in the assumption that development occurs across the life span and is not confined to children and adolescents. Children are constantly developing and changing, but so are their parents. This assumption emphasizes the importance of adults in children's lives and reminds us of how the unmet needs of adults directly influence their children's development and academic success (Walsh et al., 1999). The traditional school, open from 8 am to

3 pm, does not readily meet the needs of parents, especially since many of them work during the school day. Comprehensive models of schooling incorporate developmental opportunities for adults as well as children. The traditional school setting is transformed into one that provides resources, services, and opportunities that meet the developmental needs of parents (e.g., English as a Second Language, Graduate Equivalency Degree, computer and job skills training, housing and/or immigration services offered by community agencies in the school building).

The assumption that development occurs over the life span also implies the collaboration of many different professional partners. Although in principle many professionals may be committed to a lifespan orientation, in practice, professionals tend to identify themselves with a particular age group. The qualifiers "pediatric," "elementary," "adolescent," "adult," and "geriatric" describe many, if not most, of the specialty practices in psychology, social work, health care, education, and even law (e.g., juvenile law). Given the level of technical expertise necessary in each of these specialty practices, one would not argue for eliminating specialties in favor of a generalist model. However, a comprehensive understanding of a child's or family's needs and assets is enhanced by a team of professionals who have expertise at different levels of development. Educators are more likely to focus on children, social workers on the family, particularly the adults, and health care providers (e.g., pediatricians or internists) on either children or adults but typically not on both. In work with children and families, the expertise of multiple professions will enhance services to the child, the parents, and the family.

Development Occurs in Multiple Domains

Educators and other professionals have long recognized the assumption that children develop simultaneously, though sometimes inconsistently, across multiple systems—biological, psychological, and social (Bronfrenbrenner, 1979; Lerner, 1978, 1986) and that attention to each system is critical to the healthy development of a child. Consistent with this assumption, community schools address the many domains of the child that affect learning (e.g., cognitive, emotional, biological, and familial). As already noted, children's health and the safety of home and school environments have a direct effect on their ability to learn (Arbona, 2000; Stallings, 1995). Numerous studies also demonstrate the negative effect of poverty on the academic outcomes of children (McLloyd, 1998; Murray & Weissbourd, this volume, chapter 9).

The assumption of multiple domains in development also supports the practice of interprofessional collaboration. Reductionist and simplistic strategies of prevention and intervention that target a narrow set of behaviors are rarely effective. The resulting delivery of services is generally uncoordinated, disjointed, and fragmented (Brabeck et al., 1997; Lerner, 1995; Schorr, 1988). Since the issues facing children and families cannot be divided into "discipline-shaped boxes," it is clear that service and resource delivery must assume a more holistic, collaborative approach. In community schools, coordinated efforts by various professionals, each with a focus on one domain of development, will promote a more comprehensive understanding of the patterns of problems and strengths exhibited by individuals, families, and groups.

The collaboration required by community schools must occur not only across professions but also across institutions. Schools and agencies must begin to see their interdependence across functional lines and place the child at the center of the organizational system. Community schools, which are designed with the student at the center, provide an infrastructure that can smoothly join schools and agencies in effective working relationships.

Development Involves Risk and Resilience

Although for many years educators and health service providers have operated within a deficit model, there is a growing recognition that the assessment of an individual's risks yields only part of the picture. Resilience is as important as risk in understanding development. Community schools recognize that growth can be impeded or facilitated by an array of risk and protective factors. Consequently, these schools are designed to address the risks faced by children and to build on children's strengths. In addition to providing services, this model of schooling offers multiple opportunities for youth development through after-school programs, educational enrichment programs, and arts, cultural education, and athletics. Community schools are similar to quality after-school programs insofar as they view youth as resources to be developed rather than as problems to be managed (Roth & Brooks-Gunn, 2000). Community schools extend the resiliency model to communities as well. Rather than focusing on the various risk factors associated with communities, these schools view communities as resources to be tapped and enhanced.

The dual task of building upon strengths and addressing deficits is extremely difficult when professionals work in isolation. In isolated practice, professionals often function as "repair people," focusing on "fixing" deficits or pathologies. However, effective interventions require not only the identification of pathology but also the assessment of strengths (Masten, Best, & Garmezy, 1991; Masten et al., 1988; Werner, 1989, 1990). In contrast to isolated practice, collaboration across professions in community schools provides a single means for identifying the patterns of strength and deficit across domains and for designing interventions that take human strengths and capacity for resilience into account. A more balanced view of a young person's capacities in a variety of settings is the result (Walsh et al., 1999).

Community schools and the interprofessional collaboration that these schools require are grounded in the major principles of developmental systems theory (Lerner, 1978, 1986), which assumes that development occurs in context, across multiple levels, over the life span, and involves both strengths and deficits. This framework provides the rationale for models of schooling that are comprehensive and for practice that is interprofessional. We will now examine the empirical evidence that supports comprehensive models of schooling.

Empirical Literature on Community Schools and Interprofessional Collaboration

The Efficacy of Comprehensive Schooling

The growing number of community schools has led to numerous calls for the evaluation of their effectiveness. There are two primary types of research that focus on comprehensive approaches to schooling: research that demonstrates the relationship between the conditions assumed to be necessary for learning and academic outcomes (Melaville, Shah, & Blank, in press), and research that examines each type of comprehensive school model.

Research on conditions necessary for learning. Research on the conditions necessary for learning and positive academic outcomes can be grouped into several categories: school engagement (Singh, Granville, & Dika, 2002; Skinner, Wellborn, & Connell, 1990); family stability (Wang, Haertel, & Walberg, 1997); strong home-school relationships (Comer & Haynes, 1991; Eccles & Harold, 1993; Epstein, 1992); positive school climate (Dunn & Harris, 1998; Esposito, 1999); adequate economic status of parents (Coley, 2002); family involvement in children's learning (Fehrmann & Reimers, 1987; Marcon, 1999); adequate medical, mental, and physical health (Connell, Turner, & Mason, 1985; Dryfoos, 1994); and core instructional programs with high standards, qualified teachers, and a rigorous curriculum (Shouse, 1998). Overall, the studies examining the impact of these conditions demonstrate either that a negative status within any of these conditions can lead to poor academic and social outcomes (e.g., poor teaching leads to low academic performance), or that interventions that address these conditions in a positive way can lead to positive academic and social outcomes (e.g., increasing school engagement through after-school programs contributes to improved academic performance).

The outcomes of these studies clearly indicate that inadequate conditions or inadequate access to necessary resources results in poor outcomes for children. Furthermore, providing individual supports in health, mental health, parental involvement, youth development, safe school climates, and community-based curriculum works to improve a range of outcomes (Melaville, Shah, & Blank, in press; Walsh & Murphy, in press). These findings also suggest that if positive conditions are operating together in an integrative way, as they do in the context of a community school, their collective impact will be significant. "When typically separate categorical approaches are integrated into a comprehensive strategy, their aggregate impact is strengthened and sustained" (Melaville, Shah, & Blank).

Research that examines the impact of community schools. Examining the impact of community schools has presented numerous hurdles for researchers. Community schools are relatively new and complex educational institutions that have been developed through a variety of models and implemented in a variety of local contexts. Although nearly all the models of this type of schooling provide extended services, increased resources, and an extended school day and year, they each place an emphasis on a particular intervention (e.g., parent involvement or after-school programming). The variability across comprehensive models, as well as their implementation in local contexts, makes comparisons among these schools difficult. Furthermore, there is general agreement that community schools have not operated over a long enough period of time to provide adequate data on long-term outcomes. Finally, the complexity of their multiple, simultaneous interventions has challenged researchers, who typically operate within a traditional experimental cause and effect research paradigm.

Most community school evaluations have been conducted within the past 5 years (Melaville, Shah, & Blank, in press; Dryfoos, 2000). Although a few have looked at individual community schools, many have examined the efficacy of particular models of community schools (Melaville, Shah, & Blank). Some evaluations have tracked data internally and others have utilized external evaluators. Collectively, these evaluations have looked at a wide range of outcome measures and have examined the impact of community schools on students, schools, families, and communities (Melaville, Shah, & Blank). In our report of the findings, we will first consider evaluations of some of the more prominent community school efforts. We will then report on what has been learned about the impact of community schools on students, schools, families, and communities. Finally, we will comment on the major lessons emerging from these evaluations.

Evaluations of Particular Models

Typically, community schools have been implemented in accordance with the philosophy and guiding principles of a community school "model" (Crowson, this volume, chapter 4; Dryfoos, this volume, chapter 7; Lawson, this volume, chapter 3). While each intervention is unique, all share common features, including the major goal of improving academic achievement by improving instructional practices and by promoting the bio-psycho-social development of students.

Comer Schools—Yale University. In 1968, James P. Comer created a School Development Program (SDP), also known as the Comer Process, at an elementary school in New Haven, Connecticut. Now in many schools across the country, SDP aims to create learning environments that support the physical, cognitive, psychological, verbal, social, and moral development of children. Studies of Comer Schools indicate that the program contributes to positive effects in school climate, student attendance, and student achievement (Haynes, 1994). Comparative studies of Comer and non-Comer schools also reveal improvement in student self-confidence, self-concept, and academic achievement for Comer students (Haynes, 1994). A recent report of a city-by-city analysis of student performance and achievement gaps on state assessments (Casserly, 2002) hailed North Carolina's Charlotte-Mecklenburg district, which has used the Comer system for a decade, for raising math scores in grades 3-8 and for narrowing the gap in achievement between white students and students of color (Yale University Bush Center in Child Development and Social Policy, 2002).

Schools of the 21st century. Edward Zigler, one of the principal founders of the nation's Head Start program, developed a model of community schools called Schools of the 21st Century (21C). Out of a need for affordable quality childcare, Zigler designed 21C schools to provide all day, year-round childcare to preschoolers, and before- and after-school and vacation care for school-age children. The Bush Center reports that children who attended a 21C school for at least 3 years had higher scores in math and reading than students in a non-21C school (Schools of the 21st Century, 2001). It also reports that the 21C schools have yielded positive results for parents, including increased investment in caring for their children, increased knowledge of child development, and improved attendance at work. Principals from the 21st Century Schools reported decreased vandalism to school property and improved relations between the community and school staff. These changes were attributed to the expanded and extended services offered in the school (Dryfoos, 2000).

The CoZi schools. In 1997, Zigler and Comer combined their programs to create the "CoZi" schools. These schools combine the early childhood aspects of Zigler's Schools of the 21st Century program with Comer's School Development Program to better meet the needs of children and families. An evaluation of the CoZi model was conducted at the Bowling Park Elementary School in Norfolk, Virginia between 1996 and 1999. Students at Bowling Park were compared with children from a control school. CoZi preschoolers and kindergarteners scored 9-15 points higher on picture-vocabulary tests than children in the control school. In addition, third and fourth graders at Bowling Park scored significantly higher than students at the control school on tests of basic skills (Stevenson & Engstrom, 1999).

Research on this model has also found that teachers are associating CoZi schools with an improved school climate, with increased levels of staff leadership and staff involvement with the students, and with more frequent communication between school staff and parents. Research has also demonstrated that CoZi teachers report communicating with parents more often and more effectively. These evaluation data also suggest that CoZi parents are becoming more engaged with their children and are displaying increased levels of school and classroom participation. The CoZi model recognizes that students are more likely to achieve academically in a favorable school climate, where staff and parents collaborate to meet educational and socioemotional goals (The Yale University Bush Center in Child Development and Social Policy, 2002).

Children's Aid Society schools. New York City's largest and oldest social service agency, The Children's Aid Society (CAS), formed a partnership in 1986 with the New York City Board of Education, a local school district, and participating agencies to develop community schools in disadvantaged neighborhoods.

Evaluation findings revealed that 7 years after the CAS program was established, students were displaying more positive attitudes toward school and participating more in after-school programs. Children in CAS schools were receiving much needed medical and dental care, and parents were becoming more involved in their children's schooling and reported feeling a greater sense of responsibility regarding their children's education (Dryfoos, 2000).

Academic achievement also improved, with one of the schools reporting that the percentage of students reading at grade level increased from 28% of students in grade 4 to 42% when these students reached grade 6. Likewise, math scores for the same school increased from 43% at grade level for fourth graders to 50% by the time the students were in grade 6. At another CAS in the study, the percentage of students reading at grade level increased from 39% in grade 6 to 45% by the time the students were in grade 8. Math scores in this school also increased from 49% performing at grade level in grade 6 to 52% in grade 8 (Dryfoos, 2000). Reading scores were also found to correlate positively with students' attendance at the extended-day programs.

Three major findings have emerged from the evaluations of community schools to date. First, the quality, intensity, and duration of community school programs make a substantial difference in outcomes for children and families. In programs with higher quality youth development activities, young people are more likely to report feeling better about themselves and to report fewer negative behaviors. Similarly, the duration of community school programs is related to more intensive parent involvement, with parents reporting a higher number of benefits to themselves and to their children (Melaville, Shah, & Blank, in press).

Second, participation in community schools appears to contribute to improved student attendance and increased motivation to learn as well as improved academic performance, although it is difficult to tease out the precise causal lines leading to various outcomes.

Third, it appears that community schools have the greatest impact on academic performance for those children who are in the lowest income group. It is clear that these schools are having a positive impact on the children with the greatest needs (Melaville, Shah, & Blank, in press).

Although the impact of community schools has been assessed in relation to students, families, schools, and communities, it appears that this model of schooling also affects the practice of professionals who work in or with community schools.

Research That Examines the Impact of Interprofessional Collaboration

Although there is general recognition of the need for interprofessional collaboration, its implementation is not widely described in the professional literature. Examination of the literature in several fields (psychology, education, social work, law, and health care) suggests that most of the reported collaboration has occurred between two professions (e.g., Biaggio & Bittner, 1990; Reppucci & Crosby, 1993; Staley, 1991; Thiel & Robinson, 1997; Weil, 1982) in situations where one profession (e.g., social work) functions in a setting (e.g., hospital) dominated by another profession (Abramson & Mizrahi, 1996; Allen-Meaes & Moroz, 1989; Tharinger et al., 1996). There is less reporting of three or more professions working together in a collaborative fashion (Blumberg, Deveau, & Clark, 1997; Hawaii Medical Association, 1996). Collaborations involving more than two different professionals have taken place most often in the context of school or medical settings (Illback, Cobb, & Joseph, 1997; Melaville & Blank, 1991; Payzant, 1992; Stowitschek & Smith, 1990). The limited discussion of collaborative practice in the professional literature may surprise many practitioners who see themselves as regularly consulting with colleagues in other professions, or even working on interprofessional teams. Although such practices may appear to be genuinely collaborative, a closer examination suggests that they are more aptly characterized as cooperative—a distinction that is often blurred (Lawson, this volume, chapter 3).

The empirical evidence for the effectiveness of interprofessional collaboration is somewhat limited (Corrigan, 1996). The existing data point to positive outcomes for interventions that are based on the collaborative practice of professionals from various disciplines (see Chalfant & Pysh, 1989; Dolan, 1995; Ellis, 1984; Fuchs & Fuchs, 1989; Golan & Williamson, 1994; Lawson & Briar-Lawson, 1997; Sindelar et al., 1992; Wang, Haertel, & Walberg, 1995). These findings are particularly common in school settings. This is not surprising, given that schools have been the context for a significant number of interprofessional collaboration efforts, often referred to as integrated services (Illback, 1994). Wang et al. (1995) reviewed and synthesized a number of existing evaluations of interprofessional collaborative programs. Their summary included data about collaborative school-linked services from 44 sources. Of the six programs in the integrated service category, most reported positive effects on students' achievement tests, grades, drop-out rates, and attendance. The authors acknowledged, however, that because evaluations with positive results were more likely to be published, any conclusions regarding level of effectiveness may have been inflated.

Bearing in mind the possible inflation of efficacy results, individual studies are worth reviewing. Golan and Williamson (1994) examined the involvement of teachers in school-linked service efforts in California and found that teacher involvement in these efforts resulted in increases in the following areas: contact with parents and agency professionals, sense of professional competence, and understanding of and appreciation for program services. Similarly, a series of studies examining the impact of collaboration across professions in schools (Chalfant & Pysh, 1989; Fuchs & Fuchs, 1989; Sindelar et al., 1992), found that student-support and teacher-assistance teams fostered improved student academic performance by increasing professionals' ability to understand student difficulties, to generate creative appropriate interventions, to assist teachers in mainstreaming students who were receiving "pull-out" services, and to help reduce the number of inappropriate referrals to special education.

New Directions for Research on Comprehensive Schooling and Collaboration

Since their emergence in the early 1990s, community schools have been challenged by the criticism that they lack rigorous empirical outcome data. For example, Crowson and Boyd (1993) and Smrekar (1996) have argued that there is little hard data to support comprehensive approaches to schooling. It is now clear that the next hurdle for advocates of comprehensive models of schooling is to empirically demonstrate their value to children, families, communities, and schools. Dryfoos (2002) and others acknowledge the critical role that evaluation data play in determining the sustainability of comprehensive schooling. Well designed research studies will (1) allow us to test and modify the theoretical framework for the design of full-service schools; (2) provide a means of assessing the effectiveness of individual intervention and prevention programs; (3) provide a mechanism of accountability to funders, administrators, and staff, as well as to child and family participants; (4) provide feedback to policymakers; (5) guide program modifications during implementation; and (6) inform the work of others constructing systemic interventions in other locations and contexts.

While there is broad agreement that research and evaluation of community schools is critical, it is important to recognize that the major reason that these evaluations have been limited is the relatively recent emergence of the model. Evaluations of community schools are in their early stages, and advocates for this type of schooling appear to know more than they can prove.

The complexity of both community schools and interprofessional collaboration is a strength, in practice, and an Achilles' heel in evaluation. The interventions of a community school exist at multiple levels and affect multiple systems simultaneously. Comparing schools, even when they are in the same geographic location or the same district, is extremely challenging for a number of reasons. School populations, school needs, school administrators, and school staff often vary dramatically within the same neighborhood. Even within the same geographic area, it is difficult, if not impossible, to locate a reasonably matched control school. Furthermore, even if a control school is available, it is impossible to look at changes in one level or system (e.g., school) and assume that changes in all other levels or systems remain constant. As Bryk reminds us, "If the new component works, all other things are not constant" (Annie E. Casey Foundation, 1997, p. 6).

One could argue that evaluating a community school presents researchers with the same challenges they face in evaluating any comprehensive community initiative (CCI). Both kinds of interventions attempt to join the resources of individuals, families, and community agencies and institutions to develop coordinated systems of support with expected positive outcomes for individuals, families, and communities. Like comprehensive community initiatives, the strategies used by community schools, as well as the goals they pursue, are flexible and evolving. In discussing and evaluating CCIs, Coulton (1998) points out that traditional efforts to isolate specific elements of an intervention seem a sterile and futile task when compared to examination of the intricate, dynamic, and subtle occurrences that are revealed in observations and interviews of complex community interventions. Dryfoos supports a similar conclusion by Schorr and Yankelovich (in Dryfoos, 2000, p. 3): "Evaluating complex social programs is not like testing a new drug. The interventions needed to rescue inner-city schools, strengthen families, and rebuild neighborhoods are not stable chemicals manufactured and administered in standardized doses. Promising social programs are sprawling efforts with multiple components requiring constant mid-course corrections, the active involvement of committed human beings and flexible adaptation to local circumstances."

Coordination and comprehensiveness are central to this model of schooling and, indeed, to systemic interventions generally. However, these two core characteristics present the greatest challenge to the longitudinal research methods that traditionally have been used to analyze the effects of individual, manipulated variables.

Given the complexity inherent in comprehensive schooling, it is increasingly clear that traditional methods of evaluation, particularly those involving cause and effect research models, are inadequate. In speaking of CCIs, Bryk argues that "The complex, multi-layered character of comprehensive community initiatives and the dynamic nature of relationships between people, systems, and communities make it very difficult to know the exact cause of an outcome" (Annie E. Casey Foundation, 1997, p. 21). The scientific method—the use of random assignment of the treatment with an experimental and control group—has often been utilized to resolve the complexity issue. Given that this is impossible in complex community initiatives, it appears that we are at the stage where our traditional methodological tools do not meet our current empirical needs. Schorr argues, "We simply cannot fit the square peg of conventional evaluation into the round hole of comprehensive community based efforts" (1997, p. 141).

Considering the methodological limitations involved in conducting research on these types of interventions, there are a number of requirements for any new methodology that attempts to effectively evaluate them. New research methods must take into account the effects of compounding services; must be able to analyze the nature of effects; must incorporate research designs that are flexible; must be ethically sound; and perhaps most importantly, must be grounded in a theoretical framework. We will examine each of these requirements in turn.

The Effects of Compounding Services

Perhaps one of the first steps in beginning a community school evaluation is to expand and transform the concept of evaluation, in relation to making credible, unbiased judgments about causality (Annie E. Casey Foundation, 1997). Researchers must use methodologies that can examine the effects of the compounding of services and resources with specific attention paid to finding out which combinations of interventions work for which children under what conditions. The necessity for this level of specificity is related to understanding context, since questions of how contextual factors influence service strategies, goals, and outcomes are central to evaluations of community schools. Community schools are implemented in a local context, which both shapes and is shaped by the model. Like any comprehensive initiative, community schools are vehicles for individual change as well as agents of community change. Furthermore, this change operates in two directions: community schools change people, and people change community schools. Methodology must examine not only the nature of change but also the direction of change.

The Nature of Effects

It is also critical to examine the nature of the effects (e.g., individual, organization or community) and the scale and distribution of the effects. For example, great effects on an individual may yield a small effect when averaged across a community, leading to questions such as: What are recognized standards for the cause of specific changes? What are the ingredients of a comprehensive community initiative that cause changes? According to Granger (Annie E. Casey Foundation, 1997), it is "illusory" to believe that the individual elements that cause key changes can be clearly identified; in addition, unpacking the causes of changes is less important, because comprehensive initiatives are built around the belief in "synergistic intervention … across levels of individuals [and] organizations." In fact, building "a sense of compellingness" that can be used to demonstrate credibility may be just as important as demonstrating causality (Annie E. Casey Foundation, 1997, p. 23).

Flexible Research Designs

Methods of research and evaluation of complex interventions such as community schools must also be flexible and inclusive of a variety of perspectives, and thus capable of capturing the full story. Evaluations are comprehensive when they use what Bryk referred to as "a very eclectic and flexible" set of methods and approaches that capture real effects and differences at the communal and institutional levels (Annie E. Casey Foundation, 1997, p. 10). Flexibility may also include research on process as well as on outcomes. In community school evaluations, it is as important to measure the activity as it is to measure the outcomes. The timing of the outcome measurement is an arbitrary date set by the researcher. A student may experience significant positive changes well before the time the outcome is measured. Furthermore, evaluations must also incorporate qualitative data, because it is as important to know *why* a child changed as it is to know *how much* a child has changed. This kind of data can answer questions regarding how or why an intervention produced or did not produce the expected outcome.

Ethical Considerations

Being willing to use flexible methods carries over into the ethical issues involved in this kind of research. Given the multiple sets of stakeholders involved, each with their own ethical standards, individual members need to be openminded in collectively resolving ethical dilemmas. It is important for all collaborators to recognize that data from these kinds of interventions are very difficult to collect, in part, because of the ethical issues involved. For example, it is unethical to randomly assign children to conditions that would have deleterious effects (e.g., a school with no support services). Support and consent from all stakeholders—administrative staff, community members, and parents—are needed before any research agenda proceeds, so that the privacy and confidentiality of individuals involved in the research is protected. However, collecting consent from all stakeholders adds to the evaluation timeline.

The Importance of Theory

Finally, one of the most important requirements of a community school evaluation is that it be theory-driven. While evaluations of community schools can develop new methods that address complexity and flexibility, the process and methods of such evaluations must be grounded and guided by a theoretical framework that honors the complexity and flexibility needed. Despite the growing number of evaluations of community schools and collaborative practice, many of these research projects continue to rely on program content to guide their research questions, rather than an applicable theory meant to ground the evaluation. For example, some evaluations of after-school programs have examined the positive impact of service learning activities on children's academic performance. Although these program evaluations may be able to highlight the efficacy of a particular intervention, they may not be able to explain how or when or why it worked (Weiss, 1995). Theory, practice, and research are inextricably linked, forming a feedback loop in which each component provides essential information and knowledge that strengthens the other components. Weiss (2002) eloquently explains this process: "As we answer questions, new ones open up for inquiry; as we accumulate knowledge, we begin to connect the information to deepen our understanding, and also to identify the gaps that need to be investigated in future research and evaluation" (p. 3).

Given the critical role of theory in the generation of new research related to community schools, it is important to have not only more process and outcome evaluations, but also evaluations that are theory-based and theory-driven. Knapp (1995) explains the link between theory and research and argues that in comprehensive initiatives, so much is going on that data on change or improvement tell us little about what to attribute changes to. He argues that we must construct conceptual maps linking one thing to another to protect from evaluation chaos. Knapp believes that when it comes to teasing out complex phenomena (e.g., the effects of neighborhoods on individuals), our most effective tools are not statistical, but conceptual, and this is why it is essential to ground both design and measurement in theoretical orientations. Theory-driven evaluations are more likely to provide useful information to practitioners as well as policymakers regarding the effectiveness of comprehensive school programs in various contexts and the conditions under which they were most effective.

In the area of comprehensive community evaluations, many researchers are calling for a theory of change approach toward research and evaluation (Weiss, 1995). A theory of change offers a conceptual explanation of why a particular intervention should work in situations where statistical analysis alone cannot provide the needed answers. Demonstrating statistically significant differences between children in an after-school program versus those who are home alone is insufficient to explain why differences have occurred. Although a theory of change approach is not new, it has come to be seen as a valuable asset to the researchers of community schools, because this approach specifies the input, outcomes, and intermediate changes that are predicted to occur from an intervention. Theories of change are statements of proposed linkages between the intervention and the outcome, and are themselves grounded within larger, more comprehensive theories. In short, theories of change help to describe changes that occur, but do not fully explain the mechanisms of change. For this information, we look to broader theories.

Given our belief that developmental systems theory provides a comprehensive and flexible rationale to ground the practice of comprehensive schooling and interprofessional collaboration, we also suggest the use of this theory to guide and support research that examines the efficacy of both of these practices. Therefore, we will now examine how the four principles of developmental systems theory reviewed earlier in this paper can guide and support new directions in future research on community schools, as well as enhance the use of a variety of different designs and analysis procedures. These four principles of human development assume that development occurs in contexts and in multiple domains across the life span, and involves both risks and resilience.

Any significant human change occurs within a context, and therefore, research that examines the impact of practice must also take into consideration the environmental factors that contribute to both individual and systemic change. In the case of a community school, the intervention is schoolwide and aims to transform the school context. Because of the potentially varied impact this kind of systemwide intervention can have on the community and its individual members, there are a number of challenges to this line of inquiry that need to be acknowledged and addressed.

Research and evaluation of community school initiatives need to address individual and contextual variables. Since each school has its own unique culture, identity, demographic variables of students and staff, and neighborhood characteristics, it would be difficult to obtain meaningful results using comparisons of different schools in different communities. For some purposes, designing studies that can yield information about how an individual changes within a given context over time may be a more productive avenue for researchers interested in evaluating these schools. Instead of pretest-posttest studies comparing individuals across contexts, studies can be designed so that both individuals and schools serve as their own controls. In this way, research can highlight changes in either individuals or contexts while appreciating the mutual relationship of individuals and their contexts.

However, examining the effects of context is ultimately a complicated endeavor. The significance of contextual factors in determining the outcomes of community schools quickly leads to a recognition that simplistic statistical methods do not suffice. Sophisticated statistical models are required to adequately assess the interplay between the individual and various contextual factors and various levels of influence (e.g., individual, school, and community). Procedures such as Hierarchical Linear Modeling (HLM) are better able to capture the complexity of this type of intervention. Given that community school data are collected from individuals, who are nested within schools, which are nested within various levels of communities (e.g., neighborhood, city, state), information regarding individual outcomes without recognition of the wide range of contexts that affect the individual would not be particularly helpful. Procedures like HLM allow the researcher to examine each level in the data structure (e.g., individual, school, community, city, state); the results of this kind of analysis provide information about student-level variables and school-level factors, etc. (Raudenbush, Bryk, Cheong, & Congdon, 2000).

Multiple Domains

Given the multiple goals of community schools and interprofessional collaboration, research assessing the impact of this practice should also examine change at various levels (e.g., bio-psycho-social). Within these various domains (health, social, psychological, cognitive), there are a number of important factors that can be examined. For example, within the area of health and academic success, research could explore the impact of nutrition, mental health, dental health, pre- and post-natal health, and health education on academic success. Evaluations that are broad-based and include both academic and nonacademic variables will provide a more balanced and accurate picture of outcomes.

Examining multiple outcomes represents another challenge for researchers. For children, research must explore the academic and nonacademic variables that contribute to healthy developmental pathways. For families, outcome measures include well being, particularly stability and nurturance. Beyond individual and family outcomes, research must also focus on community impact, in order to demonstrate that communities have developed the ability to provide supports and resources that families need to successfully raise their children. Finally, researchers must also measure the changes in public policy and practices that result from community schools.

From a methodological point of view, it becomes clear that simple one-way interactions between variables will not yield a comprehensive picture of what happens in a community school. Statistical methods such as canonical analysis and path analysis are extremely useful in developing a fuller and clearer picture of the pattern of relationships among variables. With the use of canonical analysis, we are able to uncover the linear combinations of independent variables and the linear combinations of dependent variables so that the correlations between both kinds of variables are maximized (Lomax, 1992). For example, within a community school model, one might be interested in finding out what pattern of academic variables (e.g., cognitive ability, school grades, homework, teacher report) tends to be related to what pattern of health variables (e.g., mental health, self-esteem, physical health).

Across the Life Span

Community schools address a wide range of outcomes from a life span perspective and therefore focus on both immediate and long-term outcomes as they seek to educate healthy and productive future citizens. These schools address the needs of children and families at different developmental stages. A life span orientation also emphasizes the need for evaluations to include student measures and student expected outcomes that are developmentally appropriate.

In evaluation efforts, short-term and long-term outcome goals need to be specified, and the link between intermediate and long-term goals clearly delineated. Therefore, rather than relying too heavily on research designs that are cross-sectional, researchers should use longitudinal analyses that can track an individual or a school over time. This principle also encourages the researcher to measure change at many different points rather than at one end point, since change can occur throughout the process and is not limited to a once in a lifetime moment captured at an arbitrary evaluation date. A life span perspective also expands the research agenda to include the effects of comprehensive schooling and interprofessional collaboration on adults, community members, teachers, administrators, and others.

Risk and Resilience

A developmental systems approach to research would require a balanced view that includes an individual's areas of risk and resilience. Assessment of the efficacy of comprehensive schooling would examine how this model of schooling helped to reduce risk behavior and promote resilient behavior. Many evaluations tend to focus on either risk behavior (increased rates of school violence) or resilient behavior (rise in test scores), rather than on both. Such evaluations can provide only part of the outcome picture. The importance of recognizing, addressing, and assessing risk and resiliency factors also applies to communities. Communities offer substantial assets that promote resilience and reduce risk.

In brief, research on the impact of community schools requires the researcher to deal with the complexity of these interventions, necessitating new understandings of causality in research as well as utilization of recent methodological advances and statistical techniques. Employing these newer methodological approaches within the theoretical framework of developmental systems theory will serve to provide a conceptual rationale for understanding and explaining the empirical findings.

Conclusion

The greatest challenge facing educators today is closing the achievement gap. Over the last two decades, educational reform efforts have addressed this challenge with a laser-like focus on academic achievement.

It is now becoming increasingly clear to parents, educators, health and human service professionals, and policymakers that families, neighborhoods, and communities play key roles in students' educational success. Students need a range of supports—academic, physical and socio-emotional—in order to become educated and productive adults. Improving academic outcomes will require not only high-quality instructional practices, but also a qualitative and quantitative increase in the services and resources that support healthy development in students. Joining that the traditional boundaries between schools and community agencies and institutions give way to new models of partnership. Community or full-service schools represent one developing and expanding form of school-community partnership, in which universities have played a key role.

Improving academic outcomes will also require that diverse professionals who until now have worked in relative isolation design new models of service delivery in which interprofessional collaboration becomes the norm. Professionals within the school and community-based professionals can work together to create a system in which each profession collaborates with others to provide coordinated and comprehensive services to students and families. Community schools have provided one setting in which interprofessional collaboration not only is essential to the operation of the school, but also seems to flourish.

In order to be sustained, these newly emerging practices must be grounded in a theoretical framework that contributes to a comprehensive understanding of how various prevention and intervention strategies lead to healthy development and academic achievement. Developmental systems theory provides one such framework, insofar as it accounts for the interaction between development and context, for the multiple domains of development, for the continuation of development over the life span, and for the role of both risk and resilience in development.

Furthermore, the effectiveness of these new models of practice must be examined empirically through rigorous research and evaluation. The task of evaluating large-scale efforts such as the community school is challenging. Researchers are encouraged to explore new methods and analytic procedures that more aptly capture the complexity of these schools. Given the multiple stakeholders involved, evaluations need to be sensitive to all of the ethical issues involved in investigating these complex community interventions. Finally, evaluations that are theory-based and theory-driven will provide more useful information for practitioners as well as future researchers.

References

Abramson, J., & Mizrahi, T. (1996). When social workers and physicians collaborate: Positive and negative interdisciplinary experiences. *Social Work, 41*(3), 270-281.

Airasian, P.W., & Walsh, M.E. (1997). Constructivist cautions. *Phi Delta Kappan, 78*(6), 444-449.

Allen-Meares, P., & Moro, K.J. (1989). Interfacing the professions of social work and education. *Arete, 14,* 22-31.

American Academy of Pediatrics. (1994). Integrated health services. American Academy of Pediatrics Task Force on integrated school services. *Pediatrics, 94,* 400-402.

American Association for Counseling and Development, American School Counselor Association, National Association of School Psychologists, & National Association of Social Workers. (1990). *Pupil services essential to education: A position statement.* (Available from the National Association of Social Workers, 750 First Street, NE Suite 700, Washington, DC 20002-4241.)

American Bar Association. (1993). *America's children at risk: A national agenda for legal action.* Chicago: Author.

American Psychological Association. (1997). *Final report of the American Psychological Association working group on the implications of changes in the health care delivery system for the education, training and continuing professional education of psychologists: Discussion of knowledge and skills and selected readings.* Washington, DC: Author.

Annie E. Casey Foundation. (1997). *Evaluating comprehensive community change: Report of the Annie E. Casey Foundation's March 1997 Research and Evaluation Conference.* Baltimore: Author. Retrieved October 25, 2002 from www.aecf.org/publications/evaluation/

Annie E. Casey Foundation. (1999). *Kids count data book.* New York: Carnegie Foundation.

Annie E. Casey Foundation. (2000). *Kids count data book.* New York: Carnegie Foundation.

Arbona, C. (2000). The development of academic achievement in school aged children: Precursors to career development. In S.D. Brown and R.W. Lent (Eds.), *Handbook of counseling psychology* (3rd ed., pp. 270-309). New York: John Wiley & Sons, Inc.

Barton, P.E. (2001). *Facing the hard facts in education reform: A policy information perspective.* Princeton, NJ: Educational Testing Service.

Beaton, A.E., & O'Dwyer, L.M. (2002, April). *Separating school, classroom and student variances and their relationship to socio-economic status.* Paper presented at the American Association of Educational Researchers, New Orleans, LA.

Benson, L., & Harkavy, I. (2003). The role of the American research university in advancing system-wide education reform, democratic schooling, and democracy. In this volume—M.M. Brabeck, M.E. Walsh, & R. Latta (Eds.), *Meeting at the hyphen: Schools-universities-communities-professions in collaboration for student achievement and well being. The 102nd yearbook of the National Society for the Study of Education,* Part II (pp. 94-116). *Chicago, National Society for the Study of Education.*

Berliner, D.C. (1993). International comparisons of student achievement. *National Forum: Phi Kappa Phi Journal, 73*(4), 25-29.

Biaggio, M.K., & Bittner, E. (1990). Psychology and optometry: Interaction and collaboration. *American Psychologist, 45,* 1313-1315.

Bibace, R. (1999). Partnerships: What's in a name? In R. Bibace, J. Dillon, & B.N. Dowds (Eds.), *Partnerships in research, clinical, and educational settings* (pp. 307-312). Norwood, NJ: Ablex Publishing Corporation.

Blumberg, P., Deveau, E.J., & Clark, P.G. (1997). Describing the structure and content of interdisciplinary collaboration in an educational center on aging and health. *Educational Gerontology, 23*(7), 609-629.

Brabeck, M., Walsh, M.E., Kenny, M., & Comilang, K. (1997). Interprofessional collaboration for children and families: Opportunities for counseling psychology in the 21st century. *The Counseling Psychologist, 25,* 615-636.

Brandon, R.N., & Knapp, M.S. (1999). Interprofessional education and training: Transforming professional training to transform human services. *American Behavioral Scientist, 42*(5), 876-891.

Bronfenbrenner, U. (1979). *The ecology of human development.* Cambridge, MA: Harvard University Press.

Casserly, M. (2002). *Beating the odds II: A city-by-city analysis of student performance and achievement gaps on state assessments.* Washington, DC: Council of the Great City Schools.

Casto, R.M., & Julia, M.C. (Eds.). (1994). *Interprofessional care and collaborative practice.* Belmont, CA: Brooks/Cole.

Centers for Disease Control and Prevention. (2002). Surveillance summaries. *Morbidity and Mortality Weekly Report* 2002:51 (No. SS-4).

Chalfant, J.C., & Pysh, M.V. (1989). Teacher assistance teams: Five descriptive studies on 96 teams. *Remedial and Special Education, 10*(6), 49-58.

Cochran-Smith, M. (2001). Higher standards for prospective teachers: What's missing from the discourse? *Journal of Teacher Education, 52*(3), 179-81.

Coleman, J., Campbell, E.Q., Hobson, C.J., McPartland, J., Mood, A.M., Weinfeld, F.D., & York, R.L. (1966). *Equality of educational opportunity.* Washington, DC: National Center for Education Statistics, 746.

Coley, R.J. (2002). An uneven start: Indicators of inequality in school readiness. Princeton, NJ: Educational Testing Service.

Comer, J.P., & Haynes, N.M. (1991). Parent involvement in schools: An ecological approach. *Elementary School Journal, 91*(3), 271-77.

Comer, J.P., & Woodruff, D.W. (1998). Mental health in schools. *Child & Adolescent Psychiatric Clinics of North America, 7*(3), 499-513.

Conger, R.D., Conger, K.J., & Elder, G. (1997). Family economic hardship and adolescent academic performance: Mediating and moderating processes. In G. Duncan & J. Brooks-Gunn (Eds.), *Consequences of growing up poor* (pp. 228-310). New York: Russell Sage Foundation.

Connell, D.B., Turner, R.R., & Mason, E.F. (1985). Summary of findings of the school health education evaluation: Health promotion effectiveness, implementation, and cost. *Journal of School Health, 55*(8), 316-321.

Corrigan, D. (1996). Teacher education and interprofessional collaboration: Creation of family-centered, community-based integrated service systems. In L. Kaplan & R.A. Edelfelt (Eds.), *Teachers for the new millennium: Aligning teacher development, national goals, and high standards for all students* (pp. 142-171). Thousand Oaks, CA: Corwin.

Coulton, C.J. (1998). *Restoring communities within the context of the metropolis: Neighborhood revitalization at the millennium.* (ERIC Document Reproduction Service No. ED 439 207.)

Crowson, R. (2003). Empowerment models for interprofessional collaboration. In this volume—M.M. Brabeck, M.E. Walsh, & R. Latta (Eds.), *Meeting at the hyphen: Schools-universities-communities-professions in collaboration for student achievement and well being. The 102nd yearbook of the National Society for the Study of Education,* Part II (pp. 74-93). Chicago: National Society for the Study of Education.

Crowson, R.L., & Boyd, W.L. (1993). Coordinated services for children: Designing arks for storms and seas unknown. *American Journal of Education, 101,* 140-179.

Darling-Hammond, L. (2000). Teacher quality and student achievement: A review of state policy evidence. *Education Policy Analysis Archives, 8*(1), 4-41.

Dolan, L.J. (1995). An evaluation of family support and integrated services in six elementary schools. In L.C. Rigsby, M.C. Reynolds, & M.C. Wang (Eds.), *School-community connections: Exploring issues for research and practice* (pp. 395-420). San Francisco: Jossey-Bass.

Dryfoos, J.G. (1990). *Adolescents at risk: Prevalence and prevention.* New York: Oxford University Press.

40   COMPREHENSIVE SCHOOLING

Dryfoos, J.G. (1994). *Full service schools: A revolution in health and social services for children, youth, and families.* The Jossey-Bass health series, The Jossey-Bass social and behavioral science series and The Jossey-Bass education series. San Francisco: Jossey-Bass.

Dryfoos, J.G. (2000). *Evaluation of community schools: Findings to date.* Retrieved July 8, 2002 from http://www.communityschools.org/evaluation/eval2.html

Dryfoos, J.G. (2003). Community schools. In this volume—M.M. Brabeck, M.E. Walsh, & R. Latta (Eds.), *Meeting at the hyphen: Schools-universities-communities-professions in collaboration for student achievement and well being. The 102nd yearbook of the National Society for the Study of Education,* Part II (pp. 140-163). Chicago: National Society for the Study of Education.

Dunn, R., & Harris, L.G. (1998). Organizational dimensions of climate and the impact on school achievement. *Journal of Instructional Psychology, 25*(2), 100-114.

Eccles, J.S., & Harold, R.D. (1993). Parent-school involvement during the early adolescent years. *Teachers College Record, 94*(3), 568-587.

Eckenrode, J., Laird, M., & Doris, J. (1993). School performance and disciplinary problems among abused and neglected children. *Developmental Psychology, 29,* 55-62.

Ellis, N.B. (1984). Sustaining frail disabled elderly in the community: An innovative approach to in-home services. *Journal of Gerontological Social Work, 7*(4), 3-15.

Epstein, J. (1992). School and family partnerships. In M.C. Alkin, M. Linden, J. Noel, & K. Ray (Eds.), *Encyclopedia of educational research,* 6th ed., 1139-1151. New York: McMillan.

Epstein, J. (2001). *School, family, and community partnerships: Preparing educators and improving schools.* Boulder, CO: Westview Press.

Esposito, C. (1999). Learning in urban blight: School climate and its effect on the school performance of urban, minority, low-income children. *School Psychology Review, 28*(3), 365-377.

Fact Sheet on School-Age Children's Out-of-School Time. (2001). National Institute for Out-of-School Time. Retrieved September 30, 2002 from www.niost.org

Fehrmann, P.G., & Reimers, T.M. (1987). Home influences on school learning: Direct and indirect effects of parental involvement on high school grades. *Journal of Educational Research, 80,* 330-337.

Fuchs, D., & Fuchs, L.S. (1989). Exploring effective and efficient pre-referral interventions: A component analysis of behavioral consultation. *School Psychology Review, 18,* 260-283.

Furstenberg, F.F., Cook, T.D., Eccles, J., Elder, G.H., & Sameroff, A. (1999). *Managing to make it: Urban families and adolescent success.* Chicago: University of Chicago Press.

Gergen, K. (1985). The social constructionist movement in modern psychology. *American Psychologist, 20,* 266-275.

Golan, S., & Williamson, C. (1994, April). *Teachers make school-linked services work.* Paper presented at the annual meeting of the American Educational Research Association, New Orleans, LA.

Haney, W. (2000). The myth of the Texas miracle in education. *Education Policy Analysis Archives, 8*(41). Retrieved February 6, 2002 from http://epaa.asu.edu/epaa/v8n41/

Hart, B., & Risley, T. (1995). *Meaningful differences in the everyday experiences of young American children.* Baltimore: Brookes.

Haveman, R., & Wolfe, B. (1995). The determinants of children's attainments: A review of methods and findings. *Journal of Economic Literature, 33,* 1829-1878.

Hawaii Medical Association. (1996). *Building bridges. Lessons learned in family-centered inter-professional collaboration: Year II.* Washington, DC: Health Resources and Services Administration, Maternal and Child Health Bureau.

Haynes, N. (Ed.). (1994). *Selected excerpts from School Development Program Research Monograph.* New Haven, CT: Yale Child Study Center School Development Program.

Hernandez, D. (Ed.). (1999). *Children of immigrants: Health, adjustment, and public assistance.* Washington, DC: National Academy Press.

Hill, M.S., & Duncan, G. (1987). Parental family income and the socioeconomic attainment of children. *Social Science Research, 16,* 39-73.

Hord, S.M. (1986, February). A synthesis of research on organizational collaboration. *Educational Leadership, 43,* 22-26.

Illback, R.J. (1994). Poverty and the crisis in children's services: The need for services integration. *Journal of Clinical Child Psychology, 23,* 413-424.

Illback, R.J., Cobb, C.T., & Joseph, H.M., Jr. (Eds.). (1997). *Integrated services for children and families: Opportunities for psychological practice.* Washington, DC: American Psychological Association.

Institute of Medicine. (2002). Health insurance is a family matter. Retrieved October 4, 2002 from www.nap.edu/books/0309085187/html/

Knapp, M.S. (1995). How shall we study comprehensive, collaborative services for children and families? *Educational Researcher, 24*(4), 5-16.

Koretz, D.M., & Barron, S.I. (1998). *The validity of gains in scores on the Kentucky Instructional Results Information System (KIRIS).* Santa Monica, CA: RAND.

Lawson, H.A. (2003). Pursuing and securing collaboration to improve results. In this volume—M.M. Brabeck, M.E. Walsh, & R. Latta (Eds.), *Meeting at the hyphen: Schools-universities-communities-professions in collaboration for student achievement and well being. The 102nd yearbook of the National Society for the Study of Education,* Part II (pp. 45-73). Chicago: National Society for the Study of Education.

Lawson, H.A., & Briar-Lawson, K. (1997). *Connecting the dots: Progress toward the integration of school reform, school-linked services, parent involvement and community schools.* Oxford, OH: Danforth Foundation & Institute for Educational Renewal.

Lerner, R.M. (1978). Nature, nurture, and dynamic interactionism. *Human Development, 21,* 1-20.

Lerner, R.M. (1984). *On the nature of human plasticity.* New York: Cambridge University Press.

Lerner, R.M. (1986). *Concepts and theories of human development* (2nd ed.). New York: Random House.

Lerner, R.M. (1995). *America's youth in crisis: Challenges and options for programs and policies.* Thousand Oaks, CA: Sage.

Lerner, R.M., & Simon, L.A.K. (Eds.). (1998). *University-community collaborations for the twenty-first century: Outreach scholarship for youth and families.* New York: Garland.

Lerner, R.M., Walsh, M.E., & Howard, K.A. (1998). Developmental-contextual considerations: Person-context relations as the bases for risk and resiliency in child and adolescent development. In T. Ollendick (Ed.), *Comprehensive child psychology: Vol. 5. Children and adolescents: Clinical formulation and treatment* (pp. 1-24). New York: Elsevier.

Lomax, R.G. (1992). *Statistical concepts. A second course for education and behavioral sciences.* White Plains, NY: Longman Publishing Group.

Maeroff, G.I. (1998). *Altered destinies: Making life better for schoolchildren in need.* New York: St. Martin's.

Marcon, R.A. (1999). Positive relationships between parent-school involvement and public school inner-city preschoolers' development and academic performance. *School Psychology Review, 28*(3), 395-412.

Martin, M.O., Mullis, I.V.S., Gonzalez, E.J., O'Connor, K.M., Chrostowski, S.J., Gregory, K.D., Smith, T.A., & Garden, R.A. (2001). *Science benchmarking report TIMSS 1999—Eighth grade: Achievement for U.S. states and districts in an international context.* Chestnut Hill, MA: International Study Center, Lynch School of Education, Boston College.

Masten, A.S., Best, K.M., & Garmezy, N. (1991). Resilience and development: Contributions from the study of children who overcome adversity. *Development and Psychopathology, 2,* 425-444.

Masten, A.S., & Coatsworth, J.D. (1998). The development of competence in favorable and unfavorable environments: Lessons from research on successful children. *American Psychologist, 53*(2), 205-220.

Masten, A.S., Garmezy, N., Tellegen, A., Pellegrini, D.S., Larkin, K., & Larsen, A. (1988). Competence and stress in school children: The moderating effects of individual and family qualities. *Journal of Child Psychology and Psychiatry, 29,* 745-764.

McCroskey, J., & Einbinder, S.D. (Eds.). (1998). *Universities and communities: Remaking professional and interprofessional education for the next century.* Westport, CT: Praeger.

McLaughlin, M.W. (2000). *Community counts: How youth organizations matter for youth development.* Washington, DC: Public Education Network.

McLaughlin, M.W. (2001). Community counts. *Educational Leadership, 58*(7), 14-18.

McLloyd, V.C. (1998). Socioeconomic disadvantage and child development. *American Psychologist, 53*(2), 185-204.

Melaville, A.I., & Blank, M.J. (1991). *What it takes: Structuring interagency partnerships to connect children and families with comprehensive services.* Washington, DC: Education and Human Services Consortium.

Melaville, A.I., Shah, B., & Blank, M.J. (in press). Making the difference: Research and practice in community schools. Washington, DC: Coalition for Community Schools, Institute for Educational Leadership.

Murray, J., & Weissbourd, R. (2003). Focusing on core academic outcomes: A key to successful school-community partnerships. In this volume—M.M. Brabeck, M.E. Walsh, & R. Latta (Eds.), *Meeting at the hyphen: Schools-universities-communities-professions in collaboration for student achievement and well being. The 102nd yearbook of the National Society for the Study of Education,* Part II (pp. 179-200). Chicago: National Society for the Study of Education.

Nansel, T.T., Overpeck, M., Pilla, R.S., Ruam, W.J., Simons-Morton, B., & Scheidt, P. (2001). Bullying behaviors among U.S. youth: Prevalence and association within psychosocial adjustment. *Journal of the American Medical Association, 285*(16), 2094-2100.

National Association of School Nurses. (1995). *Integrated service delivery* (Issue brief). Scarborough, ME: Author.

National Center for Educational Statistics. (2002). Indicators of school crime and safety, 2001: Victimization of students at school and away from school. Retrieved September 30, 2002 from http://nces.ed.gov/pubs2002/crime2001/2.asp?nav=1

Overton, W.F. (1998). Developmental psychology: Philosophy, concepts, and methodology. In W. Damon (Series Ed.) & R.M. Lerner (Vol. Ed.), *Handbook of child psychology: Vol. 1. Theoretical models of human development* (5th ed., pp. 107-188). New York: Wiley.

Patterson, C.J., Kupersmidt, J.B., & Vaden, N.A. (1990). Income level, gender, ethnicity, and household composition as predictors of children's school-based competence. *Child Development. Special Issue: Minority children, 6*(2), 485-494.

Payzant, T.M. (1992). New beginnings in San Diego: Developing a strategy for interagency collaboration. *Phi Delta Kappan, 74,* 139-146.

Petrie, H.G. (1992). Interdisciplinary education: Are we faced with insurmountable opportunities? *Review of Research in Education, 18,* 299-333.

Prawat, R.S. (1992). Teachers' beliefs about teaching and learning: A constructivist perspective. *American Journal of Education, 100,* 354-395.

Quinn, J. (2003). An interprofessional model and reflections on best collaborative practice. In this volume—M.M. Brabeck, M.E. Walsh, & R. Latta (Eds.), *Meeting at the hyphen: Schools-universities-communities-professions in collaboration for student achievement and well being. The 102nd yearbook of the National Society for the Study of Education,* Part II (pp. 164-178). Chicago: National Society for the Study of Education.

Raudenbush, S., Bryk, A., Cheong, Y., & Congdon, R. (2000). *HLM5: Hierarchical linear and nonlinear modeling.* Chicago: Scientific Software International, Inc.

Reppucci, N.D., & Crosby, C.A. (1993). Law, psychology and children: Overarching issues. *Law and Human Behavior, 17,* 1-10.

Riley, R. (1998, January 8). *School/community/university partnerships.* Conference on Connecting Community Building and Education Reform: Effective School, Community, University Partnerships. Joint forum of the U.S. Department of Education and the U.S. Department of Housing and Urban Development, Washington, DC.

Roth, J., & Brooks-Gunn, J. (2000). What do adolescents need for healthy development? Implications for youth policy. *Social Policy Report, 14*(1), 3-19.

Sailor, W., & Skrtic, T.W. (1996). School/community partnerships and educational reform: Introduction to the topical issue. *Remedial and Special Education, 17*(5), 267-270, 283.

Schmitz, C.L., Wagner, J.D., & Menke, E.M. (1995). Homelessness as one component of housing instability and its impact on the development of children in poverty. *Journal of Social Distress and the Homeless, 4*(4), 301-317.

Schools of the 21st Century. (2001). *How do we know that 21C works?* New Haven, CT: Yale University.

Schorr, L.B. (1988). *Within our reach: Breaking the cycle of disadvantage.* New York: Doubleday.

Schorr, L.B. (1997). *Common purpose: Strengthening families and neighborhoods to rebuild America.* New York: Anchor.

Shouse, R.C. (1998). Restructuring's impact on student achievement: Contrasts by school urbanicity. *Educational Administrative Quarterly, 34*(Supplemental), 677-699.

Singh, K., Granville, M., & Dika, S. (2002). Mathematics and science achievement: Effects of motivation, interest, and academic engagement. *Journal of Educational Research, 95*(6), 323-332.

Sindelar, P.T., Griffin, C.C., Smith, S.W., & Watanabe, A.K. (1992). Pre-referral intervention: Encouraging notes on preliminary findings. *The Elementary School Journal, 92,* 245-259.

Skinner, E.A., Wellborn, J.G., & Connell, J.P. (1990). What it takes to do well in school and whether I've got it: A process model of perceived control and children's engagement and achievement in school. *Journal of Educational Psychology, 82*(1), 22-32.

Smith, A.J., & Hutchinson, B. (1992). *An analysis of human service practitioner competencies necessary for effective interprofessional collaboration.* Seattle, WA: University of Washington, Human Services Policy Center.

Smrekar, C. (1996). The influence of the family services coordinator on family-school interactions in school-linked social service programs. *Elementary School Journal, 96*(4), 453-467.

Staley, J.C. (1991). Physicians and the difficult patient. *Social Work, 36,* 74-79.

Stallings, J.A. (1995). Ensuring teaching and learning in the 21st century. *Educational Researcher, 24*(6), 4-8.

Steffe, L.P., & Gale, J. (Eds.). (1995). *Constructivism in education.* Hillsdale, NJ: Erlbaum.

Stevenson, M., & Engstrom, D. (November, 1999). Evaluation of the Comer-Zigler (CoZi) Initiative 1996-1999, final report submitted to the Carnegie Corporation.

Stowitschek, J.J., & Smith, A.J. (1990). *Implementing the C-STARS interprofessional case management model for at-risk children.* Washington, DC: Department of Education. (ERIC Document Reproduction Service No. ED 333 307).

Tharinger, D.J., Bricklin, P.M., Johnson, N.F., Paster, V.S., Lambert, N.M., Feshbach, N., Oakland, T.D., & Sanchez, W. (1996). Education reform: Challenges for psychology and psychologists. *Professional Psychology: Research and Practice, 27,* 24-33.

Thiel, M.M., & Robinson, M.R. (1997). Physicians' collaboration with chaplains: Difficulties and benefits. *Journal of Clinical Ethics, 8,* 94-103.

U.S. Public Health Service. (2000). *Report of the Surgeon General's conference on children's mental health: A national action agenda.* Washington, DC: Department of Health and Human Services.

Walsh, M.E., & Anderson, D.G. (in press). University-school-community partnerships. In R. Bibace, J. Dillon, and B.N. Dowds (Eds.), *Partnerships in research, clinical, and educational settings*. Mahwah, NJ: Lawrence Erlbaum.

Walsh, M.E., Brabeck, M.M., & Howard, K.A. (1999). Interprofessional collaboration in children's services: Toward a theoretical framework. *Children's Services: Social Policy, Research & Practice, 2*(4), 183-208.

Walsh, M.E., & Murphy, J. (in press). *Children, health, and learning*. Westport, CT: Greenwood.

Wang, M.C., Haertel, G.D., & Walberg, H.J. (1995). The effectiveness of collaborative school-linked services. In L.C. Rigsby, M.C. Reynolds, and M.C. Wang (Eds.), *School-community connections: Exploring issues for research and practice* (pp. 283-309). San Francisco: Jossey-Bass.

Wang, M.C., Haertel, G.D., & Walberg, H.J. (1997). Fostering educational resilience in inner-city schools. In H.J. Walberg, O. Reyes, & R.P. Weissberg (Eds.), *Children and youth: Interdisciplinary perspectives*. Thousand Oaks, CA: Sage.

Warner, B.S., & Weist, M.D. (1996). Urban youth as witnesses to violence: Beginning assessment and treatment efforts. *Journal of Youth and Adolescence, 25*, 361-377.

Weil, M. (1982). Research on issues in collaboration between social workers and lawyers. *Social Service Review, 56*, 393-405.

Weiss, C.H. (1995). Nothing as practical as good theory: Exploring theory-based evaluation for comprehensive community initiatives for children and families. In J.P. Connell, A.C. Kubisch, L.B. Schorr, & C. Weiss (Eds.), *New approaches to evaluating community initiatives: Concepts, methods, and contexts* (pp. 65-92). Washington, DC: The Aspen Institute.

Weiss, H. (2002). Beyond basic training: Advice from the experts on nurturing strong full service schools. *The Evaluation Exchange, 8*(2), 1-4.

Werner, E.E. (1989). Children of the garden island. *Scientific American, 206*, 106-111.

Werner, E.E. (1990). Protective factors and individual resilience. In S.J. Meisels & M. Shonkoff (Eds.), *Handbook of early intervention* (pp. 97-116). New York: Cambridge University Press.

Werner, H. (1948). *Comparative psychology of mental development*. New York: Science Editions, Inc.

Werner, H., & Kaplan, B. (1956). *Symbol formation: An organismic-developmental approach to language and the expression of thought*. New York: Wiley & Sons.

Whitaker, K.S., & King, R.A. (1994). Moving from cooperation to collaboration for improved service delivery for children. In R.A. Levin (Ed.), *Greater than the sum: Professionals in a comprehensive services model* (pp. 1-18). Washington, DC: ERIC Clearinghouse on Teacher Education.

White, K. (1982). The relation between socioeconomic status and academic achievement. *Psychological Bulletin, 91*, 461-481.

Wood, D.J., & Gray, B. (1991). Toward a comprehensive theory of collaboration. *Journal of Applied Behavioral Science, 27*, 139-162.

Yale University Bush Center in Child Development and Social Policy. The school of the 21st century. Retrieved February 17, 2002 from http://www.yale.edu/bushcenter/21C/about/about.html

CHAPTER 3

Pursuing and Securing Collaboration to Improve Results

HAL A. LAWSON

Collaboration is a unique strategy with enormous potential for schools, community agencies, and school-agency relationships. Unfortunately, collaboration's full potential remains untapped because its unique features, requirements, benefits, and contingencies have not been described precisely and coherently. This chapter addresses this need and provides a conceptual framework for collaboration. The framework is pragmatic; its aim is to improve practice, policy, and research. For example, readers can use this framework to develop planning inventories and evaluation checklists.

Although collaboration yields important benefits, it is not a panacea for schools and community agencies. Collaboration is difficult to secure and maintain, and exacts what economists call "transaction costs." For example, collaboration takes a long time to develop, and it consumes precious resources. Because it involves many people, professions, and organizations, collaboration is not always the most efficient way for professionals to work and interact. Furthermore, when key people leave a school or an agency, the collaboration may stall or even unravel, and then relationships need to be rebuilt. In other words, collaboration is not a once and for all achievement. It must be stewarded, supported, and rewarded, which involves additional transaction costs.

So, why pursue collaboration? This chapter's title provides the simple answer, and the ensuing analysis offers some details. When the conditions and problems for which collaboration is tailor-made are evident, it is a practical necessity. More specifically, in some school communities, collaboration is an example of competent practice. Basic competence related to collaboration entails doing the correct things, at the proper times, in the appropriate places, and for justifiable reasons, and achieving the desired results.

Hal A. Lawson is Professor of Educational Administration and Policy Studies and Professor of Social Welfare and Special Assistant to the Provost and Vice President for Academic Affairs at The State University of New York at Albany.

In school communities challenged by poverty, social exclusion and isolation, inequality, and other correlates, collaboration may provide the *only* way to improve results. Absent collaboration, neither schools nor community agencies achieve the results for which they are responsible and accountable. Here, collaboration is an optimal practice. The failure to collaborate may be indicative of malpractice and negligence. Children are left behind, and professional educators, service providers, parents, and community leaders ultimately shoulder some of the consequences.

In this chapter, I first identify collaboration's "sister strategies" (e.g., cooperation, coordination). These other "c-words" comprise a developmental progression for collaboration and help define it. Then I present examples of the needs, problems, and conditions that invite and require collaboration. Next I identify different kinds of collaboration, revealing choices and suggesting combinations. Then I present examples of collaboration's essential features and requirements. I conclude with questions about the institutional aims of collaboration and school-linked services. Is the aim to fortify and maintain existing institutions? Or is the aim to transform them and create new ones? I sketch responses to both questions, and I include higher education's roles.

A Developmental Progression for Collaboration

To reiterate, collaboration entails a never-ending developmental process. Sometimes this process is linear, involving sequential steps that may be prescribed and mandated. However, collaboration often is difficult to prescribe and control. In many school communities, it evolves over time through daily interactions. In these cases, collaboration develops in nonlinear, interactive phases. Here, parents, educators, service providers, and community leaders "learn their way through" these successive phases and the attendant challenges.

Other "c-words" identify key processes that serve as defining steps or phases in the development of collaboration. These c-words are connecting and communicating, cooperating, coordinating, community building, and contracting. Together, these c-words serve as trail markers on the journey toward collaboration.[1] All involve expanding the boundaries of school improvement.

- *Connecting and communicating* activities may be voluntary or involuntary and involve interpersonal, interprofessional, and interorganizational bridge-building among educators, schools, families, and future community partners. This primary step (or phase) provides the foundation for collaboration. Connecting and communicating begin the process of developing a shared language and attendant requirements such as standardized forms.

- *Cooperation* is a voluntary activity that builds on new connections and communication mechanisms. Norms of reciprocity and mutually beneficial exchanges reflect and promote cooperation. As participants begin to work together, trust develops and communication improves.

- *Coordination* builds on cooperation, and includes deliberate efforts aimed at harmonizing and synchronizing the missions and efforts of specialized people and organizations. Shared goals begin to emerge as partners realize that they depend on each other.

- *Community building* proceeds beyond the technical aspects of coordination. It involves consensus building, developing awareness of reciprocity and mutual need, and developing the capacity for collective action. Community-building activities in and around schools are vital to family support initiatives (e.g., Delgado-Gaitan, 2002) and comprehensive community development initiatives (Crowson, this volume, chapter 4).

- *Contracting* involves both legal and social agreements. Examples of legal contracts include interagency agreements and university-school community partnership agreements, which outline the specific responsibilities and accountabilities of each school, agency, and community. At the same time, social contracts develop. Social contracts are unwritten understandings and agreements that develop and are maintained as parties participating in the collaboration develop social trust. Together these legal contracts and social contracts bond and bind participants.

Collaboration encompasses all of these c-words. However, collaboration is something more than the sum of these other c-words. It will not evolve automatically from the developmental progression they comprise.

Conditions Inviting Collaboration

Genuine collaboration is both a process and a product (Corrigan, 2000). Effective, sustainable collaboration usually results from special designs (or "interventions"). These designs include implementation, learning, and evaluation supports; incentives and rewards; organizational infrastructures; and other features detailed later in this chapter. These special designs are linked to the following claim: Collaboration works best when special conditions and circumstances are evident.

Examples of Unique Conditions and Circumstances

Interdependence, complexity, and the powerful combination of *novelty* and *uncertainty* are the three most important conditions that lead to collaboration. Each is explored briefly below.

Interdependence is evident when no individual, group, family, profession, or organization is able to achieve its goal(s) and demonstrate its effectiveness when it operates independently and autonomously.[2] Collaboration is responsive to these interdependent relations; interdependent, equitable relations are, in turn, defining features of collaboration.

More specifically, collaboration is usually a competent practice or an optimal practice in the following cases, all of which manifest interdependent relationships.

- Children's needs and problems (e.g., delinquency, school-related problems, substance abuse, abuse and neglect, mental health challenges) co-occur, interact, and interlock. Find one, and sooner or later, you will find others. To effectively address one, you also must address the others.

- Professionals representing the areas of juvenile justice, special education, mental health, substance abuse, domestic violence, child welfare, and health care may serve the same family. However, these professionals often operate without knowledge of each other, and so they may unintentionally and inadvertently work at cross-purposes. The family experiences stress amid competing and sometimes contradictory advice and requirements. Professionals do not achieve the improved outcomes for which they and agencies are accountable.

- Professionals serving the same family do not understand the intricate details of the child's presenting problem and its relationship to this child's family system, home environment, and neighborhood community. The child and the parents resist and sabotage professionals' recommended "solutions." Results do not improve, and the problem may become exacerbated.

- Professionals serving the same family operate with competing frames of reference. Some use a deficit frame; they talk only about problems that they must solve for this family. Others are strengths-based; they talk about solution-focused and aspiration-oriented actions that the family must help plan, implement, produce, and evaluate.

- Teachers report that they are unable to make significant progress with children and youth challenged by poverty, parental unemployment, family stress, and unsafe neighborhoods, and that parents are not involved in their child's education. The main need, according to these teachers, is for enhanced student opportunities for academic learning and healthy development. With the principal, they claim that the school alone cannot possibly meet this need and others. They must be able to capitalize on family and community resources for learning, healthy development, and success in school.

In all such cases, the development of collaboration is warranted. Stand-alone organizations in which individual professionals work independently simply will not serve children, families, educators, and social/health service providers in a comprehensive manner.

Complexity also compels collaboration, as the following case examples indicate.

- A low-performing school is located in a pocket of concentrated urban poverty, with high levels of family transience, housing stress, environmental health hazards, abandoned buildings, and high unemployment. The school building is aging, and its facilities are in disrepair. The textbooks are outdated and in short supply. Building-centered school improvement plans do not result in improvements in learning and academic achievement, and staff turnover and morale have become vexing problems.

- Problems are not limited to one school. The entire feeder pattern of schools and early childhood centers serving the same neighborhood community evidence multiple needs and problems. Strong families committed to their children's well being increasingly exit the neighborhood, or they opt for private schools.

- Students representing 48 different nationalities attend the same school, and English is not their first language. Most of their parents do not speak English. The majority of the veteran teachers speak only English, and most are of European-American descent. Ninety percent of the staff and the principal live outside the school's neighborhood community.

- Social and health services offered by schools and community agencies are fragmented. Professionals offering these services compete for resources and political supports. System fragmentation and interprofessional competition produce system cracks and service delivery gaps. Consensus is reached that social/health

service systems are irreparably broken and that the time has
arrived to effect systems change and cross-systems change (Gardner, 1999). Improvement strategies must be developed, implemented, harmonized, and synchronized at several levels of
individual organizations (e.g., front line practice, middle management) and between and among organizations.

- A community school, or a so-called "full-service school," is created.[3] Diverse professionals are relocated at the school, and
  people from all walks of life are linked to it. Educators must develop effective working relationships with these newcomers.

As suggested by the old adage "two heads are better than one," collaboration is a practical necessity to respond to these complex challenges.

Uncertainty and *novelty* also compel collaboration. This is especially
true when existing systems are in crisis, and awareness grows that new
organizational and institutional designs are needed. For example:

- Vocal parents and powerful community leaders challenge educators' power and autonomy as they stake territorial claims on
  the school, its teaching and learning processes, and its overall
  operations. They want to appoint their own principal, and they
  announce to the school board that their ultimate goal is to
  appoint a superintendent of their choice and get their own representatives elected to the board of education.

- The limitations of simple, linear, single-issue school improvement
  strategies become apparent as academic achievement remains low;
  staff and student morale is poor; staff turnover is high; recruitment
  poses as much of a challenge as retention; and safety and security
  pose problems. Schools suffering from these difficulties appear
  destined for the roster of chronically underperforming schools.

- A new class of problems arises (e.g., Dunn, 1997). These problems are ill defined or pose tremendous challenges to existing
  schools and agencies. For example, young peoples' perspectives,
  identities, aspirations, and values change so much that they are
  not invested in succeeding in school and following a subsequent
  career pathway (e.g., Wyn & Dwyer, 2000). Here, the challenge
  is not merely to solve neatly defined problems that fit conventional categories. With this new class of problems, people need
  to figure out what it is they need to figure out. Complex multi-
  tasking capacities are required here.[4] People must plan, do something, gain knowledge, learn, improve, and adapt—interactively.

Clearly, uncertainty and novelty are conditions that can necessitate collaboration. In turn, collaboration may foster innovation (Corrigan, 2000). For example, interprofessional teams, interorganizational partnerships or alliances, and broad-based community collaboratives or coalitions are innovations that comprise elements of a collaborative infrastructure. In addition to the benefits they provide for children, youth, and families (see Dryfoos and Quinn, this volume, chapters 7 and 8), they also benefit practicing professionals and their organizations (see Crowson, this volume, chapter 4). However, the complexity of these cases can be overwhelming.

Transaction Costs and their Implications

The aforementioned cases, with their complexity, uncertainty, novelty, and interdependent relationships, substantiate a claim made at the outset: Collaboration generally exacts steep transaction costs. Developing and maintaining collaborative practices can consume a great deal of people's time and energy, spotlight individual and professional weaknesses, and consume valuable resources, while taking years to develop.

Steep transaction costs can be avoided when precise determinations are made about the feasibility and appeal of other alternatives. These alternatives include the other c-words—connecting and communicating, cooperating, etc. For example, a suburban school may be able to accomplish its goals merely by communicating more effectively with a local child welfare agency. Improvements in their referral and information management systems and coordination of foster care services with special education services could ease many burdens and streamline procedures. Full-fledged collaboration as defined in this chapter is not needed here, and its transaction costs cannot be justified.

Thus, collaboration is a highly contingent strategy, one that is tailor-made for conditions manifesting high levels of interdependence, complexity, uncertainty, and novelty. It is not a panacea for schools, agencies, and their relationships. Arguably, it should not be pursued in instances where improved communications and connections, cooperation, coordination, community building, or contracting will suffice to improve results. This claim is strengthened when the varieties of collaboration are examined.

Varieties of Collaboration

This yearbook focuses on interprofessional collaboration as a critical means of improving services to children, families, and schools and to enhance teaching and learning. However, interprofessional collaboration is just one kind of collaboration; nine others also are defined below:

- *Interprofessional collaboration*—includes educators, social workers, psychologists, nurses, counselors, and other helping professionals who comprise sustainable teams.

- *Youth-centered collaboration*—requires professionals to view youth as experts and partners who are essential co-producers of principles, action theories, programs, and results, and who share responsibility and accountability for results.

- *Parent-centered collaboration*—requires professionals to view parents as experts and partners who are essential co-producers of principles, action theories, programs, and results, who share responsibility and accountability for results, and whose engagement and well being influence and determine their children's well being.

- *Family-centered collaboration*—requires professionals to view family systems as partners and essential co-producers of principles, action theories, programs, and results who share responsibility and accountability for results, and whose engagement influences and determines the well being of children, parents, and grandparents as well as the future of the family.

- *Intra-organizational collaboration*—secures the engagement and co-production capacities of people in the same organization, many of whom must share responsibility and accountability for results. This might entail, for example, collaboration among school professionals, secretaries, custodians, cafeteria workers, bus drivers, and community leaders, who may serve on site-based teams.

- *Inter-organizational collaboration*—secures the engagement, shared responsibility and accountability, and co-production capacities of a group of organizations (e.g., a school, a boys and girls club, a family-supportive faith-based organization, a social service agency, a health clinic), formalizing their relations and aligning their policies and practices as they pursue shared results.

- *Community collaboration*—secures the engagement, mutual responsibility and accountability, and co-production capacities of all of the legitimate stakeholders in a workable geographic area. This involves developing their collaborative capacities; focusing on educational-economic pathways for children, parents, and residents; strengthening relationships among early childhood programs and schools in the same feeder pattern; and synchronizing school-related improvements with improvements in social and health service systems, neighborhood organizations, and the private sector.

- *Intra-governmental collaboration*—secures the engagement, mutual accountability, and co-production capacities of several governmental sectors and offices (e.g., education, health, justice, child and family services, and economic development) and aligns policies and practices.[5]

- *Inter-governmental collaboration*—secures the engagement, mutual accountability, and co-production capacities of local, state, and national governments and aligns policies.

- *International collaboration*—secures the engagement, shared responsibility, mutual accountability, and co-production capacities of the educators and schools that serve children and youth living in two worlds, i.e., persons who migrate back and forth between the United States and the originating, or sender, nation.

Each type of collaboration offers something different to the individuals and organizations working to improve results. Some practical implications of employing different types of collaboration follow.

Interprofessional collaboration often is a necessary improvement strategy, but by itself, it is insufficient. Interprofessional collaboration, as defined in this chapter, excludes important stakeholder groups—children, parents, families, and community leaders—and tends to maintain professional power and authority dynamics. "Professionals know best" remains the institutional rule, and children, parents, families, and community members often remain dependent clients, or consultants at best. Professionals also assume most of the responsibility and accountability for results.

For this reason, some collaboration initiatives—namely, youth-centered, parent-centered, family-centered, and community collaboration—are empowerment-oriented. These empowerment-oriented collaboration initiatives threaten the dominant idea of professionalism (Crowson, 1998). They also provide timely opportunities for helping professionals to replace elite professionalism with a more democratic style of professionalism (Lawson, 2000).

In addition, these empowerment-oriented initiatives alter the balance of responsibility and accountability. Kids, parents, families, and entire neighborhood communities are expected to assume responsibility for improved outcomes, to co-produce these outcomes, and to share accountability. Notably, educators no longer have to do it all alone, nor do they have to shoulder all of the blame when academic achievement does not improve. Furthermore, the school is no longer a stand-alone institution, one that relies exclusively on "walled-in collaboration" (Lawson, 2001).

Youth-centered, parent-centered, family-centered, and community collaboration often prioritize and address contextual issues such as race and ethnicity, social class, sexual orientation, poverty, social exclusion and isolation, and their interaction. For example, empowered "nonprofessional" participants raise important issues about equality of opportunity, because they know that many children and families confront inequitable and intolerable conditions. These collaboratives also generate innovative solutions and provide new pathways to resources and results (Delgado-Gaitan, 2002; Shirley, 1998).

Most importantly, results improve because educators and schools benefit from family and community resources for learning, healthy development, and success in school (e.g., Delgado-Gaitan, 2002; Dryfoos & Knauer, 2002; Hatch, 1998a). Reciprocally, families are supported and neighborhood communities are strengthened when these kinds of collaboration are implemented (e.g., Delgado-Gaitan).

Collaboration's Essential Features and Requirements

Until collaboration's essential features and unique qualities are identified, described, and explained, its full potential will remain untapped. The next section is structured to address this critical need, beginning with the relationship between collaboration and comprehensive services.

Collaboration and Comprehensive Services

As this yearbook's title indicates, interprofessional collaboration and comprehensive services frequently are joined in conversations, policy, and practice. The fact remains, however, that collaboration initiatives can be launched without any reference to comprehensive services. In other words, these two ideas may be related, but the terms are not synonyms. Their respective differences must be emphasized and maintained.

For example, talk about "services" often reveals a deficit-oriented view of human problems and needs.[6] In this model, someone (usually a child and frequently the parents) or something (e.g., service systems configurations) is deficient, meaning that they have problems that need to be fixed. In contrast, collaboration is not restricted to a deficit-oriented frame.

Collaboration initiatives make important contributions to teaching and learning in ways that may have nothing to do with providing comprehensive services. Frequently, these other initiatives are aspiration-based and opportunity-oriented. Some offer enrichment. Examples include after-school programs, parent empowerment programs, service learning initiatives, youth development programs, comprehensive health promotion initiatives, university-school partnerships, and school and business partnerships (including school-to-work and school-and-work programs). All are vital to holistic school improvement initiatives and can be developed and analyzed apart from comprehensive services.

Furthermore, countless comprehensive service initiatives never manage to achieve the promised land of collaboration. This observation is not a criticism, nor does it imply that these services are ineffective; rather, it suggests that collaboration is just one alternative for service providers, educators, and other partners. To reiterate, the other alternatives include combinations of c-words mentioned earlier in this chapter.

Special Features of School-Community Collaboration

The research literature on collaboration includes both field-specific and interdisciplinary analyses. This chapter draws on both kinds of literature, and practical examples are provided as space permits.

Interdependent working relationships, collective action, and shared resources. Collaboration is evident when *interdependent working relationships* are developed among various combinations of children, parents, other adults, groups, families, professions, organizations, and governments. These diverse participants are able to work collaboratively to meet the interdependent needs of their community and to solve interdependent, complex problems. Vital to this process is participants' mutual awareness of their interdependence. From these interdependent working relationships, participants are able to organize and mobilize for effective, collective action. Here, collaboration's cultural and political aspects are elevated to a status alongside its instrumental, practical aspects. The ability to pool and share resources is the acid test for every collaboration.

A shared, collective identity. Through collaboration, participants may develop a shared identity. For example, collaborating parties develop a new name for themselves (e.g., The Albany Collaborative for Children and Families), and often, participants actively identify with it. Individual and collective identities change interactively (Delgado-Gaitan, 2002). Teams and other partnerships that derive from collaboration may become vibrant communities of practice (Wenger, 1999).[7] These unique relationships often enjoy staying power; they are not limited to special projects.

Sound intervention logic. When collaboration is evident, teams of people often rely on valid interventions, and "intervention logic" is evident. Intervention logic refers to selecting the best solution, often an evidence-based intervention, to solve an identifiable problem. The intervention also addresses the cause(s) of the problem. In simple terms, participants organize decisions, actions, and events in logical, causal chains (Taylor-Powell, Rossing, & Geran, 1998).

Equitable relationships obtained through negotiations. Collaboration involves equitable, working relationships and some conditional equality. Most people do not collaborate with superiors; they obey them. Nor do superiors collaborate with inferiors; they command them (adapted from Duncan, 1962). Clearly, hierarchical relationships must be equalized as much as possible for collaborative relationships to form and to be sustained. However, power differentials do not disappear. Power is the subject of continuous negotiations (McCann & Gray, 1986), and so are unavoidable conflicts and competitions.

Benefiting from conflict and competition. Collaboration also entails continuous negotiations in relation to inherent conflicts and propensities to compete; these negotiations animate collaboration. Carefully negotiated conflict provides unique opportunities and, indeed, distinct benefits (Coser, 1956). For example, participants build on their respective strengths as they negotiate the boundaries of their respective jurisdictions. Often, they volunteer to modify their respective job descriptions, especially as their joint work enables them to develop new competencies.

A collective voice and unity of purpose. Collaboration is evident when *one voice has been created from many.* The collective voice of the collaboration becomes a powerful instrument for school improvement and community development (Shirley, 1998). This voice is created as diverse participants are able to describe, explain, and build on their commonalities and their shared destinies. They know that they comprise interdependent, overlapping communities of fate (Held, 1997). For example, teachers know and openly acknowledge that they depend on social workers, parents, juvenile justice specialists, and mental health workers (Lawson & Briar-Lawson, 1997). Through this acknowledgment, one voice emerges, representing the collective voice of the collaborative.

Clarity and unity of purpose, another essential feature of collaboration, also emerges. A clear, shared purpose is related to a shared vision or view of the future in which current problems are addressed and shared aspirations are realized. This shared vision results in the interweaving of participating professionals' and organizations' missions.

Shared language. Collaboration is, in one sense, a way of talking, making a common language a practical necessity. This means getting everyone "on the same page," with shared language being both a method and a result. When people collaborate, they are able to "walk the talk" and "talk the walk" (Elias, 1994). They know collaboration when they see it and do it, because they have a precise language for describing, implementing, and evaluating it. Shared language allows for effective communication focused on essential information. Only when diverse people, professions, and organizations have harmonized and synchronized their missions, core technologies, action theories, operating principles, core values, and ethical-moral imperatives (Briar-Lawson, Lawson, Hennon, & Jones, 2001; Walsh, Brabeck, & Howard, 1999) can they come together in collaboration.

Accepting diversity. This shared language does not preclude acknowledgment and acceptance of diversity. The belief that diversity is an asset to be maximized, not a problem to be managed, is essential for sustainable collaboration and paves the way for effectiveness. For example, diversity prevents "groupthink," that is, narrow, deceptive, and self-sealing orientations and behavior (Janis, 1972).

Shared responsibility and accountability. When collaboration is in place, participants accept shared responsibility and accountability for results. Responsibility and accountability are constantly negotiated, and determinations are made in relation to specialized missions, core technologies, and resource flows. These negotiations proceed as participants recognize their interdependence, on the one hand, and their unique capacities and specializations, on the other. In other words, specialization remains when collaboration occurs, but it is bracketed by interdependence.

More concretely, lead responsibility is key for action planning in a collaboration. For example, educators have lead responsibility for children's academic achievement, and social workers have lead responsibility for family preservation. At the same time, they share responsibility for the well being of the children and families they work with and, over time, they begin to share accountability as well.

Trusting relationships. When responsibilities and accountabilities are firmly delineated, roles and duties also are clear. This produces mutual understandings, many of which are unwritten. Trusting relationships that cement collaboration are founded on these mutual understandings (e.g., Tschannen-Moran & Hoy, 2000).

Governance structures and processes. Collaboration depends on governance structures and processes. To govern is to steer—to provide direction, structure, and guidance for negotiations, problem-setting, and problem-solving. Discussions of governance introduce other features found in collaborations. These features signal design-related needs in developing collaborations.

The first feature is intermediary people and organizations (Lawson & Barkdull, 2000). Intermediary people may be called facilitators, interprofessional leaders, resource coordinators, community developers, boundary spanners and crossers, cultural brokers (Delgado-Gaitan, 2002), or linkage agents. They are essential for successful collaborative practices. In the same vein, an existing organization may provide neutral and facilitative conditions for collaboration. Universities often play this role, and so do local chapters of The United Way. In principle, a school also can perform these convening and linkage functions if it is able to satisfy an important requirement—for collaborative efforts to work, partners must avoid any semblance of a "guest-host relationship." Community partners cannot be viewed as outsiders who are tenants of the school (Edelman, 2001). This feature has particular relevance for community schools and multi-service schools, because they bring "outsiders" into the school. Arguably, this requirement has been one of the most difficult features of collaboration to develop and sustain.

Another governance feature is a "go-between" organization. This feature is needed when two or more organizations collaborate (i.e., in inter-organizational collaboration). For example, when schools collaborate with many other community agencies and neighborhood organizations, community-based collaboratives are a practical necessity. These collaboratives develop as intermediary organizations and provide governance for entire feeder patterns of early childhood education centers; elementary, middle, and secondary schools; and higher education institutions (Lawson, 1999b). These community collaboratives may belong to everyone with no evident guest-host relationship.

Collaborative leadership is an essential aspect of governance (Lawson, 1998). Rubin (2002) describes collaborative leaders as optimistic people who are also optimizers, combining veracity and tenacity. This description is especially pertinent to principals (Goldring & Hausman, 2001) and superintendents (Lawson, 1999b), who serve as advocates for children and their families in schools and in the surrounding communities. An effective balance of leadership and management is critical. Collaborative leaders and entire collaboratives are strategic in what they prioritize and accomplish, and they do so with quality in mind. They do the right things (leadership) in the right ways (management). They promote honesty, integrity, and norms of reciprocity.

Inclusion of the relevant stakeholders. In an effective collaboration, all of the legitimate stakeholders are included (McCann & Gray, 1986; Rubin, 2002). Stakeholders must be active members of the collaboration. Results are not likely to improve without their inclusion (Cahn, 2000), and they share responsibility and accountability for these results. When they are excluded from decision making, stakeholders can cause problems, ultimately impeding the effectiveness of the collaboration.

Two key questions drive decisions about stakeholder participation: Who decides who is a legitimate stakeholder? And who decides who decides? These two questions are addressed constantly in collaborations, and the answers determine a collaboration's constituency, the range of its operations, and its effectiveness. These questions highlight the need for a coherent, effective design for improvement, which is vital to collaboration.

A coherent design for school improvement. Many school-linked and school-based plans have confronted barriers, and indeed, some have failed, because they were not developed as essential components in the school's (or the district's) improvement plans (Lawson & Briar-Lawson, 1997). Comprehensive services, after-school programs, and other initiatives often have been tacked on to the margins of school operations.

A requirement for a coherent improvement plan does not imply rigidity and automatic compliance. When collaboration is pursued, improvement plans are extended, revised, and validated even as they guide the collaboration. Collaboration, in this view, is like simultaneously designing, building, flying, and steering an airplane. Adaptability, learning, and development proceed simultaneously, and provide opportunities and structures for creativity and "generativity" (Lawson & Sailor, 2000). This openness and innovation does not suggest disorganization. Rather, a steady pragmatism guides successful collaboration. Participants "keep their eyes on the prize." Therefore, they know when they are making demonstrable progress toward improved results. Data systems are thus vital to effective collaborations.

Data-driven, results-oriented evaluation and improvement systems.
Results-oriented assessment and performance evaluation systems produce data sets, which are used for continuous improvement, learning,
and collaborative capacity building. For example, interprofessional
teams rely on data and adapt their operations as required (Bronstein, in
press). Data-based and results-oriented decision making are often associated with high-performing learning communities and organizations
and with total quality management (Rubin, 2002).

Continuous improvement also is facilitated by troubleshooting and
barrier-busting procedures. Breaking down obstacles and removing barriers often become short-term goals (Briar-Lawson, Lawson, Hennon, &
Jones, 2001). As barriers are removed, goals are more easily achieved. As
participants begin to see progress and success indicators, individual and
collective efficacy and a sense of empowerment build. A "can-do" attitude
is pervasive and often infectious (Delgado-Gaitan, 2002). These "conta-
gion" effects often accompany collaboration; for example, success in one
school in a feeder pattern leads to success in another (Shirley, 1998).

Implications

Countless school and community initiatives call their efforts collaborations, and many of these initiatives are exciting and promising.
However, if this chapter's conceptual framework for collaboration is
used to evaluate these initiatives, many do not qualify as collaboration.
In Johnson's (1993) words, "everybody talking 'bout collaboration ain't
collaborating" (p. 1).

People often use the adjective "collaborative" to describe their
work—for example, they talk about "collaborative practices" and "collaborative relationships." Unfortunately, these loose descriptors con-
note an infinite variety of practices and strategies. They dilute the precise meaning of collaboration and compromise its enormous potential.
The implication is: Beware of the adjective "collaborative" and focus
instead on "collaboration."

This line of criticism is not meant as an indictment. It is a call for a
precise language for practice, research, and policy, for more rigorous
intervention logic, for research evidence, and for coherent, effective
improvement models.

Institutional Aims of Collaboration

Social institutions have rule systems and histories. As the preceding
discussion indicates, successful collaboration changes the rules (Gardner,

1999). It has the potential to reform and transform social institutions. This potential raises critical questions: What, then, is the institutional aim for collaboration? For comprehensive services? Is the aim to fit children and youth into existing schools and existing social and health service agencies? Is it to adapt and transform schools and agencies? A mixture of both? Especially for educators, the answers depend on the framework for school improvement. For facility of analysis, I present two frameworks, and I conclude with a sketch of their features.

Tinkering Toward Utopia: An Industrial Bureaucratic Framework

The *industrial bureaucratic framework* is a legacy from the past, developed when most schools were organized like assembly lines and factory systems. Although much has changed, aspects of industrial age thinking and practice remain, such as linear thinking and buildings with "egg crate" classroom designs.

In this frame, collaboration is incorporated in an identifiable kind of improvement plan. The main strategy, aptly described by Tyack and Cuban (1995), is to "tinker toward utopia." For some schools and agencies, this limited-reform strategy may be both necessary and sufficient, and such "tinkering" may be entirely appropriate. For example, data regarding school performance indicate that conventional schools are continuing to produce acceptable, even desirable, results. Nevertheless, this reformist strategy merits critical analysis, especially as the demographic profile of the U.S. continues to change rapidly and dramatically.

The industrial bureaucratic framework holds that the condition of children and youth is the top priority. Students need to come to school ready, willing, and able to learn. In the current reality, however, a growing number of students do not. If children are not coming to school ready to learn, someone or something must be held accountable. Because this model prioritizes linear cause-and-effect thinking, the main causes of student failure are identified as ineffective, even negligent, parents, dysfunctional families, peer groups that promote bad influences, unsupervised time, and the harmful lures of the streets.

In addition, some educators believe that social and health service providers are part of the problem. If providers are ineffective, the needs of children and their families are not addressed and children cannot come to school ready to learn. Children then, are the victims, evidencing the problems and needs that arise from the failure of adults to provide adequate care.

In this line of thinking and attribution, educators, especially teachers, cannot do their jobs and achieve results because children do not arrive prepared to learn. Educators and schools don't cause school-related performance problems. The causes can be traced to negligent parents and to social and health service providers who don't do their jobs—in short, the problems are outside the school's influence and control.

Interprofessional collaboration and comprehensive services are viewed as remedies to several key problems. Ostensibly, they allow service providers, whether inside or outside the school, to become more effective as they improve, expand, and integrate social and health services. As a result, more children will come to school ready, willing, and able to learn, and then teachers can do their jobs. "Fix, then teach" is the predominant formula for success (Honig, McLaughlin, & Kahne, 2001).

This line of thinking (i.e., intervention logic) locates the main problem as residing outside the immediate jurisdiction of a school or a school district. Service providers and parents, not educators, are expected to solve it. Services and classroom pedagogy are separate activities. A clear institutional pattern is evidenced, and this pattern explains why, in many places, classroom teachers have not been included in the design, implementation, and evaluation of interprofessional collaboration and comprehensive services (e.g., Lawson & Briar-Lawson, 1997). Teachers have not been viewed as legitimate stakeholders, and this failure reveals a great deal about internal school improvement planning and its relationship with collaboration and comprehensive services.

If teachers are not involved, everyday life in classrooms—what Tyack and Cuban (1995) call "real school"—changes little, if at all. The deep structures of schooling remain intact (Crowson & Boyd, 1996). This is not surprising if the most influential stakeholders (teachers) in real school have been left out of the mix. Little wonder that schools that fail to involve teachers in the critical work of comprehensive services "tinker" their way toward utopia.

Tinkering Toward Utopia: University Interprofessional Work

University preparation programs follow a similar pattern (Lawson, 1999a). Training for interprofessional collaboration typically is aimed at social and health service providers. Principals and teachers are not required to take these courses, which tend to be offered outside schools, colleges, and departments of education. Mirroring school practice, education faculty and students are not viewed as legitimate stakeholders in the university at large. Predictably, education faculty hold conventional views about their roles, responsibilities, and duties (see Benson & Harkavy, this volume, chapter 5; McCroskey, this volume, chapter 6).

The pattern that becomes evident suggests that an industrial bureaucratic framework is in operation, and that its effects are pervasive. It influences not only schools, colleges, and universities, but also state and federal departments of education. Tyack (1974) called this type of framework "an interlocking directorate." When a dominant, interlocking framework dictates relations among schools, college and university education departments, and governmental education departments, thinking, language, and action are predictable.

School and community governance issues provide a case in point. Many school-based initiatives, including some community schools, have struggled with governance structures and issues. Although these initiatives are often called collaborations, they are not, given that educators and their partners have not been able to resolve their governance problems. A recent study of the 21st Century Learning Center after-school program initiatives funded by the U.S. Department of Education found that participating schools had not developed the capacity for collaboration because they insisted on monopolizing governance (Blank et al., 2001). Other studies have produced similar findings (Crowson & Boyd, 1996).

In these cases, *the school rules according to the school's rules.* The school is the host and outsiders are guests. In such a scenario, it is not surprising that community-based professionals are apprehensive, cautious, and reluctant to collaborate with educators and to move their offices into schools. Brabeck, Walsh, Kenny, and Comilang (1997) label this reaction "school phobia."

Clearly, both education professionals and social service and health professionals can separately contribute to the types of institutional and cultural barriers that preclude true collaboration. When they erect these barriers, their interactions are at best superficial, and at worst dishonest.

Tinkering toward utopia through interprofessional collaboration and comprehensive services is not necessarily misdirected (Lawson, 1999a). When children and youth do not come to school ready and able to learn, this *does* cause problems. Children, youth, and families frequently need comprehensive services that require interprofessional collaboration. It is important to recognize, however, that a limited conception of collaboration and services operates in this industrial-bureaucratic framework—a conception that is insufficient to improve results for all children, youth, and families. Some of the barriers to children's learning, healthy development, and success in school may be addressed, but others are ignored (Adelman & Taylor, 2000). Furthermore, the "fix, then teach" service orientation is a limited improvement strategy in its exclusive focus on barriers to learning. Problem-oriented and deficit-oriented thinking prevail, and the influence of an industrial-bureaucratic frame remains.

Mitchell and Scott (1994) warn that even the best configuration of services will not compensate for serious structural flaws in schools and in service systems, and that an exclusive focus on services would lead to unfortunate and undesirable results. Important needs and problems in the structure and conduct of schooling would be ignored, neglected, and at worst, covered up.

If flaws are present, and indeed some are, and if service-oriented, interprofessional collaboration does not address all of these flaws, and indeed it does not, then trouble lies ahead in today's accountability-rich environment. In the words of Hill, Campbell, and Harvey (2000), people are operating in "a zone of wishful thinking" (p. 23). In today's outcome-oriented accountability environments, wishful thinking is not enough. For this reason alone, other school leaders have embarked on a course of *institutional redesign*.

Redesigning Institutions

A second framework moves beyond tinkering and involves designing and creating new institutions. This *institutional redesign framework* aims to create and support new-century school communities. Industrial age schools and social and health service agencies are not designed or equipped to meet the needs of children and youth (Wyn & Dwyer, 2000). Because this deficiency is growing, some educators, parents, and community stakeholders recognize that they must "go back to the drawing board" to redesign entire institutions.

This is not the first time in history that educators and other school leaders have confronted this issue. However, in the past, educators have been more likely to attribute problems to students and to outside influences, rather than accepting any responsibility to evaluate schools themselves (Deschenes, Cuban, & Tyack, 2001). In today's environment, this option is losing its currency, and increasing numbers of people recognize the need for institutional redesign (Crowson, this volume, chapter 4; Dryfoos, this volume, chapter 7; Quinn, this volume, chapter 8).

A new class of problems is presented by high-poverty school communities characterized by interacting and interlocking forces related

to social exclusion; geographic isolation; racial, gender, and ethnic discrimination; inequalities; and toxic environments. The difficulties and
challenges children and their families face in these communities are
complex and interwoven. As explained above, the industrial-bureaucratic model offers little hope of providing immediate and dramatic
improvements in results. Its standardized solutions are like square
pegs that do not fit round holes, and its linear, fragmented change
strategies cannot begin to address the multiplicity of difficulties and
challenges faced by children, families, educators, and others in the
community. In essence, these strategies force educators and schools to
play a never-ending game of catch up.

As some educators and other school leaders are playing this losing
game, the federal No Child Left Behind Act of 2001 and its state
counterparts have raised the stakes by mandating improved academic
results. A school's legitimacy, resource flows, and long-term survival
may be at stake. Thanks to the new legislation, local, state, and national data are being made public. Everyone now knows which schools
are succeeding and which are not, although how these data are interpreted varies. Whatever the interpretation, the data suggest that
schools can effectively serve *some* children, but not others.

The data on low-performing and underperforming schools in high-
poverty areas are especially disturbing when school performance data
are linked with other demographic data. For example, a significant
number of African American males who live in concentrated poverty
attend low-performing schools (Yohalem & Pittman, 2001). Many are
retained at grade levels, diminishing the chances that these students
will graduate from high school. In comparison to other students,
African American and Latino students are more likely to be assigned
to special education classes, and they are more likely to comprise case-
loads in the child welfare, juvenile justice, and mental health systems.
This poses an important question: Is the main problem with these students, or with the mainstream institutions that affect them, starting
with schools?

Leaders of some school community initiatives have come to the
conclusion that the main problem resides in the design of schools and
their relationships with their neighborhood communities (Dryfoos,
this volume, chapter 7). They also have concluded that business as
usual today will bring results as usual tomorrow. Consequently, they
have embarked on a course aimed at deliberate institutional redesign.
If "No Child Left Behind" is to move beyond rhetoric and become
the new, substantive vision for the United States, then educators,

social and health service providers, and other U.S. citizens must use the democratic process to make it happen. Collaboration will surely be a critical component of this process.

The multiple kinds of collaboration presented in this chapter are key components in the redesign of existing institutions and the creation of new ones. For example, site-based teams remain important, but the unit of analysis for improvement planning changes. *School improvement planning* (focused on and limited to one school) becomes *school-community* improvement planning.

While a focus on one school is maintained, relationships among community agencies and other community institutions are developed. Community collaboration links groups of schools, preschools, social and health service agencies, multiple professionals, neighborhood organizations, and community development corporations. Youth-centered, parent-centered, and family-centered collaborations are mainstays in plans designed to stabilize and strengthen children, youth, families, and communities. These community collaborations provide a vital opportunity for educators and schools to gain influence and share control over the out-of-school factors that contribute to children's learning, healthy development, and success in school, and to gain family and community resources in support of their work.

Education should be associated with anytime, anywhere learning. This perspective uncovers rich opportunities for multiple kinds of collaboration and for collaborative learning. It also opens up avenues to family and community resources to contribute to learning, teaching, and healthy development. "Walled-in" collaboration in industrial-bureaucratic schools excludes these stakeholders and their resources. A redesigned school-community collaboration takes advantage of these resources, and results improve (Dryfoos, this volume, chapter 7; Hatch, 1998a).

In this institutional redesign framework, relational thinking and practice replace categorical, linear thinking and practice. For example, in lieu of "fix, then teach," collaboration presents opportunities for social workers, psychologists, counselors, and teachers to collaborate with each other and with children and parents to co-produce new teaching and learning strategies (Honig, Kahne, & McLaughlin, 2001; Lawson & Briar-Lawson, 1997). Mooney, Kline, and Davoren (1999) provide compelling descriptions of integrated teaching and learning strategies that support teachers and yield unique benefits to children. Real school—life in classrooms—changes for the better, assisting teachers and facilitating academic achievement gains.

The results associated with school-linked and school-based collaboration certainly focus on children's performance in schools, but they reflect more than simply academic achievement. School results are inseparable from indicators of child and family well being, as these factors are interdependent. Similarly, every intervention is expected (and designed) to have more than one effect (Delgado-Gaitan, 2002) that enhances learning and students' well being.

Teachers and principals also are important beneficiaries of institutional redesign. Given the current critical need to recruit and retain educators, family and community resources and supports for teachers are vital to teacher professional satisfaction and higher retention rates (Ingersoll, 2001). In addition, teachers, children, parents, and community leaders are legitimate stakeholders in school-community improvement planning. When they are included in the educational process as contributors, students benefit from multiple educators, and teachers receive additional support. Although these community stakeholders may not have the professional language to describe their thinking, their discussions and actions reflect and promote a social-ecological view of child lifespan development and general well being.

These descriptions are not pipe dreams. Some schools and agencies are being transformed, slowly but surely (e.g., Driscoll, 2001; Dryfoos, this volume, chapter 7; Quinn, this volume, chapter 8). Arguably, the community school model provides the most visible and popular example of institutional transformation. On paper, it encourages, supports, needs, and benefits from multiple kinds of collaboration. In practice, many individual schools often struggle alone, and some groups of schools struggle together. Collaboration has not yet developed at many of these sites, in part because technical assistance and capacity building supports are in short supply (Lawson & Briar-Lawson, 1997). Even so, these schools and groups of schools are making progress as they engage in the ongoing process of institutional change. Collaboration is a practical necessity for schools choosing this path. It defines both competent and optimal practice.

Responsive and Proactive Changes in Higher Education

Institutional redesign also incorporates the colleges and universities, especially education departments and professors of education. Community schools call for new university-school community partnerships. Such partnerships cannot be restricted to relations between public schools and the university's department of education, although this department should play the role of coordinator and main support. For optimal results, "sister" schools of social work, nursing, health, public administration, and others, along with the college of arts and sciences, should be included in the partnership.

If diverse professionals are expected to work together—to collaborate successfully—then they must be prepared. Interprofessional education and training programs are a practical necessity that must include teachers, principals, and service providers. These programs should emphasize the common goal that all children and youth come to school ready and able to learn, while schools must be ready to provide optimal environments to support the learning, development, and well being of all children, youth, and families (Lawson, 1999a, 2002). In this frame, readiness is a mutual need deriving from an awareness and appreciation of the school's interdependent relations with families, agencies, and universities. The "interprofessional development schools" described by Corrigan (2000) are a prime example of institutional change that many community schools could implement. In this framework, learning, teaching, practicing, policy development, and knowledge generation are intertwined (Lawson, 2002). Higher education faculty and graduate students make a critical contribution in these school communities, as research accompanies the development of collaborative practices. In fact, college and university departments of education may ultimately assume new leadership on their own campuses as they engage in collaborative, complex change involving multiple university departments and community institutions. The notion of an engaged university is also a proposal for institutional change that can be tailored to collaboration among schools and their communities (Lawson, 2002; McCroskey, this volume, chapter 6). Professional development schools are a step in this direction.

Such collaborative possibilities require an important commitment on the part of colleges and universities—to collaborate, they must be prepared to accept joint responsibility and some accountability for the results of P-12 schools. This requirement changes the status quo and may provoke some disagreement among faculty. One important incentive may facilitate these institutional changes and promote collaboration. As schools improve results, more students will be college-ready and, therefore, will enlarge the pool of higher education candidates. When these students come from historically underrepresented populations, higher education has evidence that it is meeting its social responsibilities. Thus, this collaboration-oriented institutional redesign work corresponds to the enlightened self-interest of higher education institutions (Lawson, 2002).

Finally, the institutional redesign framework must take into account changing economic realities and related issues regarding youth identities, meanings, and life course plans. A significant number of youth in the U.S. and other countries are developing less hopeful views of schools and their contribution to economic well being (Wyn & Dwyer, 2000). These youth are affected by the loss of industrial age jobs, by the growing racial and ethnic segregation of U.S. schools and neighborhoods, and by the widening gap between the rich and poor, including an obvious "digital divide." Some of these kids opt for the shadow economies associated with drugs, gangs, and crime because they do not view schools as providing viable and relevant alternatives. In these instances, the limitations of interprofessional collaboration and comprehensive services in isolation are apparent, especially when services are limited to psychosocial interventions. Most school service initiatives are not oriented toward occupational and economic development, and this limits their effectiveness in high-poverty school communities, which are home to unemployment, low levels of educational attainment, social isolation, and economic marginalization (Crowson, this volume, chapter 4; Driscoll, 2001). The apparent lack of connection between evidence-based anti-poverty strategies and most school services configurations provides an important opportunity for institutional redesign.

Ironically, service providers and educators alike may urge talented individuals to leave their neighborhoods—indeed, they very likely offer the prospect of leaving as the just reward for success in school. While not completely unworthy, this line of thinking further weakens high-poverty neighborhoods and the schools that serve them at a time when they need to be strengthened, stabilized, and revitalized (Taylor, 2002).

In contrast, some collaboration-oriented initiatives are geared toward neighborhood revitalization and economic development. These initiatives include school-to-work and school-and-work programs. They also include statewide P-16 initiatives, so named because they emphasize an education that begins in preschool and ends with the completion of an undergraduate degree. These initiatives give priority to an integrated approach to social and economic development, with school-community collaboratives as the centerpiece. Collaboration-oriented school-community improvement planning gives priority to educational and economic opportunity pathways to higher education, pathways that provide access to healthy lifestyles and new jobs in the global economy (Yohalem & Pittman, 2001).

Some critics may view this expanded focus for school-related collaboration that integrates economic and community development as yet another instance of harnessing schools to serve markets, but it is not. It protects democracy and supports schools by providing health, educational, social, and economic opportunities and by rekindling hope. Its main assumption is that social problems such as extreme poverty, social exclusion, multiple forms of overt discrimination, and the shadow economies based on drugs and crime must be confronted because they threaten democracy and imperil schools. It also derives from an awareness that our democracy's fate lies in the hands, hearts, and minds of the nation's children and youth—its future leaders and its most vulnerable citizens. No doubt this is why the current educational slogan "No Child Left Behind" is so appealing. Genuine collaboration, precisely defined and effectively implemented, will be vital to the efforts aimed at making this appealing rhetoric an everyday reality.

AUTHOR'S NOTE

I benefited from the editorial suggestions provided by Laura Bronstein, Leslie Grout, Julie Abramson, Wayne Sailor, Michael Lawson, Joy Dryfoos, and Dawn Anderson-Butcher.

NOTES

1. For a more detailed analysis, see Rubin's (2002) 24 steps for developing collaboration.

2. Where professions and organizations are concerned, resource allocations and expert authority also are "on the line" (Scott, 1995).

3. The full-service school reflects a particular view of services and human needs (Lawson & Sailor, 2000). "Multi-service school" or "community school" is a more accurate and appropriate name.

4. See, for example, the detailed analysis of "collaborative capacity" provided by Foster-Fishman, Berkowitz, Lounsbury, and Allen (2001).

5. The state of Minnesota and the Province of British Columbia are experimenting with a new governmental structure to facilitate collaboration. In both cases, education, social services, health services, and others are now part of the same agency.

6. Social workers learn strengths-based, solution-focused language in their preparation programs. However, it is not clear that social workers "stay the course" after they graduate. Even if they do, there is no evidence that they are able to persuade people from other professions to talk and practice in strengths-based, solution-focused ways.

7. The evolution of interprofessional collaboration begins with individuals who form groups and later become teams. When teams develop into communities of practice, a special collaboration is in place.

LAWSON   71

REFERENCES

Adelman, H., & Taylor, L. (2000). Looking at school health and school reform policy through the lens of addressing barriers to learning. *Children's Services: Social Policy, Research, & Practice, 3*, 117-132.

Benson, L., & Harkavy, I. (2003). The role of the American research university in advancing system-wide education reform, democratic schooling, and democracy. In this volume—M.M. Brabeck, M.E. Walsh, & R. Latta (Eds.), *Meeting at the hyphen: Schools-universities-communities-professions in collaboration for student achievement and well being. The 102nd yearbook of the National Society for the Study of Education*, Part II. Chicago: National Society for the Study of Education.

Blank, M., Hale, E., Housman, N., Kaufmann, B., Martinez, M., McCloud, B., Samberg, L., Walter, S., & Melaville, A. (2001). *School-community partnerships in support of student learning: Taking a second look at the governance of the 21st Century Community Learning Center Program*. Washington, DC: The Institute for Educational Leadership.

Brabeck, M., Walsh, M., Kenny, M., & Comilang, K. (1997). Interprofessional collaboration for children and families: Opportunities for counseling psychology in the 21st century. *The Counseling Psychologist, 25*, 615-636.

Briar-Lawson, K., Lawson, H., Hennon, C., & Jones, A. (2001). *Family-supportive policy practice: International perspectives*. New York: Columbia University Press.

Bronstein, L. (in press). The index of interdisciplinary collaboration: The design and development of an assessment instrument. *Social Work*.

Cahn, E. (2000). *No more throw-away people: The co-production imperative*. Washington, DC: Essential Books.

Chrislip, D., & Larson, C. (1994). *Collaborative leadership: How citizens and civic leaders can make a difference*. San Francisco: Jossey-Bass.

Corrigan, D. (2000). The changing role of schools and higher education institutions with respect to community-based interagency collaboration and interprofessional partnerships. *Peabody Journal of Education, 75*, 176-195.

Coser, L. (1956). *The functions of social conflict*. London: Routledge and Kegan Paul.

Crowson, R. (1998). Community empowerment and the public schools: Can educational professionalism survive? *Peabody Journal of Education, 73*(1), 56-68.

Crowson, R. (2003). Empowerment models for interprofessional collaboration. In this volume—M.M. Brabeck, M.E. Walsh, & R. Latta (Eds.), *Meeting at the hyphen: Schools-universities-communities-professions in collaboration for student achievement and well being. The 102nd yearbook of the National Society for the Study of Education*, Part II. Chicago: National Society for the Study of Education.

Crowson, R., & Boyd, W. (1996). Achieving coordinated school-linked services: Facilitating utilization of the emerging knowledge base. *Educational Policy, 10*, 253-272.

Delgado-Gaitan, C. (2002). *The power of community: Mobilizing for family and schooling*. New York: Rowman & Littlefield Publishers.

Deschenes, S., Cuban, L., & Tyack, D. (2001). Mismatch: Historical perspectives on schools and students who don't fit them. *Teachers College Record, 4*, 525-547.

Driscoll, M.E. (2001). The sense of place and the neighborhood school: Implications for building social capital and for community development. In R. Crowson (Ed.), *Community development and school reform* (pp. 19-42). Oxford, U.K.: Elsevier Science, Ltd.

Dryfoos, J. (2003). Comprehensive schools. In this volume—M.M. Brabeck, M.E. Walsh, & R. Latta (Eds.), *Meeting at the hyphen: Schools-universities-communities-professions in collaboration for student achievement and well being. The 102nd yearbook of the National Society for the Study of Education*, Part II. Chicago: National Society for the Study of Education.

Dryfoos, J., & Knauer, D. (2002, March). The evidence and lessons learned from full service community schools. Paper presented at the Leave No Child Behind:

72   PURSUING   AND   SECURING   COLLABORATION

Improving Low-Performing Urban Schools Conference, The University at Albany, The State University of New York, Albany, NY.

Duncan, H. (1962). *Communication and social order*. New York: Oxford University Press.

Dunn, W. (1997). Probing the boundaries of ignorance in policy analysis. *American Behavioral Scientist, 40*, 277-298.

Edelman, I. (2001). Participation and service integration in community-based initiatives. *Journal of Community Practice, 9*(1), 57-75.

Elias, M. (1994). Capturing excellence in applied settings: A participant conceptualizer and praxis explicator role for community psychologists. *American Journal of Community Psychology, 22*, 293-318.

Foster-Fishman, P., Salem, D., Allen, N., & Fahrbach, K. (2001). Facilitating interorganizational collaboration: The contributions of inter-organizational alliances. *American Journal of Community Psychology, 29*, 875-905.

Gardner, S. (1999). *Beyond collaboration to results: Hard choices in the future of services to children and families*. Fullerton, CA: Center for Collaboration for Children, California State University.

Goldring, E., & Hausman, C. (2001). Civic capacity and school principals: The missing link for community development. In R. Crowson (Ed.), *Community development and school reform* (pp. 193-210). Oxford, U.K.: Elsevier Science, Ltd.

Hatch, T. (1998a). How community action contributes to achievement. *Educational Leadership, 55*(8), 16-19.

Hatch, T. (1998b). The differences in theory that matter in the practice of school improvement. *American Educational Research Journal, 35*(1), 3-31.

Held, D. (1997). Democracy and globalization. *Global Governance, 3*, 251-257.

Hill, P., Campbell, C., & Harvey, J. (2000). *It takes a city: Getting serious about urban school reform*. Washington, DC: The Brookings Institution.

Honig, M., Kahne, J., & McLaughlin, M. (2001). School-community connections: Strengthening opportunity to learn and opportunity to teach. In V. Richardson (Ed.), *Fourth handbook of research on teaching* (pp. 998-1028). New York: Macmillan.

Ingersoll, R. (2001). Teacher turnover and teacher shortages. *American Educational Research Journal, 38*, 499-534.

Janis, I. (1972). *Victims of groupthink*. Boston: Houghton Mifflin.

Johnson, O. (1993). Everybody talkin' 'bout collaboration ain't collaborating. *Georgia Academy Journal, 1*(1), 5-6.

Lawson, H. (1998). Collaborative educational leadership for 21st century school communities. In D. van Veen, C. Day, & G. Walraven (Eds.), *Multi-service schools: Integrated services for children and youth at risk* (pp. 173-193). Leuven/Apeldoorn, The Netherlands: Garant Publishers.

Lawson, H. (1999a). Two frameworks for analyzing relationships among school communities, teacher education, and interprofessional education and training programs. *Teacher Education Quarterly, 26*(4), 9-30.

Lawson, H. (1999b). Two new mental models for schools and their implications for principals' roles, responsibilities, and preparation. *National Association of Secondary School Principals' Bulletin, 83*(611), 8-27.

Lawson, H. (2000). Back to the future: New century professionalism and collaborative leadership for comprehensive, community-based systems of care. In A. Sallee, H. Lawson, & K. Briar-Lawson (Eds.), *Innovative practices with vulnerable children and families* (pp. 393-419). Dubuque, IA: Eddie Bowers Publishers, Inc.

Lawson, H. (2001, March). *Reformulating the school violence problem: Implications for research, policy, and practice*. International Conference on School Violence, UNESCO, Paris.

Lawson, H. (2002). Beyond community involvement and service learning to engaged universities. *Universities and Community Schools, 7*(1-2), 79-94.

Lawson, H., & Barkdull, C. (2000). Gaining the collaborative advantage and promoting systems and cross-systems change. In A. Sallee, H. Lawson, & K. Briar-Lawson (Eds.),

Innovative practices with vulnerable children and families (pp. 245-270). Dubuque, IA: Eddie Bowers Publishers, Inc.

Lawson, H., & Briar-Lawson, K. (1997). *Connecting the dots: Integrating school reform, school-linked services, parent involvement and community schools.* Oxford, OH: The Danforth Foundation & The Institute for Educational Renewal at Miami University.

Lawson H., & Sailor, W. (2000). Integrating services, collaborating, and developing connections with schools. *Focus on Exceptional Children, 33*(2), 1-22.

McCann, J., & Gray, B. (1986). Power and collaboration in human service domains. *International Journal of Sociology and Social Policy, 6*(3), 58-67.

McCroskey, J. (2003). Challenges and opportunities for higher education. In this volume—M.M. Brabeck, M.E. Walsh, & R. Latta (Eds.), *Meeting at the hyphen: Schools-universities-communities-professions in collaboration for student achievement and well being. The 102nd yearbook of the National Society for the Study of Education,* Part II. Chicago: National Society for the Study of Education.

Mitchell, D., & Scott, L. (1994). Professional and institutional perspectives on interagency collaboration. In L. Adler & S. Gardner (Eds.), *The politics of linking schools and social services* (pp. 75-92). Washington, DC & London: The Falmer Press.

Mooney, J., Kline, P., & Davoren, J. (1999). Collaborative interventions: Promoting psychosocial competence and academic achievement. In R. Tourse & J. Mooney (Eds.), *Collaborative practice: School and human service partnerships* (pp. 105-136). Westport, CT & London: Praeger.

Quinn, J. (2003). An interprofessional model and reflections on best collaborative practice. In this volume—M.M. Brabeck, M.E. Walsh, & R. Latta (Eds.), *Meeting at the hyphen: Schools-universities-communities-professions in collaboration for student achievement and well being. The 102nd yearbook of the National Society for the Study of Education,* Part II. Chicago: National Society for the Study of Education.

Rubin, H. (2002). *Collaborative leadership: Developing effective partnerships in schools and communities.* Thousand Oaks, CA: Corwin Press.

Scott, W.R. (1995). *Institutions and organizations.* Thousand Oaks, CA: Sage Publishers.

Shirley, D. (1998). *Community organizing for urban school reform.* Austin, TX: University of Texas Press.

Taylor, H.L. (2002, March). *Linking school reform to the neighborhood revitalization movement.* Keynote address at the Leave No Child Behind: Improving Low-Performing Urban Schools Conference, The University at Albany, The State University of New York, Albany, NY.

Taylor-Powell, E., Rossing, B., & Geran, J. (1998). *Evaluating collaboratives: Reaching the potential.* Madison, WI: University of Wisconsin-Extension, Program Development and Evaluation, Cooperative Extension.

Tschannen-Moran, M., & Hoy, W. (2000). A multidisciplinary analysis of the nature, meaning, and measurement of trust. *Review of Educational Research, 70,* 547-593.

Tyack, D. (1974). *The one best system: A history of American urban education.* Cambridge, MA: Harvard University Press.

Tyack, D., & Cuban, L. (1995). *Tinkering toward utopia: A century of public school reform.* Cambridge, MA: Harvard University Press.

Yohalem, N., & Pittman, K. (2001, October). *Powerful pathways: Framing options and opportunities for vulnerable youth.* Discussion paper presented at The Forum for Youth Investment, International Youth Foundation, Takoma Park, MD.

Walsh, M., Brabeck, M., & Howard, K. (1999). Interprofessional collaboration in children's services: Toward a theoretical framework. *Children's Services: Social Policy, Research, & Practice, 2,* 183-208.

Wenger, E. (1999). *Communities of practice: Learning, meaning, and identity.* London & New York: Cambridge University Press.

Wyn, J., & Dwyer, P. (2000). New patterns of youth in transition in education. *International Social Science Journal, 164,* 147-160.

CHAPTER 4

Empowerment Models for Interprofessional Collaboration

ROBERT L. CROWSON

This chapter discusses an emerging set of models for community empowerment in support of interprofessional collaboration. Just as there is a return to community efforts to reform/improve schools, there is simultaneously a renewed interest in what it means to bring community power to bear in the improvement of practice. Following a brief background section, this chapter evaluates some differences in and the implications of four emerging models of community-based empowerment. The chapter closes with an examination of the potential lessons for professionals working toward collaboration that are embedded within each of the four models.

Background

The welfare rights movement in the early 1960s was described by Piven and Cloward (1977) as a broad-based "rebellion of the poor against circumstances" (p. 265). Indeed, it was seen as nothing less than "a struggle by the black masses for the sheer right of survival" (p. 265). The words rebellion and struggle made perfect sense, claimed Piven and Cloward (p. 284), because this quite successful movement depended upon a vigorous mobilization of the poor—first for welfare disruption, then for added relief—as a replacement for previous, milder strategies of simply organizing shared political interests around change.

Beyond welfare, the early 1960s were also a heyday of community organizing in the style of Saul Alinsky (1946)—aggressive and confrontational. Rent strikes, boycotts, picketing, protests, marches, social-action planning, and lists of nonnegotiable demands comprised key elements of both the terminology and the technology of community

Robert Crowson is Professor of Educational Policy and Administration, Peabody College, Vanderbilt University.

empowerment in Alinsky's day (see Ecklein & Lauffer, 1972). Ecklein and Lauffer observed that an effective strategy was to engage in an array of "confrontations with the social structure," to win "organizing victories" through "concessions by the service system," for example, a new street light or an enforcement of housing codes (p. 11).

For educators, by far the most notable of the empowerment moves of the 1960s was the drive to bring community control to a number of heavily centralized large-city school districts. A particularly confrontational experiment in New York (Ocean Hill-Brownsville) received widespread attention when an elected community school board apparently went too far in challenging the authority of the teachers' union, the city's political leadership, and the school district bureaucracy. Stories of decentralization that had been tried and had failed in Detroit, Chicago, Los Angeles, and the District of Columbia joined the New York story to capture much of the limelight surrounding urban school reform into the early 1970s (LaNoue & Smith, 1973).

From the perspective of many analysts of that time, each of these movements reflected deep undercurrents of political dissatisfaction, anger, and alienation in U.S. cities. One analyst coined the phrase "alienation model of politics" and predicted that those involved in community-school relations would move from dissatisfaction, a sense of inefficacy, and an experience of rejection by the political system to a turning away from politics toward apathy. His later analysis found that what happened in the 1960s, instead, was a shift to activism and confrontation (Greenberg, 1976, p. 178). People embraced values of solidarity and participation/action as essential tools for recapturing powers of political expression and shared efficacy. They wanted to take control, and in many instances, run their local schools themselves.

By the mid-1970s, it was quite a different story. Momentum had been lost, leadership suffered, and opposition forces had coalesced. Piven and Cloward (1977) attributed this "demise" of activism to a withdrawal of leadership and support (even among the urban poor), the effects of some concessions and improved services that had resulted from the movement, and a restructuring of political authority in many cities under financial and business sources of intervention. Katznelson (1976) similarly attributed the lessening of discontent and the concomitant decrease in community activism in the 1970s to a strengthened web of control buffers, including a savvier array of city bureaucratic agencies. To other scholars, however, the loss of activism in the 1970s could be more justifiably laid at the doorstep of a renewed isolation of the underclass in the U.S. and essentially an abandonment of the poor. The poor were no longer central to our nation's political consciousness just a decade after the welfare rights movement (Karp, Stone, & Yoels, 1991; Wilson, 1987, 1996).

Whether that consciousness has been restored now, at the beginning of the 21st century, is questionable. But there is little doubt that community empowerment is once again up for debate. Far from a unidimensional movement this time, today's empowerment models incorporate a range of alternatives stretching from a new array of nonconfrontational alliances/partnerships in place of old-style mobilization to community-based economic empowerment, to an extension of concepts around the cultures of communities into empowerment opportunities, and even to choice and individual preferences as a form of empowerment. Each of these models presents its own implications for schools, professionals, and collaborative support systems for children, and each is examined in the following sections.

Alliances: A New Activism Model of Empowerment

At the height of the 1960s fascination with alienation and discontent (Gamson, 1968), today's evolution of Alinsky-style organizing for school reform would not likely have been foreseen. Modern-day activists in the Alinsky tradition, observes Dennis Shirley (1997, 2001b), have now jettisoned flamboyant radicalism in favor of a softer, more pragmatic policy of grassroots political alliances with established community organizations, such as religious institutions and neighborhood associations.

In analyzing community organizing from a post-Alinsky perspective, McKnight and Kretzmann (1995) have observed that an Alinsky strategy of targeting an enemy no longer makes much sense, as many traditional targets (e.g., factories, large retailers) in poor neighborhoods are no longer there. Furthermore, organizations that *are* there are agencies to be worked *with* rather than against (e.g., schools, churches, community police, service clubs). Thus, a collaborative and organized approach to building community through alliances has replaced old-style activism.

Much of the newly focused activism has been centered on the schools—however, not in the previous confrontational style. Rather, the new model seeks to use community alliances to "develop the civic capacity of parents, teachers, and community members to improve their public schools" (Shirley, 2001b, p. 144). Civic capacity and civic leadership have now replaced conflict and disruption, even when many of the techniques for a mobilization of the poor (e.g., public demonstrations of support, neighborhood walks for unity) remain much the same (Shirley, 1997).

The work of the Industrial Areas Foundation (IAF) in Texas is an exemplar of the new activism of alliance building. Founded as a community-action group by Saul Alinsky in the 1940s, the IAF transformed itself after Alinsky's death and over time into an organization working toward "a patient building of power through collaborations based on mutual interests" (Shirley, 1997, p. 38). The foundation launched some community organizing efforts directed heavily toward the public schools in San Antonio in 1972. By the early 1990s, the IAF "had become a powerful political force in Texas" (Shirley, 2001b, p. 143).

Among the foci of the IAF effort was the development of a network of affiliated urban schools in cities across the state, called Alliance Schools. Uniformly located in extremely low-income neighborhoods, the Alliance embodied the notion of assembling the resources and strengths of the community to improve the public schools (Shirley, 1997, 2001b). Indeed, it is a school-community relations theme turned on its head—with an emphasis on community in-reach rather than school outreach.

Shirley (1997) notes, however, that alliances starting with community in-reach have often faced difficulties. Principals and teachers can be wary and even resistant when IAF leaders and organizers bring parents into the schools. Some worry that "untrained parents can . . . destabilize the learning process" (p. 225), or that aggressive parents might "seek . . . to secure special individual favors for their children" (p. 231). Concerns are also rampant that the principal's professional authority to run the school might be compromised, the principal's own job might be at risk, and upper-level administrators would not be in favor of placing community ties above school district ties (Shirley, 1997). As a result, community and school goals may be in conflict.

By April 2001 the network of schools in Texas had grown from an initial cluster of 21 to 142 schools, all based in some of the poorest communities in Texas. Although the results thus far are mixed from site to site, Shirley's (1997, 2001b) conclusion is that there is indeed merit to the notion that community-based organizations can build strong ties to the public schools and influence those schools. Moreover, strong community ties "can support achievement rather than detract from it" (Shirley, 2001b, p. 164).

Interestingly, much of the initiative to organize the alliance approach has evolved out of the community organizing work of some faith-based institutions. The IAF exemplars Shirley (1997, 2001a) describes include some grassroots interfaith collaborations to organize poor families. They partnered with local businesses, pressed for added city services, increased neighborhood safety, and eventually developed after-school centers and collaborative relationships around curricula with the Allince schools.

It is important to note and remember, however, that the IAF saw itself as primarily a political, not a faith-based organization, even when relying on the dues paid by congregations to support community organizers (Shirley, 2001a). From this perspective, observes Shirley, "We do . . . have some evidence that congregations can be powerful allies with schools in the struggle to provide a safe environment for urban youth and to provide them with a high quality education" (p. 6).

The promising contributions from the faith side of each alliance include helping poor people view their schools as community resources; offering an array of added, neighborhood-concentrated resources to the schools (e.g., volunteers, parents, community organizers); and binding together supportive elements of engagement in the community, such as "praising students during services whose school work had improved" (Shirley, 2001a, p. 15).

Goldring and Hausman (2001) have developed some further thoughts on community engagement, or outreach to empower the community, by school principals. In exercising civic capacity, principals can help organize community alliances, motivate a shared community-mindedness, involve the schools in community-wide problems, establish a sense of reciprocity and trust across the many community institutions, and share resources.

Goldring and Hausman (2001) are by no means naïve and join Shirley (1997) in an awareness of the difficulties principals face when engaging in these community-building efforts. Principals already struggle with limited time and extraordinary demands and have few extra resources to draw upon. The standards/testing movement is pulling much administrative energy inward toward the classroom rather than outward toward the community. Indeed, when Goldring and Hausman (2001, p. 204) asked a sample of principals how they would use a "magical gift" of 10 additional work hours per week, few chose increased community outreach and parental involvement. Henig, Hula, Orr, and Pedescleaux (1999) add that civic capacity is in short supply from any source in many of our urban neighborhoods and that effective school-community collaborations and alliances remain extremely few in number.

Production: An Economic Model of Empowerment

McKnight and Kretzman (1995) have noted that at least one out-growth of the new activism is a reconceptualization of neighborhoods as centers of production, not just consumption. McKnight and Kretz-man (1996) also note that the consumption model tended to present low-income neighborhoods as full of special needs and deficiencies that must be met by outsiders bringing an array of appropriate services. The production viewpoint, alternatively, sees communities as full of capacities, resources, and internal assets, as well as opportunities to invest in themselves.

The ideas of capacity and production have been developed and extended to school-community relationships by Kerchner and Driscoll (Driscoll & Kerchner, 1999; Kerchner, 1997; Kerchner & McMurran, 2001). Their analyses closely link the education-related concept of social capital development with the processes (particularly the economic processes) of community development.

Kerchner and McMurran (2001) recognize that schools have long been magnets for people and for economic activity. Families and businesses are attracted to neighborhoods with attractive surroundings and, above all, good schools. It is logical for community activists to re-analyze the potential for every school to participate in economic growth and serve as an engine of community development. Even the poorest communities have a wealth of assets rather than an accumulation of deficits (Driscoll & Kerchner, 1999), and every neighborhood has capital and growth potential. The assets are often lodged in such building blocks for regeneration as gifted individuals, local businesses, citizens' associations, financial institutions, religious organizations, the police, libraries, parks, and schools (McKnight & Kretzman, 1996).

The idea of co-production between school and community has coincided with a relatively recent nationwide thrust toward neighborhood revitalization through the federally funded Empowerment Zone/Enterprise Communities (EZ/EC) program, inaugurated during the mid-1990s under President Bill Clinton (Boyd, Crowson, & Gresson, 1997).

At the heart of the EZ/EC effort is a belief in self-determination in place of governmental largesse (see Halpern, 1995). The key ingredients in a strategy that starts from existing strengths rather than assumed weaknesses in neighborhood renewal include the following: generating business initiatives and investments from the neighborhood, strengthening indigenous community institutions, encouraging market forces through an array of added incentives, and helping residents with many quality-of-life improvements. It is a bottom-up endeavor, depending heavily upon local entrepreneurial energies and local partnership activities as catalysts for change (Halpern).

Lizbeth Schorr (1997), among others, would place the neighborhood school at the heart of the revitalization thrust. As she cleanly frames it, improved learning opportunities in low-income neighborhoods require nothing less than a key place for the school "at the table where community reform is being organized" (p. 291). Similarly, Boyd, Crowson, and Gresson (1997) have suggested a transformation of and an extended role for the public school as an enterprise school. They argue,

An enterprise school might be expected to join an array of other neighborhood and city institutions in a much-larger-than services and a more-substantive-than-preparation participation in the development and regeneration of the school's neighborhood environment. Services to children and families should be included, to be sure, but far more fulsome and well-planned relationships may also be necessary. (p. 92)

Enterprise schooling and co-production have solid roots in the full-services movement in education (Boyd & Crowson, 2001; Dryfoos, this volume, chapter 7). But as service endeavors gained steam during the 1980s and early 1990s, a realization developed that the added delivery of professional services to low-income communities may fall far short of the full scope of efforts needed to strengthen families and whole neighborhoods. An altered paradigm emerged, one of outreach through partnerships with forces integral to both the ecology and economic development of each community—from employers to volunteers, churches, service providers, residents, retailers, community activists, the police, the parks department, etc. As noted throughout this volume, the full-service school finds much strength in a new sense of the local school as a central source of its own brand of societal investment in families, communities, and the development of children (Boyd, Crowson, & Gresson, 1997; Hawley, 1990; Kagan, 1989). Sadly, as McKnight and Kretzman (1996) observe, "Big city schools have often become so separate from local community initiatives that they are a liability rather than an asset" (p. 10).

Nevertheless, as an empowerment model with much potential, the idea that schools and communities can engage in co-production that will result in community revitalization places an emphasis on grassroots coalitions and multiple-stakeholder partnering. The need for considerable attention to empowerment issues has been more clearly recognized in the shaping of enterprise strategies than in full-service schooling. In the services movement, the assumption that professionals know best often constrained outreach programs and consequently the school's capacity to form partnerships (Boyd & Crowson, 2001).

The idea of partnering is currently in vogue in the community-relations literature, but partnering is extraordinarily hard to do (McCroskey, this volume, chapter 6; Sarason & Lorentz, 1998). For example, coalitions can develop and break apart; some participants may pursue neighborhood agendas (e.g., jobs for friends) that are not acceptable to their partners. Empowerment may mean different things to different members of the coalition. For some, broadened political participation in itself represents empowerment, while for others, empowerment can be represented only in activism and direct action (Couto, 1998). Educators quite often feel that the distribution of added information and "knowledge" is an empowering activity (Cohen & Lavach, 1995), but to other analysts, empowerment is better viewed as an extended process—e.g., overcoming a sense of powerlessness over time, developing a collective sense of purpose, recognizing some common grounds for change (Bookman & Morgen, 1988).

Not only are partnering and coalition building difficult, there has been surprisingly little research that has examined activities of educators in community-based partnering. In one of the few published studies, Knapp and Brandon (1998) observed that there are many constraints embedded in organizational structures and institutionalized forces, including differing vocabularies, reward systems, authority structures, uses of teamwork, assignment of credit or blame, and notions of what is and is not problematic. Strategies and guidelines for overcoming such constraints are currently nonexistent (Sarason & Lorentz, 1998).

Finally, the co-production model of shared empowerment through bottom-up renewal and revitalization carries baggage for the helping professions. The community development idea assumes that market forces can be effectively reintroduced to low-income communities, beginning a transformation process that trickles downward to improved opportunities for families and their children and upward to reformed and better performing schools. In contrast, the helping professions have strong Progressive-era roots in protecting poor families from the ravages of the market. Historically, healthy homes and neighborhoods and support for families and children were provided by a well-trained cadre of informed and committed people as a hedge against the horrors of sweatshop industrialism. As a result, a residue of distrust of market forces remains among human service professionals.

Regime: A Cultural Model of Empowerment

Empowerment in the form of "regime theorizing" (Elkin, 1987; Mossberger & Stoker, 2001; Ramsay, 1996; Stone, 1989) was applied originally to questions of citywide governance. Regime theorizing is beginning to be applied to individual neighborhoods and to the public schools (Ferman, 1996; Henig et al., 1999).

In simple terms, Stone (1989) defined a regime as the set of informal arrangements that surround the formal workings of government. In a more complex sense, regime theorizing represents an interpretation of politics rooted in cultural understandings of communities and peoples (Ramsay, 1996). Much influenced by Mansbridge's (1983) observation that something "beyond adversarial democracy" is often at the heart of policymaking, regime theory looks behind the scenes of politics to the informal, institutional, normative level of tacit understandings and expectations.

There are roots in the community-power studies of old (e.g., Hawley & Wirt, 1968). However, the idea of regime goes beyond earlier analyses of the local distribution of power and into the underlying foundations or substrata of power. Power is understood to be a deeply structured element of each neighborhood, existing in a reciprocal relationship with each community's culture and overall ecology (e.g., its essential lifeways, social institutions, local history, values, norms, expectations, market forces). To the regime theorist, the prime sources of empowerment in a community, and the school's role in support of its community, are to be discovered quite simply in the community's day-to-day activities and its essential way of life (Crowson & Boyd, 2001).

Just how does the day-to-day produce political power? We're not absolutely sure. Small opportunities in which people have a chance to share in some tasks and achievements that allow understanding, dependability, and trust to evolve are key, claims Stone (1989). Connections between people and institutions are essential, says Lauria (1997); connections have many sources, including spatial arrangements in a community, market relationships, service delivery relationships, and the work of local community members who represent local institutions.

Henton, Melville, and Walesh (1997) point out that grassroots leadership in civic entrepreneurship is vital—from business people, organizers, journalists, elected officials, or professionals in direct service. However, a deeper form of leadership—that of cultural broker—may also be essential (Chrispeels & Rivero, 2001). Cultural brokering can establish a bridge between the lifeways of a community and the institutions that serve it (such as schools). Indeed, empowerment is well embedded within each community's sense of social cohesion, and in that community's commitment to a uniqueness of character and/or a specialness in its way of life or culture (Ramsay, 1996).

However, regimes, like cultures, can be as resistant to change as they are engaged in change, and as impervious to empowerment as they are ready for empowerment. Tapping a culture's intrinsic bases of power is likely to bring out fear, inertia, distrust, and avoidance in addition to energy and activism (Scott, 1976).

As a construct, a sense of place (Driscoll, 2001; Driscoll & Kerchner, 1999; Philo & Kearns, 1993) captures both the activist and the non-activist sides of the regime model and the central connection between a neighborhood's culture and key supporting institutions such as schools. A sense of place, argues Driscoll, returns the public school to its neighborhood not just by respecting the values, but also through community engagement, crossing boundaries, shared community construction, and social capital development. It establishes the school, along with other community and city institutions, as part of a sustaining habitat (Duneier, 1999) in which a continuation of culture and a regeneration of community are simultaneously of value. Henig et al. (1999, p. 290) observe that the key to empowerment collaborations is to build a sustainable mobilization for reform that derives heavily from a viable regime platform of both place and participation (see also Harding, 1996).

A sense of place as a foundation to empowerment fits well with current inquiry into the new ecology of learning, much influenced by Bronfenbrenner (1979) and Goodlad (1987; see also Prawat & Peterson, 1999). The recent thrust to unpack the notion of social capital development into action at the community level also applies here (see Kahne & Bailey, 1997). Finally, the agency relationship between schools and communities (Asante, 1987; Savage, 2001) in which schools display a sense of centeredness around the ideas, values, culture, actions, psychology, and social systems of their communities (Morris, 1994, 2001) is a driving element in the renewed interest in the construct of place.

This construct of place is once again part of discussions about school curricula and pedagogy. Deweyan in its roots, the current discussion of place-based education includes attention to the study of regional and

local cultures, local natural phenomena, community issues or problems, local economies and vocations, and community processes (e.g.,
political activities, local services) (Smith, 2002). "Place-based education
holds out the potential of resituating learning within the context of
communities" claims Smith (p. 594).

Choice: A Preferences Model of Empowerment

For those people who are already empowered (usually financially),
choice has typically been a valuable tool for expressing and maintaining a set of educational advantages. Families who have a choice reside
in communities where there are schools that share their values, lifestyles, and academic expectations (Tiebout, 1956). The power to exit
(Hirschman, 1970) a school system when dissatisfied has been exer-
cised by large numbers of people on different occasions, such as the
white flight or home-school movements. This power, too, belongs to
people who already have the resources necessary to fulfill their special
desires, self-select, and choose.

Increasingly, school-improvement advocates have suggested that
families who are economically disadvantaged and insufficiently empowered to fulfill their educational preferences should be given the
power of school choice. Choice can be empowering for those who do
not have adequate resources to pursue preferences (Gorard, Fitz, &
Taylor, 2001). Choice is a basic value in a variety of increasingly popular options, including magnet schools, charter schools, and voucher
programs. The central value of choice in school improvement is that
families without sufficient power or resources are no longer locked in,
unable to avoid underperforming schools.

As a strategy for empowerment, choice is very different from the
other models described above. Choice focuses on individual or, at
most, family preferences, and not the community collectivity. Choice
is an individualistic model of empowerment that recognizes that the
dreams and drives of families in any one locale are not necessarily similar. Some families are much more education-minded than others, and
choice can serve their special interests well.

In what Smrekar (1996) labels "the paradox of choice," the benefit
to those who choose can be an empowering coalescence of "like-
minded individuals who view themselves as separate from other non-
choice individuals" (p. 156). These like-minded people are found to be
unusually committed to and satisfied with the schools they have
selected. And the very act of choosing generates a sense of power, says

Smrekar, for it "may make parents aware of benefits that would other-
wise go unnoticed" (p. 8). On the other side of the coin, however, are
non-choosing families and non-chosen schools, which can be left even
less empowered than before, as those who choose have "bailed out."

Indeed, the choice to bail out can be a key piece of the empowerment equation. In their study of the social context of choice in St.
Louis and Cincinnati, Smrekar and Goldring (1999) discovered that
"parents do not choose schools so much as they leave other schools
behind" (p. 31). In decisions to leave a school, dissatisfaction with the
consequences of staying was more important than choosing a particular school, a move *from* rather than a move *toward*. Even in very poor
neighborhoods, a social-class distinction was evident in the exercise of
choice. Lowest income parents tend to have a more restricted network
of friends and more limited information about school options than
higher income parents (Smrekar & Goldring).

Nevertheless, those who transfer to magnet settings express a sense
of empowerment concerning educational goals and beliefs. The trade-
off and paradox of empowerment is that parents who choose seem willing to suffer a loss of connection in community in exchange for a
shared empowerment of purpose and individual values and needs
(Smrekar & Goldring, 1999). Empowerment cannot be analyzed solely
at the communal level, but without a convergence of communal and
individual hopes and preferences, the likelihood is that those who can
will choose to exit.

Few studies exist on families who could choose a better school but
decide not to; however, Morris (1997, 1999) offers one instructive case
study. In St. Louis, Missouri, deep cross-neighborhood and cross-gen-
erational ties to a single public school led one inner city community to
reject all forms of choice available, including magnet schools and voluntary desegregation, in favor of maintaining the historical integrity
of their African American neighborhood. Morris (2001) suggests that
the power to reject choices to transfer African American students away
from their neighborhoods has become a rapidly emerging priority
among many Black families, educators, and community leaders.

Empowerment and Interprofessional Collaboration: Some Concluding Observations

Renewed respect for the school-community relationship and the
ecology of schooling (Bronfenbrenner, 1979) has brought empowerment
back into the discussion. No longer a unitary construct of community

activism, requiring an enemy with whom to do battle, empowerment has begun to acquire a number of forms (or "models"), with important differences among them.

The choice model and variations of collaborative empowerment fall on opposite ends of the spectrum, with individualized and collective participation marking the greatest difference. Differences also exist in matters of personal freedom, belief in market forces, self-help versus being provided for, and family-to-family autonomy. Individualism and choice appeal to parents' ability to provide nurturance, encouragement, stimulation, and oversight for their children's academic endeavors.

A direct link between collective forms of participation and student performance has not been empirically supported (Henig et al., 1999). Much of the current research on the impact of neighborhoods and communities on the development of children has concentrated on social disorganization and deficits rather than on the positive effects the people and the institutions of a neighborhood may have on achievement (Brooks-Gunn, Duncan, & Aber, 1997).

Key differences exist among the various collective models. The Alliances approach emphasizes the political actions of forging a coalition, developing a shared agenda, and gaining and using access to the schools. The Economic model focuses on building both community and school capacity for improvement and regeneration; the school is a partner in a community and its own empowerment, rather than the target of a coalition of community activists. Finally, the Regime model situates empowerment in the mobilization of some deeply embedded characteristics of community culture, relationships, values, and traditions. Bringing school and community together through such things as sharing a sense of place can in itself be empowering.

One of the most important links between empowerment and schools has yet to receive much attention in the current literature. The link between a community's service delivery systems and whatever empowerment model may be active in the community represents a neglected area. Implicitly, the coordinated-services or full-service school movement contains an empowerment theme through discussions of building social capital, meeting deep-seated needs, enhancing collaborations among professionals, and integrating services for greater effectiveness. However, there has been no explicit discussion of connecting services and community power.

White and Wehlage (1995) explored this relationship in one of the few studies on this issue. Their work criticized much of the professionalized service delivery at that time, citing the problematic assumption that professionals know best, along with the top-down identification of community needs and the neglect of the demand side of the service equation. Professional providers addressed the service needs that they themselves identified and defined, largely ignoring the service priorities identified by the communities.

If new collaborations and links and new models of alliances, regimes, and the like are to bear fruit, there must be attention to what Wynn, Meyer, and Richards-Schuster (1999) refer to as "connection impacts"—the impact of the connections among organizations on the children served, as well as on the community and on the organizations themselves. The expansion of after- and before-school programming offers significant service connections. This programming includes tutoring, recreation, and art and music education, among other things. After-school options are on the rise nationally, with public libraries, Boys and Girls Clubs, Y's, youth groups, faith-based organizations, and some private businesses leading the charge (Behrman, 1999). The impact of these connections remains to be demonstrated.

Each empowerment model carries a special and unique message, in addition to many opportunities for successful interprofessional collaborations around service delivery. A connection between services to children, families, and the community and the current strategies for empowering those communities exists, even if it still needs to be empirically demonstrated. The goal now must be to add specific connection impacts to existing practices and partnerships in each community.

The Alliances model, for example, can be an effective model for partnering with the schools to obtain needed services from the state and city, the private sector, and the school district bureaucracy. An alliance of community organizations and professionals also can help to provide the supportive conditions necessary for successful service delivery, including a safe community environment, bridging of cultural differences, rallying community participation, and blending of both school and nonschool services around common achievement objectives. Finally, as Shirley (1997) points out, a community alliance can provide services to schools even to the point of participating actively in school governance and instructional improvement.

The Production model of empowerment is heavily based on both community and school activism focused on community-led economic development. The key strategic ingredients include adding to and using effectively the strengths and assets of a community, assisting community leadership in attracting added resources to a neighborhood regeneration effort, and fostering community-wide buy-in to the power of self-determination. From this perspective, the local school may be a responsible partner in the development effort if the school acquires or is already well endowed with services as assets that are extended to the community. Employment counseling, family health services, adult literacy, before- and after-school child care, teen programs, and service-learning activities can be among the prime service assets delivered through school-based or school-linked sources.

The Regime model holds that the asset-value of collaborative professional service delivery is its brokering capacity between school and community (Cooper, Denner, & Lopez, 1999). If the services are not embedded in the community's own sense of place and do not have a close cultural connection with the community, then both the school's ability to be of service and the community's ability to benefit from that service are compromised. In Latino communities, for example (Torres & Miron, 2001), service providers must have an awareness of the dialectics of landscape. Dynamic connections among geography, family, language, neighborhood, social class, cultural identity, and employment opportunities construct the human landscape (pp. 112-113). Thus, an awareness of the human landscape of a particular community is essential in service provision.

If regime theorizing pushes service providers to be aware of cultural links, the Choice model pushes providers to create them. Empowerment through choice gives individual families an opportunity to opt out of the neighborhood collectivity. However, an array of appealing services to children and families might attract these families to opt back in. Dryfoos (1999; this volume, chapter 7), for example, has documented the attractiveness of a cafeteria of after-school, child care, enrichment, extended-day, youth development, sports, arts, and tutorial centers. Some might be school-based; others could be in partnership with community agencies. Wherever such services are located, parental preferences, parental needs and schedules, perceptions of available options, and satisfaction with each child's experiences must be at the center of a services program (Larner, Zippiroli, & Behrman, 1999).

Whatever the models of service delivery and empowerment or combinations among them, a key understanding must be established cleanly and clearly. Sarason (1995, p. 29) noted that a Custer-like stance of professionalism requiring that outsiders be kept outside must now adapt to the political principle that power is something to be shared, experienced, and protected under the aegis of community assistance and interprofessional collaboration.

Public schools have been in but not of their communities and neighborhoods for a long time. The importance and power of the neighborhood has been rediscovered as a vital complement to the work of the school, and the neighborhood has emerged as an important educator in its own right. However, for connective impacts to be developed and sustained, a service delivery tradition must evolve that is as comfortable with community engagement and the development of community capacity as it is with interprofessionalism.

REFERENCES

Alinsky, S.D. (1946). *Reveille for radicals*. Chicago: The University of Chicago Press.

Asante, M. (1987). *Afrocentricity*. Trenton, NJ: African World Press.

Behrman, R.E. (1999, Fall). When school is out. *The Future of Children, 9*(2), 1-160.

Bookman, A., & Morgen, S. (Eds.). (1988). *Women and the politics of empowerment*. Philadelphia: Temple University Press.

Boyd, W.L., & Crowson, R.L. (2001). Full-service schooling: The U.S. experience. In S. Riddell & L. Tett (Eds.), *Education, social justice and inter-agency working: Joined up or fractured policy?* (pp. 58-69). London: Routledge.

Boyd, W.L., Crowson, R.L., & Gresson, A. (1997). Neighborhood initiatives, community agencies, and the public schools: A changing scene for the development and learning of children. In M.C. Wang & M.C. Reynolds (Eds.), *Development and learning of children and youth in urban America* (pp. 81-104). Philadelphia: Temple University Center for Research in Human Development and Education.

Bronfenbrenner, U. (1979). *The ecology of human development*. Cambridge, MA: Harvard University Press.

Brooks-Gunn, J., Duncan, G.J., & Aber, J.L. (Eds.). (1997). *Neighborhood poverty: Context and consequences for children* (Vol. 1). New York: Russell Sage Foundation.

Chrispeels, J.H., & Rivero, E. (2001). Engaging Latino families for student success: How parent education can reshape parents' sense of place in the education of their children. *Peabody Journal of Education, 76*(2), 119-169.

Cohen, R., & Lavach, C. (1995). Strengthening partnerships between families and service providers. In P. Adams and K. Nelson (Eds.), *Reinventing human services: Community- and family-centered practice* (pp. 261-277). New York: Aldine De Gruyter.

Cooper, C.R., Denner, J., & Lopez, E.M. (1999, Fall). Cultural brokers: Helping Latino children on pathways toward success. *The Future of Children, 9*(2), 51-58.

Couto, R.A. (1998, November). Community coalitions and grassroots policies of empowerment. *Administration & Society, 30*(5), 569-594.

Crowson, R.L., & Boyd, W.L. (2001). The new role of community development in educational reform. *Peabody Journal of Education, 76*(2), 9-29.

Driscoll, M.E. (2001). The sense of place and the neighborhood school: Implications for building social capital and for community development. In R.L. Crowson (Ed.), *Community development and school reform* (pp. 19-41). London: Elsevier Science, Ltd.

Driscoll, M.E., & Kerchner, C.T. (1999). The implications of social capital for schools, communities, and cities: Educational administration as if a sense of place mattered. In J. Murphy & K.S. Louis (Eds.), *Handbook of research on educational administration* (2nd ed., pp. 385-404). San Francisco: Jossey-Bass.

Dryfoos, J.G. (1999, Fall). The role of the school in children's out-of-school time. *The Future of Children, 9*(2), 117-134.

Dryfoos, J. (2003). Comprehensive schools. In this volume—M.M. Brabeck, M.E. Walsh, & R. Latta (Eds.), *Meeting at the hyphen: Schools-universities-communities-professions in collaboration for student achievement and well being. The 102nd yearbook of the National Society for the Study of Education*, Part II. Chicago: National Society for the Study of Education.

Duneier, M. (1999). *Sidewalk*. New York: Farrar, Straus and Giroux.

Ecklein, J.L., & Lauffer, A.A. (1972). *Community organizers and social planners*. New York: John Wiley & Sons, Inc.

Elkin, S.L. (1987). *City and regime in the American republic*. Chicago: The University of Chicago Press.

Ferman, B. (1996). *Challenging the growth machine: Neighborhood politics in Chicago and Pittsburgh*. Lawrence: University Press of Kansas.

Gamson, W.A. (1968). *Power and discontent*. Homewood, IL: The Dorsey Press.

Goldring, E.B., & Hausman, C. (2001). Civic capacity and school principals: The missing links for community development. In R.L. Crowson (Ed.), *Community development and school reform* (pp. 193-209). London: Elsevier Science, Ltd.

Goodlad, J.I. (1987). *The ecology of school renewal: Eighty-sixth yearbook of the National Society for the Study of Education*, Part I. Chicago: National Society for the Study of Education.

Gorard, S., Fitz, J., & Taylor, C. (2001, October). School choice impacts: What do we know? *Educational Researcher, 30*(7), 18-23.

Greenberg, S.B. (1976). Political alienation and political action. In W.D. Hawley (Ed.), *Theoretical perspectives on urban politics* (pp. 176-195). Englewood Cliffs, NJ: Prentice-Hall.

Halpern, R. (1995). *Rebuilding the inner city*. New York: Columbia University Press.

Harding, A. (1996). Is there a "new community power" and why should we need one? *International Journal for Urban and Regional Research, 20*(4), 637-655.

Hawley, W.D. (1990). Missing pieces of the educational reform agenda: Or why the first and second waves may miss the boat. In S.B. Bacharach (Ed.), *Education reform: Making sense of it all* (pp. 213-233). Boston: Allyn & Bacon.

Hawley, W.D., & Wirt, F.M. (Eds.). (1968). *The search for community power*. Englewood Cliffs, NJ: Prentice-Hall.

Henig, J.R., Hula, R.C., Orr, M., & Pedescleaux, D.S. (1999). *The color of school reform: Race, politics, and the challenge of urban education*. Princeton, NJ: Princeton University Press.

Henton, D., Melville, J., & Walesh, K. (1997). *Grassroots leaders for a new economy: How civic entrepreneurs are building prosperous communities*. San Francisco: Jossey-Bass.

Hirschman, A. (1970). *Exit, voice and loyalty*. Cambridge, MA: Harvard University Press.

Kagan, S.L. (1989, October). Early care and education: Beyond the schoolhouse doors. *Phi Delta Kappan, 71*(2), 107-112.

Kahne, J., & Bailey, K. (1997, October). *The role of social capital in youth development: The case of "I have a dream."* Paper presented at the annual meeting of the University Council for Educational Administration, Orlando, FL.

Karp, D.A., Stone, G.P., & Yoels, W.C. (1991). *Being urban: A sociology of city life* (2nd ed.). New York: Praeger.

Katznelson, I. (1976). The crisis of the capitalist city: Urban politics and social control. In W.D. Hawley (Ed.), *Theoretical perspectives on urban politics* (pp. 214-229). Englewood Cliffs, NJ: Prentice-Hall.

Kerchner, C.T. (1997). Education as a city's basic industry. *Education and Urban Society, 29*(4), 424-441.

Kerchner, C.T., & McMurran, G. (2001). Leadership outside the triangle: The challenges of school administration in highly porous systems. In R.L. Crowson (Ed.), *Community development and school reform* (pp. 43-46). London: Elsevier Science, Ltd.

Knapp, M.S., & Brandon, R.N. (1998). Building collaborative programs in universities. In M.S. Knapp and Associates (Eds.), *Paths to partnership* (pp.139-164). Lanham, MD: Rowman & Littlefield Publishers, Inc.

LaNoue, G.R., & Smith, B.L.R. (1973). *The politics of school decentralization*. Lexington, MA: Lexington Books.

Larner, M.B., Zippiroli, L., & Behrman, R.E. (1999, Fall). When school is out: Analysis and recommendations. *The Future of Children, 9*(2), 4-20.

Lauria, M. (Ed.). (1997). *Reconstructing urban regime theory*. Thousand Oaks, CA: Sage Publications.

Mansbridge, J.J. (1983). *Beyond adversarial democracy*. Chicago: University of Chicago Press.

McCroskey, J. (2003). Challenge and opportunities for higher education. In this volume—M.M. Brabeck, M.E. Walsh, & R. Latta (Eds.), *Meeting at the hyphen: Schools-universities-communities-professions in collkaboration for student achievement and well being. The 102nd yearbook of the National Society for the Study of Education*, Part II. Chicago: National Society for the Study of Education.

McKnight, J.L., & Kretzman, J.P. (1995). Community organizing in the eighties: Toward a post-Alinsky agenda. In J. McKnight (Ed.), *The careless society: Community and its counterfeits* (pp. 153-160). New York: Basic Books.

McKnight, J.L., & Kretzman, J.P. (1996). *Mapping community capacity* (Neighborhood Innovations Network report). Northwestern University: Institute for Policy Research.

Morris, J.E. (1994, October). *Community in an all-black neighborhood school: Implications for immersion schools*. Paper presented at the annual meeting of the University Council for Educational Administration, Philadelphia, PA.

Morris, J.E. (1997). *Voluntary desegregating in St. Louis, Missouri: Impact on partnerships among schools, African American families and communities*. Unpublished doctoral dissertation, Peabody College, Vanderbilt University.

Morris, J.E. (1999). A pillar of strength: An African American school's communal bonds with families and communities since *Brown*. *Urban Education, 33*(5), 584-605.

Morris, J.E. (2001, September). Forgotten voices of black educators: Critical race perspectives on the implementation of a desegregation plan. *Educational Policy, 15*(4), 575-600.

Mossberger, K., & Stoker, G. (2001, July). The evolution of urban regime theory: The challenge of conceptualization. *Urban Affairs Review, 36*(6), 810-835.

Philo, C., & Kearns, G. (1993). Culture, history, capital: A critical introduction to the selling of places. In G. Kearns & C. Philo (Eds.), *Selling places: The city as cultural capital, past and present* (pp. 1-32). Oxford: Pergamon Press.

Piven, F.F., & Cloward, R.A. (1977). *Poor people's movements: Why they succeed and how they fail*. New York: Anchor Books.

Prawat, R.S., & Peterson, P.L. (1999). Social constructivist views of learning. In J. Murphy & K.S. Louis (Eds.), *Handbook of research on educational administration* (2nd ed., pp. 203-226). San Francisco: Jossey-Bass.

Ramsay, M. (1996). *Community, culture, and economic development: The social roots of local action*. Albany, NY: SUNY Press.

Sarason, S.B. (1995). *Parental involvement and the political principle*. San Francisco: Jossey-Bass.

Sarason, S.B., & Lorentz, E.M. (1998). *Crossing boundaries: Collaboration, coordination, and the redefinition of resources*. San Francisco: Jossey-Bass.

Savage, C.J. (2001). "Because we did more with less": The agency of African American teachers in Franklin, Tennessee, 1890-1967. *Peabody Journal of Education, 76*(2), 170-203.

Schorr, L.B. (1997). *Common purposes: Strengthening families and neighborhoods to rebuild America*. New York: Anchor Books.

Scott, J.C. (1976). *The moral economy of the peasant*. New Haven, CT: Yale University Press.

Shirley, D. (1997). *Community organizing for urban school reform*. Austin, TX: University of Texas.

Shirley, D. (2001a). Faith-based organizations, community development, and the reform of public schools. *Peabody Journal of Education, 76*(2), 222-240.

Shirley, D. (2001b). Linking community organizing and school reform. In R.L. Crowson (Ed.), *Community development and school reform* (pp. 139-169). London: Elsevier Science, Ltd.

Smith, G.A. (2002, April). Place-based education: Learning to be where we are. *Phi Delta Kappan, 83*(8), 584-594.

Smrekar, C. (1996). *The impact of school choice and community: In the interest of families and schools*. Albany, NY: SUNY Press.

Smrekar, C., & Goldring, E. (1999). *School choice in urban America: Magnet schools and the pursuit of equity*. New York: Teachers College Press.

Stone, C.N. (1989). *Regime politics: Governing Atlanta, 1946-1988*. Lawrence, KS: University Press of Kansas.

Tiebout, C. (1956, October). A pure theory of local expenditures. *Journal of Political Economy, 64*, 416-424.

Torres, R.D., & Miron, L.F. (2001). Economic geography of Latino Los Angeles: Schooling and urban transformations at the century's end. In R.L. Crowson (Ed.), *Community development and school reform* (pp. 101-120). London: Elsevier Science, Ltd.

White, J.A., & Wehlage, G. (1995). Community collaboration: If it is such a good idea, why is it so hard to do? *Educational Evaluation and Policy Analysis, 17*(1), 23-38.

Wilson, W.J. (1987). *The truly disadvantaged: The inner city, the underclass, and public policy*. Chicago: University of Chicago Press.

Wilson, W.J. (1996). *When work disappears: The world of the new urban poor*. New York: Alfred A. Knopf.

Wynn, J., Meyer, S., & Richards-Schuster, K. (1999). *Furthering education: The relationship of schools and other organizations*. Unpublished manuscript, Chapin Hall Center for Children at the University of Chicago.

CHAPTER 5

The Role of the American Research University in Advancing System-Wide Education Reform, Democratic Schooling, and Democracy

LEE BENSON AND IRA HARKAVY

Community-higher education-school partnerships should be the core strategy for improving schools and schooling systems from pre-K through college. We base our argument on two propositions: 1) committed, multi-sectoral community partnerships are a prerequisite for sustained school- and system-wide educational reform, and without such partnerships, meaningful educational reform will not happen, and 2) sustained, system-wide educational reform requires transforming the educational system from pre-K through colleges and universities. Therefore, higher educational institutions must be partners in and strategic components of sustained, system-wide educational reform.

Our focus on community partnerships and the central role of higher education institutions in such partnerships is based on 17 years of work with public schools in Philadelphia, with particular emphasis on West Philadelphia, the local community of the University of Pennsylvania (Penn), and regional and national efforts to replicate this work. In 1985, four of our students developed the West Philadelphia Improvement Corps (WEPIC) with our assistance. Initially a school-based youth corps, WEPIC has evolved into a comprehensive program to create higher education-assisted community schools as the social, educational, and service delivery centers for the entire community. At its core, WEPIC consists of school personnel and neighborhood residents receiving strategic assistance from Penn students, faculty, and staff. During WEPIC's first summer, we realized that focusing only on schools and teaching could not accomplish school change. As WEPIC evolved into Penn's major school reform project, we recognized that

---

Lee Benson is Professor Emeritus of History at the University of Pennsylvania. Ira Harkavy is the Associate Vice President and Director, Center for Community Partnerships, University of Pennsylvania.

94

school and school system change are connected to community change and mobilization, and that effective community change depends on transforming the local public schools into "good" public schools.

This increased recognition of the school-community connection may result from frustration with reform efforts focused on the school and/or school system as the only units of change. Certainly it is a reaction to the troubling and visible inequalities between urban, largely nonwhite school systems and communities and suburban school systems and communities.

Neither governmental policy nor U.S. higher educational institutions have systemically addressed the intersection of community and school. A strategy must be developed that connects school change to a process of democratic community change and development. The strategy should integrate and mobilize the untapped resources of communities, including colleges and universities, to improve schooling and community life.

Democratic Schooling, Democracy, and the U.S. Research University

The path toward effective democratic schooling and ongoing systemic change must run through U.S. higher education, particularly the U.S. research university. The research university's significance derives in part from its status as a powerful and resource-rich local institution. Universities have become arguably the most influential institutions in the world. In 1990, while president of Harvard, Derek Bok highlighted the growth in importance of universities since World War II:

... all advanced nations depend increasingly on three critical elements: new discoveries, highly trained personnel, and expert knowledge. In America, universities are primarily responsible for supplying two of these three ingredients and are a major source of the third. That is why observers ranging from Harvard sociologist Daniel Bell to editorial writers from the Washington Post have described *the modern university as the central institution in post-industrial society* [italics added] ... (Bok, 1990, p. 3).

Bok did not explicitly emphasize, however, the most critical reason for higher education's leadership role. The schooling system functions as the core and strategic subsystem of modern information societies. More than any other subsystem, education influences the functioning of the societal system as a whole and has the greatest direct and indirect effects. Also, universities function as the primary shapers of the overall schooling system in the United States. The strong influence of research universities stems not only from their prestige and power, but also from their role in educating teachers.

At the turn of the 20th century, William Rainey Harper, the first president of the University of Chicago (1892-1906), identified the urban "Great University" as the most strategic organizational innovation of modern society (Goodspeed, pp. 109-110, 124-125). To build a great university and help realize in practice the democratic promise of the United States, Harper argued that the University of Chicago must take responsibility for developing and implementing solutions to correct the severe problems confronting Chicago, particularly within its public school system. After a university trustee criticized him for sponsoring a journal focused on pedagogy in precollegiate schools, Harper emphatically proclaimed, "As a university we are interested *above all else in pedagogy*" [italics added] (as quoted in Wirth, 1964, pp. 47-48). Harper's devotion to pedagogy derived from two propositions central to his vision for the University of Chicago in particular, American universities in general, and universities throughout the world: "Education is the basis of all democratic progress. The problems of education are, therefore, the problems of democracy" (Harper, 1905, p. 25). More than any other institution, the university determines the character of the schooling system. Again, to quote Harper: "Through the school system, the character of which, in spite of itself, the university determines and in a larger measure controls . . . through the school system every family in this entire broad land of ours is brought into touch with the university; for from it proceeds the teachers or the teachers' teachers " (1905, p. 25).

Has Harper's vision been realized? Has the U.S. higher education system positively contributed to the successful functioning of the U.S. schooling system? To answer that question, we must first determine how best to conceive and measure "successful functioning." What do scores on standardized tests, for example, tell us about the state of schooling? What does the widening gap in the educational achievement of urban, predominantly African American and Latino youth and their largely white suburban counterparts tell us? To answer such questions requires careful thought about, and specific explanations of, the aim(s) and methods of schooling.

John Dewey's work, with its strong emphasis on education for democracy, provides a theoretical beginning. In a 1997 article on "Democracy and Inquiry," Charles Anderson perceptively summarized Dewey's position:

Dewey thought that democratic citizenship could be understood as the unifying aim of education [italics added]. But Dewey thought of democracy as but one manifestation of a power that was vested in and distinctive in humanity. That power was inquiry . . . .

Inquiry, Dewey taught, was the method of democracy. It was also the method of science. And as the century wore on, it in fact became the method of management, of the law, of education itself.

Here then is a theme that can unify education as it unifies the spheres of everyday life [italics added]. Citizenship now carries enhanced meaning. It pertains not just to public affairs but to our *performance* in every realm of life [original emphasis]. (1997a, p. 16)

Informed by Dewey's theory of inquiry-based, real-world action-oriented, participatory democratic schooling for participatory democratic citizenship—our lengthy term for Dewey's powerful set of concepts—we believe that U.S. universities have had and continue to have harmful effects on the public school system. Higher education has tended to function as an essentially Platonic, elitist, anti-democratic system. Put another way, Plato still dominates the university and contributes to public schools' inability to perform their roles well, particularly their critical role in providing schooling and pedagogy that prepares students for a democratic society (Aron, 1970; Benson & Harkavy, 1997; Harkavy & Benson, 1998). Full discussion of this theoretical proposition would require an entire chapter. Here we simply call attention to the direct and indirect harmful effects resulting from: 1) the pressures to produce high school graduates prepared for admission to prestigious colleges; and 2) the deliberate choice of leading graduate schools of education to ape the much more prestigious schools of arts and sciences, thereby "distancing themselves from both the task of training teachers for elementary and secondary schools and that of addressing the problems and needs of those schools " (Judge, 1982, p. 6).

Our position is simple and unequivocal: without democratic radical reform of higher education in the United States, there will be no successful democratic schooling reform and no truly democratic society. Participatory democratic societies require the development of participatory democratic universities. The radical reform of higher education will most likely occur in the crucible of significant, sustained engagement with public schools and their local communities. Ivory tower isolation neither sheds intellectual light nor produces societal fruit. Fortunately, a university civic responsibility movement is emerging and working toward an engaged, democratic university with intellectual and societal promise.[1]

Following Donald Kennedy (1997), we argue that higher education is in the early stages of its third "revolution." The first revolution occurred in the late 19th century. Beginning at Johns Hopkins in 1876, the uniquely U.S. adaptation of the German model of schooling revolutionized higher education. By the turn of the century, the U.S. research university had been established. The second revolution began in 1945 with Vannevar Bush's "endless [research] frontier" manifesto and produced the big science, Cold War, entrepreneurial university (Stokes, 1997, p. 9). The third revolution began about 1989. The fall of the Berlin Wall, the dissolution of the Soviet Union, and the end of the Cold War provided the necessary conditions for the emergence of the democratic cosmopolitan civic university. The democratic cosmopolitan civic university emerged a century after Harper first envisioned it as a defensive response to the increasingly obvious and embarrassing contradiction between the growing status, wealth, and power of higher education in U.S. society, particularly at its elite research universities, and the decline of U.S. cities.

The third revolution is still in its early stages. According to an old academic joke, universities constitute such self-contradictory and internally competitive institutions that they tend to move with all the speed of a runaway glacier. Nevertheless, things are changing in the right direction. One indicator of positive change is the accelerating number and variety of higher education institutions that publicly proclaim their desire to collaborate actively with neighboring public schools and local communities. Predictably, intentions to collaborate surpass mutually respectful and mutually beneficial collaboration. To move toward institutionalized change and significant results, we call for acceptance of this radical proposition: *All higher U.S. educational institutions should explicitly make solving the problem of the U.S. schooling system their highest institutional priority; their contributions to its solution should count heavily both in assessing their institutional performance and in responding to their requests for renewed or increased financial support.* Actively helping to develop an effective and integrated pre-K through university schooling system should become the collaborative primary mission of and performance test for universities and colleges in the United States.

Obviously, colleges and universities have other important missions outside of collaboratively helping to solve the problem of the schooling system. These missions, such as advancing knowledge, educating students for democratic citizenship, and developing the next generation of scholars and professionals, also would benefit from successful collaborative work on the schooling problem, although space does not permit us to explore these issues here. However, three corollary propositions are outlined briefly: (1) Given the disruptive, complex consequences of the rapid development of information societies throughout the world, and the critical role schooling must play in such societies, improving the schooling system problem should now constitute U.S. society's highest priority; (2) solving the overall problem of the schooling system must begin with changes at the university level; and (3) if universities take responsibility for solving the overall schooling system problem, they will secure greater resources than they now have to carry out their missions.

In the short term, higher education institutions may experience difficulties associated with radical change in academic priorities and cultures. In effect, we are calling on colleges and universities to reallocate the largest share of their intellectual resources to improving their neighboring public schools and communities.

Given their present competitive, "pure research" orientation, how can we expect higher education institutions to answer our call positively rather than dismissively? Since universities are not experiencing any crisis, why should "successful" universities take on the difficult job of trying to transform themselves into civic institutions that actively accept collaboration with their local schools and communities as an imperative for the new millennium? We contend that if they succeed, they will be better able to achieve their professed morally inspired and loudly trumpeted missions: To advance, preserve, and transmit knowledge, as well as to help produce the highly skilled, well-educated, moral citizens necessary to develop and maintain an optimally democratic society (Anderson, 1993, 1997b; Harkavy, 1999). In the end, universities and academics not only want to do well; they also want to do good. In a sense, how best to satisfy that desire is the principal—and principled—problem universities and academics must solve in the 21st century.

To understate the case, the radical transformation sketched above will be hard to achieve. But it is not impossible, provided that universities and academics embrace change as their categorical imperative and work creatively to develop and implement a strategy in which community-higher education-school partnerships function as the core means to realize an effective "democratic devolution revolution." To delineate that strategy, we recount some of the recent history of our own university work with public schools below. First, we describe the changes that needed to take place within Penn for it to achieve this democratic devolution revolution.

"Democratic Devolution Revolution"

Since 1985, Penn has increasingly engaged itself with local public schools in a comprehensive community-higher education-school partnership known as WEPIC. In its 17 years of operation, the project has evolved significantly. Moreover, it has helped spawn a variety of related projects engaging Penn with public schools in West Philadelphia. From its inception, Penn's work with WEPIC was designed to forge mutually beneficial and respectful community-higher education-school partnerships. In recent years, we have conceptualized the work in much broader terms, as part of a radical attempt to advance a "democratic devolution revolution " (Benson & Harkavy, 2000, p. 182; Harkavy, 1997). We believe that Penn's work (and the work of many other higher education institutions) is best understood through this concept.

For nearly a generation, John Gardner thought and wrote about organizational devolution, and the university's potential role in it. For Gardner, the effective functioning of organizations requires planned and deliberate devolution of functions:

We have in recent decades discovered some important characteristics of the large-scale organized systems—government, private sector, whatever, under which so much of contemporary life is organized. One such characteristic, perhaps the most important, is that the tendency of such systems to centralize must be countered by deliberate dispersion of initiative downward and outward through the system. The corporations have been trying to deal with this reality for almost 15 years and government is now pursuing it . . .

What this means for government is a substantially greater role for the states and cities. And none of them are entirely ready for that role. . . Local government must enter into collaborative relations with non-governmental elements. (Gardner, 1998, p. 3)

In effect, Gardner proposes that higher education become more involved in building community, convening public discussions, educating public-spirited leaders, offering continuing civic and leadership seminars, and providing a wide range of technical assistance. An effective democratic devolution revolution, he emphasizes, requires more than practicing new forms of interaction among federal, state, and local governments and among agencies at each level of government. For Gardner, government integration by itself does not make meaningful change. New cooperative forms of interaction among the public, for-profit, and non-profit sectors are also mandatory. Government must function as a collaborating partner, effectively facilitating rather than imposing cooperation among all sectors of society to support and strengthen individuals, families, and communities (Gardner, 1998).

To extend Gardner's observation about universities, and similar observations by such influential thinkers as Ernest Boyer (1994), Derek Bok (1990), and Alexander Astin (1997), we propose a democratic devolution revolution. In our proposed revolution, government serves as a powerful catalyst and provides the funds needed to create stable, ongoing, effective partnerships. But government would function only as a second-tier deliverer of services. Universities, community-based organizations, unions, churches, other voluntary associations, school children and their parents, and community members would function as the first-tier operational partners. That is, various levels and departments of government would guarantee aid and significantly finance welfare services. Local, personalized, integrated services, however, would be delivered by the third (private, non-profit, voluntary associations) and fourth (family, kin, neighbors, friends) sectors of society. Put another way, government would not be responsible for the delivery of services; it would have macro fiscal responsibilities, including fully adequate provision of funds.

This strategy requires creatively and intelligently adapting the work of local institutions to the locally determined needs and resources of communities. The strategy also assumes that colleges and universities potentially constitute powerful partners and creative catalysts for change and improvement in the quality of life in U.S. cities and communities.

For colleges and universities to fulfill their potential and contribute to this democratic devolution revolution, however, they will have to make significant changes. To begin with, higher education institutions must recognize that they contribute to the problem by disengaging from their local communities. To become part of the solution, colleges and universities must take on the hard task of transforming themselves and becoming socially responsible civic universities dedicated to advancing knowledge and education for democracy. Institutional cultures and structures must change through the development of a comprehensive, realistic strategy.

A major component of the strategy Penn and other higher education institutions are developing focuses on higher education-assisted community schools designed to help educate, engage, activate, and serve all members of the school's community. The strategy assumes that universities can help develop and maintain community schools. These schools serve as focal points in creating healthy urban environments.

This strategy asserts that, like higher education institutions, public schools can function as environment-changing institutions and become the centers of broad-based partnerships that engage a wide variety of community organizations and institutions. Public schools "belong" to all members of the community, and thus are well suited to function as neighborhood hubs where local partnerships can be generated and sustained. In this role, schools function as community institutions, providing locally-based responses to significant problems and creating the democratic, neighborly communities that Dewey envisioned.

The higher education-assisted community school reinvents and updates an old idea, that the school can effectively serve as the core neighborhood institution, providing comprehensive services and galvanizing other community institutions and groups. That idea inspired the early settlement house workers; they recognized the centrality of the neighborhood school in community life and hailed its potential as the strategic site for community stabilization and improvement. At the turn of the 20th century, socially concerned settlement house workers like Jane Addams and Lillian Wald pioneered the transfer of social, health, cultural, and recreational services to the public schools of major U.S. cities (Harkavy & Puckett, 1994). Feminist settlement leaders recognized that though there were very few settlement houses, there were many public schools. Not surprisingly, Dewey's ideas about "The School As Social Centre" (1902/1976, p. 80) had been shaped by his experiences and discussions with Jane Addams and others at Hull House. In an influential address, Dewey paid homage to them:

I suppose, whenever we are framing our ideals of the school as a social Centre, what we think of is particularly the better class of social settlement. What we want is to see the school, every public school, doing something of the same sort of work that is now done by a settlement or two scattered at wide distances through the city. (Dewey, 1902/1976, pp. 90–91)

Dewey failed to note, however, two critically important conceptions of community schools: (1) the school as the core community institution actively engaged in solving basic community problems; and (2) the school as a community institution that educates young children through engagement in real-world, community problem solving. He did recognize that if the neighborhood school were to function as a genuine community center, it needed additional support and human resources. But Dewey never identified universities as a key source of broadly based support for community schools.

Higher education institutions across the country are actively engaged in creating community schools. Undergraduates and graduate students in dentistry, medicine, social work, education, and nursing are learning to work together as they serve the public schools. Public school students are also connecting their education to real-world problem solving and providing service to other students and community members. Adults are participating in locally based job training, skill enhancement, and ongoing education. Many communities are moving toward effective integration of services for school children and their families.

But higher education-assisted community schools have a long way to go before they can mobilize the untapped resources of their communities, allowing individuals and families to function both as deliverers and recipients of local services.

Translating Ideas into Reality:
Penn and the West Philadelphia Public Schools

Following Gardner (1998), we believe that for all U.S. universities—including Penn—the greatest responsibility is to help implement the democratic promise of the Declaration of Independence and become an exemplary democratic "City on the Hill." Penn can best fulfill its democratic responsibility through effective integration and improvement of the West Philadelphia schooling system, beginning with Penn's own neighborhood but including all schools within West Philadelphia.

Penn's work with West Philadelphia public schools has been a process of painful organizational learning (Whyte, 1991, pp. 237–241). We cannot overemphasize that our understanding and activities continue to change over time. Penn is only beginning to tap its human resources in ways that will mutually benefit Penn and its neighbors, resulting in substantial school, community, and university change. Our work is a concrete example of democratic, integrated teaching, learning, research, and service. Our strategic problem has been and continues to be radically improving the quality of the West Philadelphia schooling system.

Ironically, when we first began working to change university-community relationships in 1985, we did not envision them in terms of schools, teaching, and learning. What immediately concerned us was that West Philadelphia was rapidly and visibly deteriorating, affecting the university's attractiveness, ambience, and reputation. West Philadelphia's deterioration, therefore, motivated Penn to address the problems facing urban schools. But what specifically could Penn do, and how could it be encouraged to do it?

Our experiences during the 1960s with undergraduates, who were catalytic agents of university change, led us to design a special undergraduate Honors Seminar. The seminar sought to stimulate undergraduates to think critically about what Penn should do to improve its environmental situation. The president of the university, Sheldon Hackney, a former professor of American history, agreed to join us in teaching that seminar in the spring 1985 semester. The seminar's title suggests its general focus: "Urban University-Community Relationships: Penn-West Philadelphia, Past, Present, and Future, As a Case Study."

When the seminar began, we knew nothing about Dewey's community school ideas or the history of community school experiments. We had not considered working with public schools in West Philadelphia. A complex, painful process of trial and error led us, President Hackney, and our students to see that using Penn's internal and external resources to improve West Philadelphia public schools and neighborhoods was the best strategy to address the rapid deterioration. Unwittingly, during the course of the seminar we reinvented Dewey's community school idea.

We realized that public schools could function as core community centers for organizing, educating, and transforming entire neighborhoods by serving as neighborhood sites for the West Philadelphia Improvement Corps—WEPIC. WEPIC is made up of school personnel and neighborhood residents who receive assistance from Penn students, faculty, and staff. WEPIC helped transform the traditional West Philadelphia public school system into a new system of community-centered schools with assistance from Penn.

Students in the initial seminar focused their research on a specific problem that adversely affected specific groups in West Philadelphia. During the course of the semester, four students decided to work cooperatively to study the problem of youth unemployment in the context of improving the West Philadelphia physical environment. The students did research, consulted experts in Philadelphia and elsewhere, and interviewed leaders of local groups. They then developed a proposal to create a "better and much less expensive" youth corps than currently existed. More specifically, they proposed a neighborhood-based summer-job training program focused on neighborhood improvement for at-risk youth. The possibility of expanding the program to include adults and volunteers concerned about neighborhood improvement was built into their proposal. The comprehensive nature and multiple objectives of the proposed program called for the the creation of WEPIC. WEPIC constituted a "neat" acronym, which has been retained and remains appropriate, though it now identifies a project that is radically different from the one originally envisioned.

The university was able to obtain funds for implementing the proposed youth job-training program during the summer of 1985. Contrary to the original plan, however, much of the summer activity was focused on the Bryant School, a neighborhood elementary school. Murals were painted around the school building and a nearby daycare center to cover graffiti and improve the overall appearance. The university donated a Penn landscape architect's time, and together with Penn undergraduate summer interns, the architect drafted and partially implemented a comprehensive landscaping plan for the weed-covered and rubbish-filled school grounds. Trees, shrubs, grass, and groundcover were planted, brick walks constructed and benches set in place, and a general cleanup and area improvement took place.

As work proceeded on the school building and grounds, an unforeseen development occurred. Neighbors reacted positively to the school improvements, provided some volunteer help, and undertook improvement projects on their own properties. From the positive reactions of the neighbors, Penn faculty and students saw that public schools might function as centers both for youth work experience and neighborhood revitalization. During the fall of 1985, WEPIC became an extracurricular after-school program at Bryant, funded through an outside grant. Some of the teachers linked the after-school projects to their teaching during the day. From its small beginnings at the Bryant elementary school in the summer of 1985, WEPIC has spread to an increasing number of schools in West Philadelphia during the past 17 years. WEPIC's growth and progress have been fueled by the development of academically-based community service courses at Penn. These courses integrate research, teaching, and service and focus on solving the schooling problem in West Philadelphia. At present, 126 academically-based community service courses have been developed and are "on the books" at Penn, and 43 were offered during the 2001–2002 academic year. Moreover, an increasing number of faculty members from a wide range of Penn schools and departments are considering how they might revise existing courses or develop new courses that would allow students to become active learners, creative problem solvers, and producers of knowledge.

The Center for Community Partnerships and Presidential Leadership

Encouraged by the success of the university's engagement with West Philadelphia, President Hackney created the Center for Community Partnerships in July 1992. To highlight the importance of the Center, he located it in the Office of the President. Ira Harkavy was appointed director.

Symbolically and practically, creation of the Center constituted a major change in Penn's relationship to West Philadelphia. The University formally committed itself to finding ways to use its resources to help improve the quality of public schools and the community.

The Center is putting into practice Penn's academic missions of advancing universal knowledge and effectively educating students. Penn's research and teaching focus on universal problems, such as schooling, health care, and economic development, as they are manifested in West Philadelphia/Philadelphia. By integrating general theory and concrete practice, Penn would improve both the quality of life in its local ecological community and the quality of its academic research and teaching. When Penn acts as a "cosmopolitan community school," it constitutes both a universal and a local institution of higher education.

The emphasis on partnerships in the Center's name was deliberate; it acknowledges that Penn could not work in isolation, as it had been (arrogantly) accustomed to doing. The creation of the Center meant that the university president would encourage university community members to consider the roles they could play in improving the quality of the local environment. Judith Rodin became president of Penn in 1994 and accelerated the strategy implementation. A native West Philadelphian and Penn graduate, Rodin was appointed in part because of her commitment to improving Penn's local environment and transforming Penn into the leading urban university.

Rodin made undergraduate education reform her first priority. To achieve that far-reaching goal, she established the Provost's Council on Undergraduate Education and charged it with designing a model for Penn's undergraduate experience in the 21st century. Following the lead of Penn's patron saint, Benjamin Franklin, the Provost's Council emphasized the action-oriented union of theory and practice and "engagement with the material, ethical, and moral concerns of society and community defined broadly, globally, and also locally within Philadelphia" (Provost's Council, 1995, p. S-1). The Provost's Council defined the 21st century undergraduate experience as:

. . . provid[ing] opportunities for students to understand what it means to be active learners and active citizens. It will be an experience of learning, knowing, and doing that will lead to the active involvement of students in the process of their education. (Provost's Council, 1995, p. S-1)

The Provost's Council designated academically-based community service as a core component of Penn undergraduate education during the next century, putting Benjamin Franklin's orientation into practice. Building on themes identified by the Provost's Council, Penn's 1994–95 annual report was titled *The Unity of Theory and Practice: Penn's Distinctive Character*. Describing the university's efforts to integrate theory and practice, President Rodin observed that:

. . . there are ways in which the complex interrelationships between theory and practice transcend any effort at neat conceptualization. One of those is the application of theory in service to our community and the use of community service as an academic research activity for students. *Nowhere else is the interactive dimension of theory and practice so clearly captured* [italics added].

For more than 250 years, Philadelphia has rooted Penn in a sense of the "practical," reminded us that service to humanity, to our community is, as [Benjamin] Franklin put it, "the great aim and end of all learning." Today, thousands of Penn faculty and students realize the unity of theory and practice by engaging West Philadelphia elementary and secondary school students as part of their own academic course work in disciplines as diverse as history, anthropology, classical studies, education, and mathematics.

For example, anthropology professor Frank Johnston and his undergraduate students educate students at West Philadelphia's Turner Middle School about nutrition. Classical studies professor Ralph Rosen uses modern Philadelphia and fifth century Athens to explore the interrelations between community, neighborhood, and family. And history professor Michael Zuckerman's students engage West Philadelphia elementary and secondary school students to help them understand together the nature—and discontinuities—of American national identity and national character. (University of Pennsylvania, 1996, pp. 9-10)

The 1994–95 annual report illustrated and advanced a fundamental cultural shift that had begun to take place across the university. By the end of her first year in office, President Rodin had increased the prominence of undergraduate education, defined the integration of theory and practice as the hallmark of Ben Franklin's university, and identified academically-based community service focused on West Philadelphia and its public schools as a powerfully integrative strategy to advance university-wide research, teaching, and service.

Presidents can provide leadership, but faculty members develop and sustain the courses and research projects that link a university to its local schools and community. More specifically, faculty teaching and research make the connection to local schools and communities. Penn gave high priority, therefore, to increasing the number and variety of academically-based community service courses.

Faculty-Led Projects, School Improvement, and Improved Student Learning

The development of academically-based community service learning and research courses at Penn does not in and of itself advance an ongoing democratic partnership with West Philadelphia schools and communities. The WEPIC project serves as the integrative, community-focused organizational vehicle that helps these courses make a practical difference in those schools and communities. The courses, therefore, are one key component of a wider university-school-community partnership that focuses primarily on providing neighborly assistance and, in the process, improving undergraduate and graduate education.

The growth of WEPIC and related projects, along with increasingly concrete, positive outcomes for schools and neighborhoods, has fostered community trust and participation. Two very different faculty-led projects—one in sociolinguistics, the other in classical studies—exemplify how the Center has connected the university with the community, and how both Penn students and public school students have benefited.

Linguists 161. Bill Labov, a linguistics professor and Director of the Linguistics Laboratory at Penn, leads a collaborative action research project. Professor Labov is concerned about the low reading achievement of African American youth in poor, urban school districts. To help solve that problem, he has developed a comprehensive research program that analyzes reading deficiencies and offers customized interventions to address identified deficiencies.

Professor Labov is a distinguished sociolinguist whose research interests are in African American linguistic patterns. His focus on solving "the reading problem" in West Philadelphia schools was prompted by two undergraduates who were students in our seminars. They asked Professor Labov to offer an academically-based community service course that would incorporate African American cultural and linguistic patterns in interventions designed to improve reading performance. The course, Linguistics 161: The Sociolinguistics of Reading, was first offered in the 1998 spring semester, with financial support from the Center for Community Partnerships.

Studying reading difficulties among African American children in the Wilson Elementary School, a local public school, was one of the initial goals of Linguistics 161. Undergraduates in the course met with children experiencing reading problems and tried to diagnose these difficulties. Penn students obtained samples of reading errors made by the children. The results were then compared to performance levels of children who experienced fewer reading problems. Labov, his students, and the teachers at Wilson developed a customized reading program that addressed the reading difficulties of children at the Wilson school.

Labov expanded the project considerably during the 1998–1999 academic year. He taught four linguistics courses, both undergraduate and graduate, centered on the reading improvement program. The Charles Drew School, another public school in West Philadelphia, also became part of the program. In one course, undergraduates develop linguistically and culturally appropriate narrative texts and illustrations to teach reading to inner city African American children. Another course trains students to work as tutors in the Wilson and Drew schools. Understanding the role of hip-hop music in the socialization of African American youth is an important part of being linguistically and culturally sensitive. Undergraduates study in detail how elementary school children acquire and use hip-hop language. They use hip-hop materials as part of a curriculum to teach standard English, thus incorporating cultural values into the program.

Labov's courses are connected to after-school programs at both the Wilson and Drew schools. Initially, undergraduates in one of our seminars had designed the after-school program at Wilson as a peer-tutoring program. High school students from West Philadelphia High tutored Wilson students and were supervised by undergraduates participating in the seminar.

Although the after-school program showed promise, it was initially only a modest success. In January 1997, Bettina Baker, a graduate student in Early Education, became the graduate student coordinator. Under her leadership, the program improved significantly. Baker introduced Labov to the Wilson after-school program, encouraging him to do field research. Labov implemented his reading program with an initial group of 40 students. Baker also recruited a number of Penn undergraduates through President Clinton's "America Reads" program to work with the Wilson students after school, four days a week. The early results proved to be impressive. Baker has described the findings as follows:

The program assessed the pre-and post-intervention Jerry Jons Informal Reading Inventory (IRI) scores of 40 randomly selected subjects and a matched control group. The subjects were in grades 2 through 5, and were one to two years behind in reading grade level before participating in . . . [the] extended day program . . . at Wilson . . . All of the 40 subjects' IRI scores increased by one grade level after 3.5 month's enrollment in the program, which met 4 days per week for 1.5 hours per day. Thirty-three of the 40 subjects were caught up to their classroom reading grade level (approximately 2 grade reading levels). Three of the seven subjects who were not caught up to their grade levels were recently from Ethiopia (ESL students) and one was in a learning support (IEP) program. There was a statistically significant increase in average IRI reading scores of special education participants. The 4th grade participants had statistically significant gains in SAT-9 reading scores. The student's average SAT-9 achievement test scores increased from "below basic" to "basic" levels on the test. (Baker, 1999, n.p.)

Although short-term results should be interpreted with caution, they do help explain the program's rapid expansion. As of 1998–1999 (more recent data is currently being collected), the extended day program enrolled 40 students at Wilson and 40 students at Drew. Seventy-six America Reads work-study students from Penn, 13 Penn volunteers, and 9 elementary school teachers staffed the program. Activities include literacy tutoring, homework help, and literacy-based enrichment. Labov's project and other Penn projects appear to have contributed to positive changes at the Drew School, which "showed more improvement on the state's standardized reading and math test than any other school in the state" (Snyder, 1999, p. B3).

A school-day program was soon added. Approximately 70 Penn students, supported by the America Reads funds, were placed with classroom teachers from grades pre-K through 8 at both schools, at least one day a week. The program helped significantly to reduce class size during literacy instruction and after-school activities through the addition of America Reads tutors, high school students, staff, and students from Linguistics 161. Reducing class size allows teachers to provide more attention to individual students and is one of the most significant benefits made possible by an effective higher education-school partnership.

Professor Labov's project to improve reading is extraordinarily comprehensive. This program effectively integrates a theory-based action research project, undergraduate and graduate seminars, and a volunteer program in the development of a creative and innovative model. The program exemplifies the valuable results that can be achieved through higher education-school partnerships. Given the importance of reducing the gap in reading achievement between white and nonwhite children, the findings from this project have national significance. The Interagency Educational Research Initiative, a joint project of the National Science Foundation, the Office of Educational Research and Improvement, and the National Institutes of Health, has provided $3,000,000 and the Spencer Foundation has given $320,000 to expand the reading improvement project. Thanks to this grant support, Stanford, California State Fullerton, Georgia State, and Penn are all partnered with local schools in the reading improvement program.

Classical studies 125, 240, and 352. Ralph Rosen is professor and chair of the Classics Department at Penn. He developed a series of academically-based community service courses that are quite different from the courses comprising Professor Labov's project to improve reading. Professor Rosen's work directly challenges the assumption that participatory action research is incompatible with the mission of the humanities (Harkavy, Puckett, & Romer, 2000). In the spring of 1994, he taught his first academically-based community service course, Classical Studies 125, "Community, Neighborhood and Family in Ancient Athens and Modern Philadelphia." His students worked with public school students at the Anderson Elementary School in West Philadelphia on reading as well as on discussion of similarities and differences between ancient Athens and modern West Philadelphia. Although the class was successful from the outset, Classical Studies 125 improved in spring 1996, when the Penn students began working with students from University City High School (UCHS). Not only were high school students more age-appropriate for the seminar, but UCHS borders Penn's campus, making ongoing interaction between the Penn and UCHS students relatively easy.

Classical Studies 125 invited undergraduates to study classical Greek conceptions of the city and its problems and to compare them with those of a modern city like Philadelphia. High school students were invited to share their experiences of life in Philadelphia and to join seminar undergraduates in comparing them with the concerns identified in readings about ancient Greece. Through this sharing, both the high school students and undergraduates came to see that despite all the changes in the world over the past two and a half millennia, many problems and solutions have endured.

Censorship and the arts in ancient Greece was a topic that created a sense of community in the class. Students read Plato's views on the potential hazards of poetic expression and compared these concerns with those of critics of modern rap music. The comparison led to discussion about the role of artistic expression in a free society and where, if at all, one can draw limits on this expression. The dilemmas noted by the

Greeks were not very different from those the students of today could recognize. From these discussions, Professor Rosen developed a new course titled "Scandalous Arts in Ancient and Modern Communities" (Classical Studies 240) that focused almost entirely on these dilemmas.

First taught in spring 1998 and affiliated with two humanities classes taught by a teacher at UCHS, Classical Studies 240 was modeled after Classical Studies 125, with undergraduate students sharing and working with students from the high school. Undergraduates had the opportunity to teach and learn through teaching—or to learn through "professing the liberal arts," as Lee Shulman describes it (1997, p.151-173). In a recent article, Rosen describes the positive impact the seminar had on both the UCHS and Penn students:

The students at UCHS were uniformly excited by the visits from Penn. Their teacher told me time and again that her students always eagerly looked forward to the visits from the Penn students. She found that even some of the more uninterested students felt drawn out of the experience by having Penn students visit. To my surprise (because this had not been my experience with the first course), she told me that most of the students were actually interested in the antiquarian aspects of the material; that is, they were amazed at the clear connections to be found between ancient society and our own. They got a real charge out of knowing that they were reading something that was more than two millennia old . . .

The students in my seminar at Penn were deeply committed to this project from the beginning. . . . [Students said] that working with the high school students allowed them to see just how "alive" these ancient texts still remain for our culture. I think it is not so much the case that they found anything especially unique or timeless about the ancient text, but that they simply never would have expected that something so distant and old would resonate for them in quite the way it did. I also believe that they experienced a certain comfort (and perhaps frustration!) in seeing that some of our greatest and most intractable philosophical and social problems are nothing new, that they were articulated by great writers of the past, and that placing ourselves in an intellectual tradition that extends to antiquity allows for a deeper perspective on our own real-world problems. (Rosen, 2000, pp. 181–182)

The success of Classical Studies 240 led Professor Rosen to develop a third course, "Teaching Plato's Republic" (Classical Studies 352) in the spring 2000 semester. Although the seminar has been offered only twice, reports from all participants have been positive. Professor Rosen's courses create community by helping high school and university students to see each other's worlds in the context of the classical Greek world, an unfamiliar frame of reference for both groups. Finally, each course provides an experience that allows both the undergraduates and the high school students to discover how much they can learn from each other and benefit from working together.

A National University Civic Responsibility Movement

The changes in Penn's relationship with its local schools are not atypical or unique. Similar changes throughout the country testify to the emergence of a university civic responsibility movement—a national movement to construct an optimally democratic schooling system as a means to advance democracy.[2] Our own efforts to create higher education-assisted community schools across the country illustrate the trend. Thanks to generous support from the Wallace Funds and the Corporation for National and Community Service, 22 colleges and universities are developing higher education-assisted community schools as part of a National WEPIC Replication Project.[3] Finally, the Charles Stewart Mott Foundation has provided additional support to the National Center for Community Education to work with 60 different colleges and universities and their school and community partners over a five-year period to develop higher education-assisted community schools.

Many approaches to community-higher education-school partnerships developed over the past decade could be cited, but space does not permit an exhaustive review. The Chancellor of the University System of Maryland, Donald N. Langenberg, observed that the successful collaboration between the University of Texas at El Paso and local schools exemplified a national movement. He noted that their productive collaboration had taught university observers a powerful lesson:

We have come to believe strongly, and elementary and secondary schools have come to believe, that they cannot reform without us. . . . *This is not telling them how to do it, but both of us working together to fix what's wrong with our education systems* [italics added]. . . We prepare teachers for the public schools, and we admit their students. *So it's our problem just as much as theirs* [italics added]. (Basinger, 1998, p. A28)

Summing Up and Looking Forward

Chancellor Langenberg's observation returns us to the central component of the vision sketched above: Educating young people so that they function as informed, intelligent, moral citizens in an optimally democratic society requires a collaborative and democratic schooling system, from preschool through the university. However, U.S. society is a long way from realizing the radically improved schooling system that Harper and Dewey envisioned and worked to achieve. Times *are* changing and signs of progress *can* be found across the educational landscape. The emerging revolution in U.S. higher education and society is beginning to transform the big science, Cold War university into the democratic cosmopolitan civic university—a new type of university dedicated to the development of an optimally democratic schooling system and society.

In this chapter, we have focused on the example we know best, Penn's relationship to the West Philadelphia public schools and community, to share some of the accomplishments, future goals, and lessons learned. Building democratic relationships that are mutually respectful and beneficial among communities, higher education institutions, and schools cannot be accomplished by following a standard blueprint or road map; no such map exists. But the Penn-West Philadelphia example can serve as a useful case study for other institutions as they work to fulfill the democratic promise of higher education in particular and of schooling and society in general.

NOTES

1. In our judgment, Campus Compact, a coalition of more than 750 college and university presidents committed to the civic purpose of higher education, has been central to advancing the University Civic Responsibility Movement.

2. The growth of Campus Compact from 3 founding members in 1985 to more than 750 members in 2002 is one indicator of a growing sense of university civic responsibility. Another indicator is the development of organizations and programs designed to engage colleges and universities with their local communities, including Community-Campus Partnerships for Health, which has grown to a network of over 1,000 communities and campuses in five years, and HUD's Office of University Partnerships, established in 1994 as a catalyst for joining colleges and universities with their communities, which has supported 125 university-community partnerships through its extraordinarily successful Community Outreach Partnership Centers Program (COPC).

3. Schools involved in the National WEPIC Replication Project include: Bates College, Central State University, Clark Atlanta University, Community College of Aurora, Indiana University–Purdue University in Indianapolis, Lewiston-Auburn College of the University of Southern Maine, Lock Haven State University, Mercer University, Morehouse College, New Mexico State University, Regis University, Rhode Island College, Slippery Rock University, Temple University, University of Alabama at Birmingham, University of Dayton, University of Denver, University of Kentucky-Lexington, University of Michigan-Ann Arbor, University of New Mexico at Albuquerque, University of Rhode Island, and West Virginia University.

REFERENCES

Anderson, W. (1993). *Prescribing the life of the mind.* Madison, WI: University of Wisconsin Press.

Anderson, W. (1997a). Democracy and inquiry. *The Good Society,* 7(2), 15-18.

Anderson, W. (1997b). Pragmatism, idealism, and the aims of liberal education. In R. Orrill (Ed.), *Education and democracy: Re-imaging liberal learning in America* (pp. 111-130). New York: College Entrance Examination Board.

Aron, R. (1970). *Main currents in sociological thought, volume II.* Garden City, NY: Anchor Books.

Astin, A.W. (1997). Liberal education and democracy: The case for pragmatism. In R. Orrill (Ed.), *Education and democracy: Re-imaging liberal learning in America* (pp. 203-207). New York: College Entrance Examination Board.

Baker, B. (1999). Report of findings of Penn's America Reads Program to the school district of Philadelphia. Unpublished report: University of Pennsylvania Linguistics Laboratory.

Basinger, J. (1998, November 20). University joins with entire community to raise academic standards in El Paso schools. *The Chronicle of Higher Education,* A28.

Benson, L., & Harkavy, I. (1997). School and community in the global society. *Universities and Community Schools,* 5(1/2), 16-71.

Benson, L. & Harkavy, I. (2000). Integrating the American system of higher, secondary, and primary education to develop civic responsibility. In T. Ehrlich (Ed.), *Civic responsibility and higher education* (pp. 174-196). Washington, DC: American Council on Education and Oryx Press.

Bok, D.C. (1990). *Universities and the future of America.* Durham, NC: Duke University Press.

Boyer, E.L. (1994, March 9). Creating the new American college. *Chronicle of Higher Education,* A48.

Dewey, J. (1902/1976). The school as social centre. In J.A. Boydston (Ed.), *John Dewey: The middle works, 1899-1924, 2* (pp. 80-93). Carbondale, IL: Southern Illinois Press.

Gardner, J.W. (1998, 10 February). Remarks to the Campus Compact Strategic Planning Committee, San Francisco. Unpublished remarks.

Goodspeed, T.W. (1928). *William Rainey Harper: First president of the University of Chicago.* Chicago: University of Chicago Press.

Harkavy, I. (1997). Testimony before the Subcommittee on Housing and Community Opportunity for the Committee on Banking and Financial Services of the House of Representatives (105 Cong. 1 Sess.). Washington, DC: U.S. Government Printing Office.

Harkavy, I. (1999). School-community-university partnerships: Effectively integrating community building and education reform. *Universities and Community Schools,* 1(2), 7-24.

Harkavy, I., & Benson, L. (1998). De-Platonizing and democratizing education as the basis of service learning. In R.A. Rhodes & J. Howard (Eds.), *Academic service learning: A pedagogy of action and reflection* (pp. 11-19). San Francisco: Jossey-Bass.

Harkavy, I., & Puckett, J.L. (1994). Lessons from Hull House for the contemporary urban university. *Social Service Review,* 68(3), 299-321.

Harkavy, I., Puckett, J.L., & Romer, D. (2000). Action research: Bridging service and research. *Michigan Journal of Community Service Learning,* 7, 113-118.

Harper, W. R. (1905). *The trend in higher education.* Chicago: University of Chicago Press.

Judge, H. (1982). *American graduate schools of education: A view from abroad.* New York: Ford Foundation.

Kennedy, D. (1997). *Academic duty.* Cambridge, MA: Harvard University Press.

Provost's Council on Undergraduate Education. (1995, May). The 21st century Penn undergraduate experience: Phase one (Suppl.1). University of Pennsylvania, pp. S-1-S-4.

Rosen, R. (2000). Classical studies and the search for community. In I. Harkavy & B. Donovan (Eds.), *Connecting past and present: Concepts and models for service learning in history* (pp. 173-183). Washington, DC: American Association for Higher Education.

Schulman, L. (1997). Professing the liberal arts. In R. Orrill (Ed.), *Education and democracy: Re-imaging liberal learning in America* (pp. 151-173). New York: College Entrance Examination Board.

Snyder, S. (22 October 1999). Philadelphia schools awarded $3.5 million for improvements. *Philadelphia Inquirer*, B3.

Stokes, D. (1997). *Pasteur's quadrant: Basic science and technological innovation*. Washington, DC: The Brookings Institution Press.

University of Pennsylvania. (1996). *Annual report 1994/1995*. Philadelphia: University of Pennsylvania, pp. 1-11.

Whyte, W. F. (Ed.). (1991). *Participatory action research*. Newbury Park, CA: Sage.

Wirth, A.W. (1964). *John Dewey as educator: His design for work in education (1894-1904)*. New York: Wiley and Sons.

CHAPTER 6

Challenges and Opportunities for Higher Education

JACQUELYN McCROSKEY

The builders of the modern university expected that the research conducted within it would solve moral problems. The research would
provide authoritative instruction on how to live and how to shape a
more perfect society. But within a generation, it became clear that this
expectation would not easily be fulfilled. Indeed, many of the faculties
housed in these new universities were ready to wash their hands of
moral concerns. The university faced a crisis: Did it serve to advance
morality? And if so, how? The success of the university in producing
knowledge and training skilled professionals has compensated for and
masked the moral crisis. But nonetheless, the problem of morality
continues to plague American higher education. Universities have
been unable either to fully incorporate morality or to comfortably
abandon a moral mission. This is the unresolved legacy of the creation of the modern research university. (Reuben, 2000, pp. 72–73)

In communities around the country, increasing numbers of people
believe that the education, health, social services, and early childhood
development systems designed to support families with children are
broken and desperately in need of repair (Schorr, 1997). Efforts to fix
these systems—restructuring education, managing health care, reform-
ing social services, and developing comprehensive early childhood systems—have been fragmented and inadequate. Because each arena of
service has developed a complex array of constituencies, interest groups,
professional guilds, privileges, and organizational structures, it has been
difficult to make significant changes within traditional disciplinary and
institutional boundaries. Reports about systematic efforts to reform
service delivery systems from within are generally quite discouraging
(Hagedorn, 1995; Sarason, 1990; Tyack & Cuban,1995).

Rather than working within traditional boundaries, interprofessional collaboration and comprehensive services strategies purposefully

Jacquelyn McCroskey is the John Milner Associate Professor of Child Welfare at the
University of Southern California School of Social Work.

engage mixed groups of professionals and community residents in planning for systems change based on community resources and needs. These strategies are based on core values and beliefs that families know themselves best. Interprofessional collaboration assumes that experts do not have all the answers, and community members should have a much stronger voice in decision making at all levels. Experience from work using collaborative strategies in communities around the country suggests that such groups can successfully identify shared goals, use data to guide community-wide planning, and improve outcomes for children and families (Adams & Nelson, 1995; Bruner et al., 1998; Cutler, 1997; Gardner, 1998; Los Angeles County Children's Planning Council, 1998; Nelson, 1996). Similar efforts are underway in other Western countries with comparable populations and systems (Boocock, Barnett, & Frede, 2001; Department of Health, 2000; Smale, 1995).

Whether people begin by working together to improve a specific neighborhood or school or to integrate services across jurisdictions, participants ultimately need to address many of the same challenges. Both approaches require significant public engagement in complex change processes and knowledge of policies and practices across organizational systems. They also call for people to develop new relationships, to learn to trust each other, and to work in teams made up of people with very different backgrounds, training, and perspectives, including parents, businesspeople, civic leaders, and various professionals.

The systems now serving families and children are fragmented, categorical, and cumbersome, and are generally more invested in treatment than in prevention. These systems are difficult for outsiders—whether they are community members or professionals from other systems—to understand and negotiate, often requiring technical knowledge of administrative guidelines, funding streams, acronyms, and jargon. Very few professionals have the necessary interprofessional skills or ability to work effectively across community and organizational boundaries.

As described throughout this volume, faculty and administrators from a number of far-sighted colleges and universities have worked on interprofessional collaborative initiatives. Some faculty and staff from institutions of higher education entered into partnerships with community groups to develop more effective approaches to support children and families, improve schools, and enhance communities (Walsh et al., 2000). Individuals affiliated with local colleges or universities have also devoted themselves to local change efforts through their personal commitments to improving conditions for children and families (Gardner, 1998).

People from higher education have played different kinds of roles in these community and systems change initiatives. Some individuals affiliated with local colleges and universities have served on leadership teams that have developed visions, directions, and strategies such as service learning (for example, see Benson & Harkavy, this volume, chapter 5; Casto, Harsh, & Cunningham, 1998). Others have played supportive roles by analyzing data, supervising students in internships and community service activities, or providing interprofessional training (Foley, 1998; Knapp & Associates, 1998). Still others have evaluated or documented core issues and lessons learned from successful initiatives (Crowson, this volume, chapter 4; Murray & Weissbourd, this volume, chapter 9; Stone, 1996).

However, many partnerships have not included participants from higher education, even when local institutions had faculty with related expertise. In some cases, the community groups did not know how to get through to the right people or shift university attention toward community-based discussions. Others did not even try to connect because of past experiences in which ivory tower experts did not return their phone calls, engage in discussion, respect their ideas, or stay engaged long enough to become a true partner. Some question the relevance of higher education for such community-based change efforts: Are faculty really interested in what communities want? Are university administrators committed to community engagement? To what extent do people who spend their lives studying under disciplinary and professional boundaries have something to offer strategies of change devoted largely to breaking down these and other boundaries?

The complexity and diversity of higher education systems offer unique possibilities for partnerships with community groups at multiple levels. This chapter focuses on the challenges and opportunities faced by research universities engaged in this kind of collaborative work. Walshok (1995) describes the unique role that research universities play in developing and communicating knowledge. She notes that although there are more than 3,500 postsecondary institutions in the United States, only 100 of these are major research universities that give priority to the formation and development of knowledge, as well as to the preservation and communication of knowledge through teaching (Walshok, p. 3).

The next section of this chapter examines sources of dissonance between research universities and community-based efforts to implement interprofessional collaboration and comprehensive services. Subsequent sections describe perspectives on university engagement and examine the unique challenges universities face when engaged in these collaborative practices. The chapter concludes with ideas about bridging the gap and bringing the potential power of higher education more centrally into the emerging interprofessional movement to improve the lives of children and families in communities across the nation.

Working at the Boundaries: Sources of Dissonance Between Interprofessional Collaboration, Comprehensive Services, and Research Universities

In a *New York Times* article about test results for city schools, Traub (2000) suggested that sometimes the experts on school reform ignore the obvious correlation between test scores and socioeconomic status. Traub notes that all but one of New York City's 32 school districts' scores could have been predicted based on socioeconomic status. Only a few dozen of the city's 675 elementary schools performed better than expected based on poverty level. Fortunately, some people do see the obvious and have begun long-term multifaceted efforts to address deep-seated community problems such as family poverty, violence, substance abuse, and racism. They are working to help families support their children so that they can be successful in school. These efforts focus on developing relationships among community leaders, local decision makers, visionary change agents, and professionals who run key institutions. Based on a set of values that have become a mantra for the emerging comprehensive services movement (Bruner, 1996), the principles guiding most collaborative efforts state that supports for children and families should be *community-based, comprehensive, family-centered, culturally competent, strengths-based,* and *outcomes-driven.*

In brief, community differences should be understood and respected, and planning should be organized around communities as children and families experience them, rather than around administrative districts designed for institutional convenience. A comprehensive array of flexible supports and services should be available and accessible in local communities and provide a seamless fit for each family. Professionals should be culturally competent and respectful in working with families from different racial, ethnic, and cultural backgrounds and with other types of diversity (Chang, 1997). People should respect and build on family and community strengths rather than focusing solely on deficits and problems. Service providers and systems should be accountable for outcomes or results, rather than just complying with criteria, guidelines, and rules (Hogan, 1999; McCroskey, 1999).

Professional Preparation

The core principles noted above are at odds with usual professional practice, current university structures, and the values of many faculty members. University-based professional preparation programs often teach that services are—and should be—determined from the top down by knowledgeable and experienced professionals. In practice, service delivery structures generally reflect professional specialization, magnifying the autonomy and control of key professional groups. They are not designed holistically to support families, to respect differences between communities, to serve children and adults in one location, or even to serve individuals with complex overlapping problems.

Service delivery systems are too often unclear about the outcomes they are seeking, either positing vague hopes or leaving it up to individuals to judge success. Unclear goals and outcomes are further complicated by the reality that professionals and clients tend to see things differently. These differences may be a consequence of professional training, different roles and perspectives, or a variation in perceptions of complicated human interactions (Achenbach, McConaughy, & Howell, 1987; McCroskey & Meezan, 1997).

Many professional preparation programs pay relatively little attention to the values that are most important to potential clients—respect for the strengths of the people they are trying to help, encouragement of the client's autonomy, and respect for cultural and family differences. In his 1995 book, *The Careless Society: Community and Its Counterfeits*, John McKnight argues that U.S. society does not recognize caring for others as an essential component of the social contract. Paying professionals in the service economy relieves the general public of the need to care for one another as fellow citizens in shared communities. He describes reactions to his description of the harm done by professionals and the overall problem of a society grown overly reliant on professional services. In meeting after meeting, McKnight found that people did not ask how they could work to reform their jobs or systems, but instead acknowledged the problems associated with professional roles and asked what alternative kinds of helpful work they could pursue. Sadly, McKnight points out that, with the exception of physicians, the professionals he interviewed basically said, "I thought that professional training would lead me to good work, but it has led me to live off some people who don't need me and others I can't help" (p. 25).

In response to such difficult questions about the value of professional helpers and the fragmentation of their efforts, Schorr (1997) observes that comprehensive community-based efforts are giving rise to a new type of practical professionalism. This emerging professional practice consciously emphasizes the strengths of children, families, and adults and focuses on clients' ability to take control of their own lives. This kind of practice requires new skills, norms, power relationships, and different ways of thinking about professionalism (Schorr, p. 12).

Strategies for Systems Change

Similar ideas are guiding many comprehensive community-based systems change strategies. Participants are urged to share their stories, build on local strengths, organize communities to solve their own problems, and include economic and community development strategies along with comprehensive services (Cutler, 1997; Medoff & Sklar, 1994).

Change-oriented groups in many inner city communities are working to strengthen local neighborhoods and link schools to a broad range of partners and community groups. Schools and local businesses, civic groups, allied public agencies, nonprofit agencies, and community-based organizations are building connections with each other (Briar-Lawson & Lawson, 1997; Cibulka & Kritek, 1996; Dryfoos, 1994, 1998). Such school-linked systems change initiatives differ from previous generations of school reform efforts because they start at the boundaries of school and community. Rather than looking inside the schoolhouse, engaging the usual players in the usual discussions, and focusing on the balance of power among school boards, superintendents, and unions, these strategies bring something new to predictable and well-worn arguments about low-performing schools. They engage stakeholders in strategic efforts to improve schools through partnerships with other local stakeholders, adding supports for children and families at little or no additional cost to schools.

Although comprehensive services hold a great deal of promise, they are hard to define and difficult for many people to understand. Because they work at the boundaries of established institutions, they make intuitive sense to many community residents who deal with all of these institutions separately. However, many professionals have difficulty understanding or embracing such strategies. Crossing these boundaries can be especially difficult for professionals who have been trained, licensed, or certified in a profession, and have garnered personal privilege and power by staying well within prescribed boundaries.

People in research universities may have even more difficulty appreciating the power of this boundary-spanning approach. The principles that guide comprehensive community initiatives are at odds with academic values such as disciplinary specialization and intellectual autonomy, which can create dissonance for everyone involved. For example, many of the most effective school principals say that their success is based on willingness to "bend" the rules. While Howard Lappin was a principal at Foshay, a school in south central Los Angeles that has received national recognition for its extraordinary turnaround, he used to say that his operating principle was that it was easier to ask for forgiveness than to wait for permission. Lappin brought health and dental services onto campus, created a parent center, and integrated a broad range of services for children and families with the help of faculty from the Schools of Education, Social Work, Dentistry, and Public Administration and the Department of Nursing at the nearby University of Southern California. Coordinating the efforts of these academic units raised numerous challenges for USC participants (McCroskey & Einbinder, 1998; McCroskey, Robertson, & Associates, 1999). While each unit "owned" its own knowledge and skills, none were used to working together toward a shared goal, especially when that goal was defined by the school and not by the university.

Perspectives on the Engaged University

The premises of collaboration probably fit most comfortably with the historic roots of land-grant universities initially established during the post-Civil War period (Bender & Schorske, 1997). Land-grant colleges and universities were designed to serve practical purposes by helping to solve pressing agricultural and community problems. Research universities were initially based on a different set of traditions linked to 19th-century European models of higher education (Reuben, 1996). Current urban social problems are serious enough that they require the best efforts of people throughout the entire system of higher education, including both land-grant institutions and research universities.

Several authors have suggested that higher education may once again be facing a time of intense scrutiny and change (Boyer, 1990; Kellogg Commission on the Future of State and Land-Grant Universities, 1999; Kennedy, 1997). For example, the fall 2000 issue of *The Hedgehog Review* poses a basic question in the title, "What's the university for?" While the achievements of research universities have been substantial, there are still unanswered questions about whether and to what extent they should be pursuing moral purposes, helping to search for solutions to society's most troubling civic and social problems.

Roles of Faculty

In his book *Return to Reason*, Toulmin (2001) describes how scholars became preoccupied with the concept of "rationality," restricting their focus to content and losing hold of the more practical concept of "reasonableness," or the ways that situations modify and interact with content. Not surprisingly, research universities value rationality, rewarding most highly those faculty members whose scholarship is based on empirical methods. What is surprising to many outside the university, however, is the extent to which even professional education programs prize "rationality" and empirical science over "reasonableness" and practical application.

Specialization has been widely credited with increasing productivity through division of labor in the industrial era. Disciplinary specialization, however, can also limit intellectual vision and perception. Toulmin (2001) describes the arguments associated with disciplinary specialization. Those who concentrate solely on one aspect of production can be more efficient, reducing the time and energy wasted through distraction. This narrowing of one's intellectual responsibilities led to "what Anthony Flew christened the Specialist Fallacy: a belief that the words 'I am only *paid* to know about these things' meant the same as 'I am paid to know *only* about these things'" (p. 41).

The last decade has been marked by numerous calls to rethink some of the basic premises of academia (Anderson, 1993; Damrosch, 1995; Kennedy, 1997; Walshok, 1995). For example, Boyer (1990) called for "a new vision of scholarship" (p. 13) that would help maintain the vitality of U.S. colleges and universities by rethinking the priorities of the professoriate. The need for connection between the ivory towers and the social and environmental realities that exist outside of academia has never been greater. Narrowly defined missions and faculty reward systems limit the potential roles of universities in addressing national problems. Boyer notes "while research is crucial, we need a renewed commitment to service, too" (p. xii).

It has proven extraordinarily difficult to alter many of the time-honored paradigms of higher education, including the individual intellectual journey of the solitary scholar, the protection of the ivory tower from the intrusions of daily life, and the value of theory over mundane practical experience. Damrosch (1995) has described some of the mechanisms that weigh against change in the academy. For example, faculty selection and promotion processes help to filter out new approaches, assuring that only those with acceptable ideas within the "generally given parameters of a given discipline" (p. 63) pass through each stage of the process. Faculty who accept these established paradigms settle into academic life and those who question them "are weeded out during the process, usually by their own decision" (p. 63).

Trower and Chait (2002) describe how similar processes have affected ethnic and gender diversity of university faculties:

Despite 30 years of affirmative action … the American faculty profile remains largely white and largely male. Women currently represent 36 percent of full-time faculty compared to 23 percent in the early 1970s. Although this represents a very substantial gain nationwide, women constitute only 25 percent of the full-time faculty at research universities, versus 10 percent in 1970. Faculty of color remain a very small part of the professorate. (Whites constituted 95 percent of all faculty members in 1972 and 83 percent in 1997.) Most of the growth in minority participation has been by Asian Americans, from 2.2 percent in 1975 to 4.5 percent in 1997. The percentage of African-American faculty members at all levels has been remarkably stagnant—4.4 percent in 1975 and 5 percent in 1997—and almost half of all black faculty teach at historically black colleges. The increase in Hispanic faculty has also been slow: from 1.4 percent in 1975 to 2.8 percent in 1997. (pp. 33–34)

University Engagement

The Kellogg Commission on the Future of State and Land-Grant Universities (1999) has urged universities to go beyond outreach and service to engagement. According to the Commission, "engaged universities" are those that redesign their "teaching, research, and extension and service functions to become even more sympathetically and productively involved with their communities" (p. 9). Their report suggests a seven-part "test" of engagement:

1. *Responsiveness*. We need to ask ourselves periodically if we are listening to the communities, regions and states that we serve.

2. *Respect for partners*. … the purpose of engagement is not to provide the university's superior expertise to the community but to encourage joint academic-community definitions of problems, solutions, and definitions of success.

3. *Academic neutrality*. The question we need to ask ourselves here is whether outreach maintains the university in the role of neutral facilitator and source of information when public policy issues, particularly contentious ones, are at stake.

4. *Accessibility*. Our institutions are confusing to outsiders. We need to find ways to help inexperienced potential partners negotiate this complex structure so that what we have to offer is more readily accessible.

5. *Integration*. Our institutions need to find ways to integrate their service mission with their responsibilities for developing intellectual capital and trained intelligence.

6. *Coordination*. A corollary to integration, the coordination issue involves making sure the left hand knows what the right hand is doing.

7. *Resource partnerships*.The final test asks whether the resources committed to the task are sufficient. Engagement is not free; it costs. The most obvious costs are those associated with the time and effort of staff, faculty and students. But they also include curriculum and program costs, and possible limitations on institutional choices. (Kellogg, 1999, p.12)

Very few research universities could successfully meet all parts of this test, though some have made great efforts toward becoming engaged universities. For example, Benson and Harkavy (this volume, chapter 5) describe long-term systematic efforts by the University of Pennsylvania to become a "democratic cosmopolitan civic institution" that is "both a universal and a local institution of higher education" (p. 106). Ohio State University (Casto, Harsh, & Cunningham, 1998; Casto & Julia, 1994) and Boston College (Walsh et al., 2000) have made comparable long-term efforts. However, many research universities could not meet more than two or three of these tests.

The former president of Stanford University, Donald Kennedy, (1997) notes that universities suffer in large measure from their own failures to "exercise leadership in areas that a thoughtful public believes to be important" (p. 278). Although universities' influence may not be as great as it once was, an important role will be served, "if, and only if, they can reconnect to the society that nurtures them" (p. 278). Improving the lives of children and families in communities around the country is one of the important arenas where universities could make a much bigger contribution through reconnection.

Special Challenges for Research Universities

Almost all of the principles guiding comprehensive community-based service strategies pose difficulties for research universities. These principles require collaborative efforts to be community-based, comprehensive, family-centered, culturally competent, strengths-based, and outcome-driven. Key challenges appear in four primary arenas: supporting applied scholarship, linking scholarship and teaching to meaningful community service, sustaining interprofessional education efforts, and developing responsive community partnerships.

Challenges in Supporting a Scholarship of Application

Boyer (1990) suggests that a new definition of scholarship should focus more practically on "the full range of academic and civic mandates" (p. 16), calling the scholarships of integration and application as important as the more traditional scholarships of discovery and teaching. The scholarship of integration, according to Boyer, puts isolated facts into perspective, and requires interdisciplinary work and holistic approaches to research and service. Faculty involved in the scholarship of integration have to work "at the boundaries where fields converge" (p. 19), integrating context, practical experience, and intellect.

Boyer's (1990) definition of the scholarship of application goes well beyond lackadaisical interest in community service and involves a dynamic process of applied service work. Such scholarship cannot separate "discovery" and "application"; rather, it blends the two in a dynamic process that proves "its worth not on its own terms but by service to the nation and the world" (p. 23).

Although scholarship in many of the professions and disciplines concerned with families and children addresses practical problems, there are still very few widely known instances of this kind of serious, demanding, rigorous work. Faculty reward systems are based on traditional academic values. Junior faculty members in the social sciences are expected to publish numbers of peer-reviewed pieces in the single-discipline journals most highly regarded in their fields. The most valued publications are written by a single author and if the publication is co-authored, the faculty member applying for promotion should be listed as the first author. Interdisciplinary journals are likely to be judged as less prestigious, especially by faculty members serving on promotion and tenure committees. Working with teams in complex collaborative initiatives is considered risky business for junior faculty, both because it takes too much time to allow for the requisite number of publications and because an individual cannot claim full credit for new insights. If their work fails to meet the usual university standards for tenure, some who have been engaged in interprofessional collaborations may lose their jobs.

After tenure has been awarded—often based on 6 years of individual research in studies yielding multiple publications based on the least publishable unit (garnering the largest possible number of publications from each study)—faculty work habits are usually set. While some senior faculty members do decide to put aside their own career interests to work on interprofessional initiatives, they may be giving up raises, grant opportunities, and promotions to pursue this path.

Challenges in Linking Scholarship and Teaching
to Meaningful Community Service

Although practical relevance was one of the core purposes underlying development of the land-grant universities (and a number of
other academic institutions), commitment to service or application of
practical knowledge has little scholarly cachet today. Tenure-track faculty members are required to do a modicum of community service as a
regular part of review and promotion, but most realize that two core
functions—scholarship and teaching—will determine their progress.
Data from the Holmes Partnership on tenure standards in schools of
education, for example, suggest that research is most highly valued,
with teaching ranking second. Service, however, is not given much attention (Blackwell, 2002, p. 16).

Requirements for community service can generally be met by extremely modest investments of time and energy. For example, faculty
can serve the university community by sitting on committees and task
forces, their professions by presenting papers to professional groups
(for which they may also receive scholarship credit), or the local community by sitting on committees or making speeches. A level of service
well beyond current expectations is clearly required when faculty
members take meaningful roles in interprofessional and comprehensive
services initiatives. While there have been some efforts to reform promotion criteria to include new forms of collaboration (for example, at
Montclair State University), whether and how promotion and tenure
committees in the highest level research universities will reward such
work in the future is unknown.

Challenges in Developing Sustainable Approaches
to Interprofessional Education

While university faculty and the professionals they train work autonomously and independently, most families interact with a number
of different kinds of professionals. Families with troubled children
may see an even greater number of highly specialized professionals.
The university-based professional preparation programs whose graduates work with families and children include (at a minimum) education, social work, psychology, counseling, early childhood development, law, medicine, nursing, public health, public administration,
physical therapy, occupational therapy, dentistry, and pharmacy. Professional programs are organized in different schools or departments,
are accredited by different specialty bodies, and respond to different

regulatory, licensing, or credentialing bodies (Zlotnik et al., 1999). By definition, each profession lays claim to its own specialized body of knowledge and skills, and over time, each has developed its own key concepts, assumptions, and jargon. Different professional groups are guided by different sets of values and ethics (Wood, 1998) and have established different norms and expectations. Professional preparation programs are designed not only to transmit knowledge and skills to potential practitioners but also to socialize students in the specialized cultures, values, and ethics of their prospective guilds.

Experience with interdisciplinary education has provided some of the groundwork for interprofessional education programs, which are distinguished by their added focus on preparing students to apply skills and knowledge in professional service delivery organizations. Interprofessional approaches are designed to complement professional education programs—adding to the perspectives, values, and norms that guide practice in specialized professional arenas. Such programs broaden the student's exposure to other professionals, providing a better understanding of different professional roles and skills needed for cross-professional collaboration. Interprofessional education programs encourage students to focus on the whole person in familial, community, and societal settings. Students learn to appreciate the skills, knowledge, and expertise held by others, respecting and valuing their input in teams and multidisciplinary settings. They develop interpersonal skills for practice in a multidisciplinary context and learn about group dynamics, teamwork, conflict resolution, and interpersonal, group, and organizational communication.

Given the proliferation of professions and specialties, there is little point in moving toward a generalist professional model (McCroskey 1998). A framework that allows professionals to share their specialized knowledge, however, is desperately needed so that different kinds of professionals can work together in response to changing situations. This model would allow families to receive services and care that are best suited to their needs.

There have been a number of experiments with interprofessional education, but these programs have been difficult to implement and sustain because they challenge so many aspects of regular functioning in universities (Foley, 1998; Knapp & Associates, 1998; McCroskey & Einbinder, 1998). Working interprofessionally challenges both institutional structure and culture. Collaboration across departments also challenges the individualized identities that fields in general, and faculty members in particular, work hard to maintain.

Problems can include everything from decisions about curriculum to university financial structures, as illustrated by the following examples based on the author's experiences at the University of Southern California (McCroskey, Robertson, & Associates, 1999). Curriculum committees often are organized by undergraduate and graduate divisions, making it difficult to get approval for courses designed to mix graduate and undergraduate students. If the front-line workers who will need to work together include B.A.-level teachers and nurses, M.S.W.-level social workers, Ph.D.-level planners and postgraduate medical fellows, this makes it even more complicated to get new courses approved.

Current practices also make it difficult to award different numbers of credits or unit hours for an integrative internship or lab course even when students invest different amounts of time or energy at practice sites. Requiring each group of students to register under a different course number can help, but it also necessitates additional paperwork, tracking, and monitoring by personnel in different departments. Also, negotiating experiential internships across units with different expectations and assumptions is an ongoing challenge. Coordinating schedules to allow students enrolled in different professional preparation programs to work together in the classroom or at a community-based practice site can be extremely difficult.

While onsite teamwork is especially rewarding for students, it requires adequate supervision by faculty from different units. Each profession has different expectations about the credentials of supervisors, acceptability of onsite or offsite supervision, number of supervised hours required for degree completion, and the level of interaction and reporting required. High-quality supervision is essential in developing professional skills, but it can require extraordinary amounts of time and coordination from all involved.

Foley (1998) reports that time was one of the key issues in a collaborative initiative involving nine university interprofessional preparation programs in the mid-1990s. Faculty reported that the sheer number of meetings needed to plan joint sessions was overwhelming, and institutional rewards were few. Overall, involved faculty felt that the costs associated with interprofessional training were prohibitive (p. 223).

Some universities are changing the structure of their financial systems to give more financial autonomy to schools and departments. Picus (1998) describes three models of resource allocation commonly used by universities: centralized line-item budgeting, performance-responsibility budgeting, and revenue-responsibility budgeting. According to his analysis, only a hybrid system of value-responsibility budgeting would really support interdepartmental efforts, because of the lack of incentives available under the other models.

Given all of the challenges and difficulties involved in getting university-based interprofessional education programs off the ground, it is especially discouraging that several authors have reported serious challenges related to maintaining and sustaining these complex programs (Knapp & Associates, 1998; McCroskey, Robertson, & Associates, 1999). Judging from such reports, two things appear to be essential to ensure the institutional stability of these programs: a flexible and responsive organizational home base and continuing core financial support that is not dependent on soft money.

*Challenges in Developing Responsive Partnerships
with Communities*

Development of responsive community partnerships can be especially challenging for research universities. The academic time frame is future-oriented, requiring time to plan and submit proposals, gather and analyze data, and write up results. Community problem solvers work in the present to resolve immediate crises or respond to current needs, and conditions can change quickly. Academics usually focus on the theoretical and conceptual, while community problem solvers tend to be practical and results-oriented. The conditions that stimulate rewards are also different. For academics, success is usually based on individual achievement in a discipline or specialty area. Community problem solvers often work together across geographic and organizational boundaries because the problems they face are not unidimensional but complex and multifaceted.

Defining community for purposes of university-community partnerships is an essential but difficult task. Clearly, there are different kinds of communities. The definition may be based on geography, emotional ties or affiliations, or government or public institutional determinations. University and community groups not only face conceptual and geographic challenges in reaching agreement on the focus of their energies, but may also have to reconcile differing perceptions of community and university-community partnerships. Issues of power will undoubtedly arise in trying to negotiate such a relationship. Universities must be willing to negotiate equitable relationships, giving up some of their autonomy and power so that community groups sit at the table as equal partners. As Tippins, Bell, and Lerner (1998) note, "University-based participants have a fundamental decision to make about their role in the community: to seek to 'empower' the community to take charge of their own fate and problem-solving, or to 'better' the community through university-controlled services and other improvement activities" (p. 181).

Empowering others in a shared initiative requires that university representatives give up some of their authority and relinquish some institutional controls. Giving up institutional control may be harder for universities than for service-delivery agencies because universities generally have less stake in responding to community voices. Most of the public agencies that serve families and children regularly struggle with tensions among elected officials, professional managers, bureaucrats, and community-based constituencies.

Administrators in many highly ranked research universities are used to more individual authority and control than public agency managers have, and eminent faculty members sometimes display little tolerance for being publicly questioned. It is considerably easier to accept the abstract notion that community residents know their own conditions best than to acknowledge that there are other kinds of expertise more valuable than one's own. Sometimes practical experience does trump theory and a national reputation. Community members may also have difficulty believing that universities really want to partner, particularly if they have been left out of previous decisions.

Comprehensive community-based initiatives may require that colleges and universities from different systems (e.g., community colleges, state colleges, and private universities) work together toward common purposes. Coordinating the efforts of a diverse collection of community colleges, liberal arts colleges, land-grant universities, and research universities to serve a specific locality is extremely challenging.

People from higher education, who tend to place extraordinary value on rationality, may have particular difficulty understanding and appreciating political approaches to changing current conditions. Otis Johnson, Dean of the College of Liberal Arts and Social Studies in Savannah, Georgia and former Executive Director of the Chatham-Savannah Youth Futures Authority, suggests that everyone needs to acknowledge the complexity of the work and to be clear about the politics involved (Walsh, 1999). Johnson outlines three different process models used by people developing community partnerships. The collaborative model brings together the different stakeholders who are working toward a shared cause with the assumption that they will want and know how to work together. The professional planners' model relies on experts and professionals to diagnose the problems and offer solutions. Finally, the conflict model assumes that the powerful and the powerless have different interests, and that resolution will be reached only through conflict and struggle (p. 38).

Bridging the Gaps: Opportunities and Benefits

By and large, neither service-delivery agencies nor universities ask communities what they want from professionals, nor do they ask whether clients benefit from the services of trained professionals. Movement toward interprofessional collaboration and comprehensive services requires that everyone begin asking these difficult questions. It is hoped that collaboration will contribute to the development of new skills for professionals, who will learn to improve their practices according to the wishes and desires of the people they serve.

Universities involved in comprehensive community-based partnerships will gain benefits for students, faculty, and administrators. Students can benefit from enhanced learning opportunities, new skills and knowledge, better preparation for the practical challenges of collaborative practice, and deeper understanding of community connections and networks. Faculty can benefit from the wisdom of different voices and concerns, better connections to local communities, exploration of new methodologies, multidimensional approaches to scholarship, and more dynamic relational views of knowledge. University administrators can benefit from increased and diversified enrollment in professional preparation programs. When universities are known and admired as resources for local communities, fundraising, marketing, and public relations opportunities increase.

The literature reviewed above suggests that authentic engagement in university-community partnerships challenges leaders in higher education to address five operational challenges:

1. Weave community engagement issues into all three of the core academic activities—teaching, scholarship, and community service—rather than viewing these issues as falling primarily under the category of service.

2. Encourage broad-based student participation in community engagement efforts by designing a range of possible options, including service learning, research assistantships, classroom experiences, and volunteer community service experiences.

3. Match faculty interests with community needs identified through engagement with neighborhoods, civic groups, businesses, nonprofit organizations, and other public institutions.

4. Respond to the highest priority issues and needs raised by community partners and link them to issues of interest to faculty investigators.

5. Commit to serious and sustained efforts to help resolve the practical problems identified by local community representatives.

To respond effectively, most universities will need to address underlying structural issues, reordering priorities and providing ongoing support for university-community partnerships through the following four steps.

Develop better structures to span the boundaries of knowledge reified by disciplines and professions. Universities should learn from the multidisciplinary structures in the hard sciences that address issues such as information sciences and brain research. Parallel structures should be developed to address the issues facing children, families, and communities.

Address critiques of professional education. According to critics, many disciplines and professions are focused exclusively on creating and transmitting knowledge in their specialty area, without adequate attention to holistic theories or comprehensive approaches (Kellogg Commission, 1999). These programs do an inadequate job of incorporating theoretical and scientific advances from other fields into curricula (see, for example, National Reading Panel, 2000; National Research Council Institute of Medicine, 2000).

Track and coordinate community partnerships. Many universities host large numbers of community-based projects developed by individual faculty and staff members. The time and resources involved in such community partnerships represent a significant, but often fragmented, investment. A coordinated university-wide strategic agenda would address this fragmentation. University leaders should encourage faculty to learn about each other's efforts, working together where possible to assign priorities to a small number of focused efforts.

Secure stable funding to support engagement in long-term, multifaceted university-community partnerships. Universities must provide core support to sustain these partnerships. Administrators need to think about reallocating existing funds, establishing new public and private matching funds, and other long-term financial mechanisms. They will also need incentives to encourage ongoing faculty involvement in such efforts.

This is a complex, long-term agenda that goes well beyond improving public relations and sharing information about all the great things that universities already do on behalf of communities. The challenges of genuine engagement require that universities make significant changes in their approaches to building and sharing knowledge. Since universities bear a good deal of responsibility for the entrenched barriers between community-based institutions that make interprofessional collaboration and comprehensive strategies so compelling, they should be involved in finding new and better ways to work. We have a long way to go, but there is much to be gained on all sides.

REFERENCES

Achenbach, T.M., McConaughy, S.H., & Howell, C.T. (1987). Child/adolescent behavioral and emotional problems: Implications of cross-informant correlations for situational specificity. *Psychological Bulletin, 101*(2), 213-232.

Adams, P., & Nelson, K. (Eds.). (1995). *Reinventing human services: Community- and family-centered practice.* Hawthorne, NY: Aldine de Gruyter.

Anderson, C.W. (1993). *Prescribing the life of the mind: An essay on the purpose of the university, the aims of liberal education, the competence of citizens, and the cultivation of practical reason.* Madison, WI: University of Wisconsin Press.

Bender, T., & Schorske, C.E. (1997). *American academic culture in transformation: Fifty years, four disciplines.* Princeton, NJ: Princeton University Press.

Benson, L., & Harkavy, I. (2003). The role of the American research university in advancing system-wide education reform, democratic schooling, and democracy. In this volume—M.M. Brabeck, M.E. Walsh, & R. Latta (Eds.), *Meeting at the hyphen: Schools-universities-communities-professions in collaboration for student achievement and well being. The 102nd yearbook of the National Society for the Study of Education,* Part II (pp. 94-116). Chicago: National Society for the Study of Education.

Blackwell, P.J. (2002). *Where's the change? Deans' views of the Holmes Partnership tenure standards.* Monograph published by the Holmes Partnership. Milwaukee, WI: Chancellor's Office, The University of Wisconsin-Milwaukee.

Boocock, S.S., Barnett, W.S., & Frede, E. (2001, September). Long-term outcomes of early childhood programs in other nations: Lessons for Americans. *Young Children, 56*(6), 43-50.

Boyer, E.L. (1990). *Scholarship reconsidered: Priorities of the professorate.* San Francisco: Jossey-Bass.

Briar-Lawson, K., & Lawson, H. (1997). *Connecting the dots: Progress towards the integration of school reform, school-linked services, parent involvement and community schools.* St. Louis, MO: The Danforth Foundation.

Bruner, C. (1996). *Realizing a vision for children, families and neighborhood: An alternative to other modest proposals.* Des Moines, IA: National Center for Service Integration/Child and Family Policy Center.

Bruner, C., Cahn, E.S., Gartner, A., Giloth, R.P., Herr, T., Kinney, J., Nitoli, J.M., Reissman, F., Trent, M., Trevino, Y., & Wagner, S.L. (1998). *Wise counsel: Redefining the role of consumers, professionals, and community workers in the helping process.* Des Moines, IA: Child and Family Policy Center.

Casto, R.M., Harsh, S.A., & Cunningham, V. (1998). Shifting the paradigm for interprofessional education at the Ohio State University and beyond. In J. McCroskey & S.D. Einbinder (Eds.), *Universities and communities: Remaking professional and interprofessional education for the next century* (pp. 54-64). Westport, CT: Praeger Publishers.

Casto, R.M., & Julia, M. (1994). *Interprofessional care and collaborative practice.* Pacific Grove, CA: Brooks/Cole.

Chang, H.N. (1997). *Community building and diversity: Principles for action.* San Francisco: California Tomorrow.

Cibulka, J.G., & Kritek, W.J. (Eds.). (1996). *Coordination among schools, families and communities: Prospects for education reform.* Albany, NY: SUNY Press.

Crowson, R. (2003). Empowerment models for interprofessional collaboration. In this volume—M.M. Brabeck, M.E. Walsh, & R. Latta (Eds.), *Meeting at the hyphen: Schools-universities-communities-professions in collaboration or student achievement and well being. The 102nd yearbook of the National Society for the Study of Education,* Part II (pp. 74-93). Chicago: National Society for the Study of Education.

Cutler, I. (1997). *Learning together: Reflections on the Atlanta Project.* Atlanta, GA: The America Project.

Damrosch, D. (1995). *We scholars: Changing the culture of the university.* Cambridge, MA: Harvard University Press.

Department of Health. (2000). *Framework for the assessment of children in need and their families.* Monograph produced by the British Department of Health, Department for Education and Employment and Home Office. London: The Stationery Office. (Available from The Stationery Office, PO Box 29, Norwich NR3 1GN, England).

Dryfoos, J.G. (1994). *Full service schools: A revolution in health and social services for children, youth and families.* San Francisco: Jossey-Bass.

Dryfoos, J.G. (1998). *Safe passage: Making it through adolescence in a risky society.* New York: Oxford Press.

Foley, E.M. (1998). Lessons learned: A three-year project to advance interprofessional education in nine universities. In J. McCroskey & S.D. Einbinder (Eds.), *Universities and communities: Remaking professional and interprofessional education for the next century* (pp. 221-228). Westport, CT: Praeger Publishers.

Gardner, S. (1998). *Beyond collaboration to results: Hard choices in the future of services to children and families.* Phoenix, AR and Fullerton, CA: Arizona Prevention Resource Center and the Center for Collaboration for Children.

Hagedorn, J.M. (1995). *Forsaking our children: Bureaucracy and reform in the child welfare system.* Chicago, IL: Lake View Press.

The Hedgehog Review. (2000, Fall). *What's the university for?* [Special Issue]. *2*(3).

Hogan, C. (1999). *Vermont communities count: Using results to strengthen services for families and children.* Baltimore: Annie E. Casey Foundation.

Kellogg Commission on the Future of State and Land-Grant Universities. (1999). *Returning to our roots: The engaged institution, third report.* Retrieved September 24, 2002, from http://www.nasulgc.org/publications/Kellogg/engage.pdf

Kennedy, D. (1997). *Academic duty.* Cambridge, MA: Harvard University Press.

Knapp, M.S., & Associates. (1998). *Paths to partnership: University and community as learners in interprofessional education.* Lanham, MD: Rowman & Littlefield Publishers.

Knapp, M.S., Barnard, K.E., Bell, M., Brandon, R.N., Gehrke, N.J., Smith Jr., A.J., Teather, E.C.T., & Lerner, S. (1998). Lessons learned and enduring challenges. In M.S. Knapp & Associates, *Paths to partnership: University and community as learners in interprofessional education* (pp. 193-216). Lanham, MD: Rowman & Littlefield Publishers.

Los Angeles County Children's Planning Council. (1998). *Laying the groundwork for change: Los Angeles County's first action plan for its children, youth and families.* Los Angeles: Author.

McCroskey, J. (1998). Remaking professional and interprofessional education. In J. McCroskey & S.D. Einbinder (Eds.), *Universities and communities: Remaking professional and interprofessional education for the next century* (pp. 3-24). Westport, CT: Praeger Publishers.

McCroskey, J. (1999). *Getting to results: Data-driven decision-making for children, youth, families and communities* (A what works policy brief). Sacramento, CA: Foundation Consortium.

McCroskey, J., & Einbinder, S.D . (1998). *Universities and communities: Remaking professional and interprofessional education for the next century.* Westport, CT: Praeger Publishers.

McCroskey, J., & Meezan, W. (1997). *Family preservation and family functioning.* Hawthorne, NY: Aldine de Gruyter.

McCroskey, J., Robertson, P.J., & Associates. (1999). Challenges and benefits of interprofessional education: Evaluation of the Inter-Professional Initiative at the University of Southern California. *Teacher Education Quarterly, 26*(4), 69-87.

McKnight, J.L. (1995). *The careless society: Community and its counterfeits.* New York: Basic Books.

Medoff, P., & Sklar, H. (1994). *Streets of hope: The fall and rise of an urban neighborhood.* Boston, MA: South End Press.

Murray, J., & Weissbourd, R. (2003). Focusing on core academic outcomes: A key to successful school-community partnerships. In this volume—M.M. Brabeck, M.E. Walsh, & R. Latta (Eds.), *Meeting at the hyphen: Schools-universities-communities-professions in collaboration for student achievement and well being. The 102nd yearbook of the National Society for the Study of Education*, Part II (pp. 179-200). Chicago: National Society for the Study of Education.

National Reading Panel. (2000). *Teaching children to read: An evidence-based assessment of the scientific research literature on reading and its implications for reading instruction.* NIH Pub. No. 00-4769.

National Research Council & Institute of Medicine. (2000). From neurons to neighborhoods: The science of early childhood development. J.P. Shonkoff & D.A. Phillips (Eds.), Committee on Integrating the Science of Early Childhood Development, Board on Children, Youth, and Families. Washington, DC: National Academy Press.

Nelson, D.W. (1996). The path of most resistance: Lessons learned from "New Futures." In A.J. Kahn and S.B. Kammerman (Eds.), *Children and families in big cities: Strategies for service reform* (pp. 163-184). New York: Columbia University School of Social Work.

Nelson, K., & Allen, M. (1995). Family-centered social services: Moving toward system change. In P. Adams & K. Nelson (Eds.), *Reinventing human services: Community- and family-centered practice* (pp. 109-125). Hawthorne, NY: Aldine de Gruyter.

Picus, L.O. (1998). University fiscal management structures and interprofessional collaboration among faculty. In J. McCroskey & S.D. Einbinder (Eds.), *Universities and communities: Remaking professional and interprofessional education for the next century* (pp. 245-256). Westport, CT: Praeger Publishers.

Reuben, J.A. (1996). *The making of the modern university: Intellectual transformation and the marginalization of morality.* Chicago: University of Chicago Press.

Reuben, J.A. (2000). The university and its discontents. *The Hedgehog Review, 2*(3), 72-91.

Sarason, S.B. (1990). *The predictable failure of educational reform: Can we change course before it's too late?* San Francisco: Jossey-Bass.

Schorr, L.B. (1997). *Common purpose: Strengthening families and neighborhoods to rebuild America.* New York: Anchor Books, Doubleday.

Smale, G.G. (1995). Integrating community and individual practice: A new paradigm for practice. In P. Adams & K. Nelson (Eds.), *Reinventing human services: Community- and family-centered practice* (pp. 59-80). Hawthorne, NY: Aldine de Gruyter.

Stone, R. (Ed.). (1996). *Core issues in comprehensive community-building initiatives.* Chicago: Chapin Hall Center for Children at the University of Chicago.

Tippins, P., Bell, M., & Lerner, S. (1998). Building relationships between university and community. In M.S. Knapp & Associates, *Paths to partnership: University and community as learners in interprofessional education* (pp. 165-192). Lanham, MD: Rowman & Littlefield Publishers.

Toulmin, S. (2001). *Return to reason.* Cambridge, MA: Harvard University Press.

Traub, J. (2000, January 16). What no school can do. *New York Times Magazine,* 52-67.

Trower, C.A., & Chait, R.P. (2002, March/April). Faculty diversity: Too little for too long. *Harvard Magazine,* 33-37.

Tyack, D., & Cuban, L. (1995). *Tinkering toward utopia: A century of public school reform.* Cambridge, MA: Harvard University Press.

Walsh, J. (1999). The eye of the storm: Ten years on the front lines of New Futures. An interview with Otis Johnson and Don Crary. Baltimore: The Annie E. Casey Foundation.

Walsh, M.E., Brabeck, M.B., Howard, K.A., Sherman, F.T., Montes, C., & Garvin, T.J. (2000). The Boston College-Allston/Brighton partnership: Description and challenges. *Peabody Journal of Education, 75*(3), 6-32.

Walshok, M.L. (1995). *Knowledge without boundaries.* San Francisco: Jossey-Bass.

Wood, G.J. (1998). An analysis of professional values: Implications for interprofessional collaboration. In J. McCroskey & S.D. Einbinder (Eds.), *Universities and communities: Remaking professional and interprofessional education for the next century* (pp. 25-35). Westport, CT: Praeger Publishers.

Zlotnik, J., McCroskey, J., Gardner, S., Gil de Gibaja, M., Taylor, H.P., George, J., Lind, J., Jordan-Marsh, M., Costa, V.B., & Taylor-Dinwiddie, S. (1999). *Myths & opportunities: An examination of the impact of discipline-specific accreditation on interprofessional education* (Preparing human service workers for interprofessional practice: Accreditation strategies for effective interprofessional education project report). Alexandria, VA: Council on Social Work Education.

CHAPTER 7

Comprehensive Schools

JOY G. DRYFOOS

"Comprehensive" is not an unfamiliar term to educators, but it has many meanings. In this chapter, comprehensive describes schools that offer a range of social, medical, enrichment, family, and recreational services through partnerships with other agencies. These schools "comprehend" much more than traditional curricula in services offered, hours open, parent involvement, community focus, and forms of governance (Southwest Educational Development Laboratory, 1989). They address the social and economic barriers to learning so prevalent across this nation. What makes these schools unique is that they are based on collaborations between schools and community agencies, functioning best when school faculty, outside agency personnel, parents, and students demonstrate high levels of interprofessional collaboration and emphasize the integration of support services and academics to enhance the whole school climate. The phrase I use to classify such efforts is "full-service community schools" (Dryfoos, 1994).

Interprofessional collaboration in schools is not a new concept, and many of the examples cited in this text have been around for a long time. School buildings have been open to the community for educational and recreational purposes for probably as long as public schools have existed. The one-room schoolhouse was the center of early community life in this nation, often with one teacher who offered advice, comfort, and attention. But life is very different today, and children and families have complex needs that must be met in new ways if the children are going to be able to learn and function in the demanding 21st century economy. Many of these needs can be met within the confines of the schoolhouse, but not by one teacher and not without the participation of agencies other than the schools.

This chapter describes various approaches to comprehensive efforts, and presents a typology that sorts the emerging models according to

Joy G. Dryfoos is an independent researcher and writer.

the degree of interprofessional collaboration. The chapter focuses on the full-services community school model using the Quitman Street Community School in Newark, New Jersey, as an example. Lessons about collaboration and interprofessional relationships are extracted from the experience at Quitman and at other sites around the country.

Comprehensive School Models: A Typology of Interprofessional Collaboration

Currently in the United States, about 117,000 school buildings are in use, and 89,500 are defined as public (U.S. Census Bureau, 2000). Some 13,726 local education authorities govern what goes on in U.S. classrooms. Thus, the characteristics of schools are widely divergent in service configurations. One can find a wide range of school-based services—everything from communal laundries to dog-training facilities—located in school buildings (Dryfoos & Maguire, 2002). Some schools house literally hundreds of ancillary programs brought in by community groups, while others stand quite isolated, with little relationship to local agencies.

Service Provision in Traditional Schools

Most school systems hire a variety of pupil support personnel, with wide variations from state to state and system to system. In 2000, the Centers for Disease Control and Prevention (CDC) conducted a School Health Policies and Programs Study in all states, sample districts, and schools (Kolbe, Kann, & Brenner, 2001). This study found that more than three fourths of all schools have a part-time or full-time school nurse, although only one half of schools have the 1:750 nurse-to-student ratio recommended by the CDC (U.S. Department of Health and Human Services, 2000). Also, about three fourths of schools have a mental health and social services coordinator and/or a part-time or full-time guidance counselor. While two thirds of schools reported a part-time or full-time school psychologist, only about 44% of schools have a part-time or full-time social worker. Special education funds allow schools to employ additional student support services, such as audiologists and other specialists.

Service personnel employed by school systems are generally well integrated and perform their jobs within school regulations. Many serve on various school teams reviewing problems of high-risk children or figuring out how to implement mandated health education programs, such as violence prevention, among other things. In disadvantaged communities, school nurses and counselors are not always available, although the demand is great. Some schools augment their support systems with interns and field placements in service professions through university connections.

Schools With Links to Other Agencies

Most schools have contacts with community agencies. School nurses and counselors typically keep lists of resources for referral to mental health counseling, substance abuse treatment, family services, or reproductive health care, among other services. If a student presents a problem that cannot be addressed by school staff, the parent is contacted and referred by school personnel to an appropriate community agency. Follow-up is usually limited, and the school has no further role in the transaction. About one third of schools have arrangements with off-site health care providers, including health departments, mental health and social service agencies, and private practitioners, to provide services to students.

Schools With Add-On Services

As schools increasingly recognize the difficulties families encounter and the resulting problems children face, school administrators and educators are focusing on bringing additional services into schools. Thus, they are ensuring that service provision will actually take place and that follow-up will be maintained by an on-site service provider.

School-based primary health clinics are an excellent example of add-on services, with approximately 1,400 schools operating clinics within the school building (Making the Grade, 2000). An outside agency develops the clinic, which is then established in an available space in the school, such as an unused classroom. The clinic is typically staffed with a licensed nurse practitioner, a social worker, a health educator, and a clinic aide, with medical backup provided by a part-time pediatrician. In some places, a dentist and a dental technician are also on the staff. Students can obtain medical examinations, psycho-social evaluations, emergency care, medications, treatment for minor illnesses, and pregnancy tests.

Most school-based clinics are operated by local health departments, health centers, and university hospitals, and all services are free. Most clinics are funded through outside sources, including state grants, Maternal and Child Health Funds, Medicaid reimbursements, and HMO contracts.

In some schools, the school nurse is central to the school-based health program and is physically stationed at the front of the clinic to act as a triage nurse. Students start with a visit to the school nurse, who then refers them to the clinic, if necessary. In other schools, the school nurse maintains a separate office and performs mostly nonmedical functions, such as attendance phone calls.

Interprofessional relationships are not necessarily built into these kinds of efforts. The primary relationship in most school-based clinics is between the principal and the director of the clinic, who may be on-site or located at the provider agency. This relationship sets the tone for the level of integration among clinic staff and school administrators and educators. For example, school-based clinic personnel are often part of site-based management and pupil personnel service teams. They may also provide classroom-based health courses, such as sex education, drug and violence prevention, and life skills training.

Family resource centers, like school-based clinics, are designated areas in school buildings where parents can go for help with an array of problems. Several states have rather extensive family center programs, each with different elements and different grant criteria, but all with linkages to schools. For example, Kentucky's Family Resources were established as part of the state's educational reform efforts. Almost all schools with at least 20% of the students eligible for free or reduced school meals have received grants from the state, resulting in 774 centers serving 1,145 schools (Kentucky Office of Family Resource and Youth Services Centers, 2002). Connecticut's Family Resource Centers are found in 61 schools selected for their capacity to replicate the Schools of the 21st Century concepts, including preschool and child care, home visiting, and other components, of Dr. Edward Zigler of Yale University (America's Family Support Magazine, 2002). At the national level, Family Support America is working to encourage the creation of family-supportive community schools. It is estimated that the number of schools housing family support programs may already be as high as 5,000 (Blank & Melaville, 1999).

Family resource centers do not follow any prescribed pattern. At some schools with fully developed programs, the centers are operated by staff (usually including a full-time coordinator), parents, and other volunteers. Parents can learn what is going on in the school and how they can become involved. Support services such as emergency assistance, food, housing, legal aid, and assistance with employment, benefits, and immigration are also available. Parents are welcome to socialize and hang out together, either informally or through planned events. The centers offer parenting skills workshops with information about family life and sex education, entrepreneurial skills, nutrition, and child-rearing, and courses to improve parents' ability to assist their children with schoolwork. Computer technology, GED, ESL, and other adult education courses are held afternoons and evenings, and higher education courses are also offered through partnerships with local colleges and universities.

School social workers or school counselors are expected to work with the community agency personnel staffing the family resource center. Center staff should be included in pupil personnel teams and family-centered discussions. In the past, school social workers and school counselors have not been trained to deal with problems such as housing, immigration, and employment; rather, the focus has been on attendance and behavioral issues within the school environment. With the advent of family support services, outreach to families is strongly promoted. In some school communities, every family receives a home visit by the center outreach worker or volunteer, while in other places, teachers are expected to perform that task.

After-school programs are the fastest growing add-on component, substantially extending the hours schools are open across the country. The Department of Education's 21st Century Community Learning Centers (21st CCLC) initiative has given grants to more than 6,800 local schools and spurred the growth of after-school programs (Department of Education, 2002). Some states and foundations are also supporting after-school initiatives, making it possible for an increasing number of schools to extend their hours. Up until recently, all 21st CCLC grants went directly to school districts and required collaborative arrangements with community-based organizations in after-school services. Under the No Child Left Behind Act of 2002, funds will now go to state departments of education, which will fund either schools or community-based organizations in low-income areas to set up collaborative efforts to operate after-school programs in school buildings (Department of Education, 2002).

The program requirements for 21st CCLC grants are quite flexible. An array of inclusive and supervised services must include expanded learning opportunities such as enriched instruction, tutoring, or homework assistance. Also, 21st CCLC programs may provide youth development activities; drug and violence prevention programs; technology education; nutrition and health; art, music, and recreation programs; counseling and character education; children's day care services; and parenting skills education. Many different kinds of personnel could be involved in after-school services; for example, health services suggests collaboration with a medical provider, while the child care component might require youth development workers. However, enhanced learning has been the primary thrust for most after-school work, and teachers have been hired to fill many of the jobs in this burgeoning industry. The focus of these programs is clearly to expand academic enrichment opportunities and to bring up standardized test scores in low-performing schools.

Tension exists concerning the purpose of after-school programs in general. Are these programs merely babysitting, an extension of school classroom hours, or an opportunity to provide enrichment and youth development? The best examples have aspects of all three elements: parents are able to work through the afternoon hours with the assurance of quality child care; students can do their homework under teachers' supervision; and the after-school program material extends the curriculum and offers creative, cultural, and recreational experiences. The level of integration between the after-school program and the school program is a key element. Several examples of integrated programs can be found in this volume (see the Quitman example below; Quinn, this volume, chapter 8).

The desired integration cannot take place without close association between the school staff and the after-school staff. The transition at 3 p.m. from teachers and other school staff to after-school program staff can be difficult. For example, in a New York City middle school, an established community-based organization provided case management workers during extended hours through a grant from the city that funded after-school Beacon programs. However, the principal would not allow the after-school staff into the school building during regular school hours, thus prohibiting the staff from meeting the school counselors or any of the other school personnel. Arrangements between school and community-based organizations must be worked out before the program is initiated to ensure that after-school staff have full access to the students and families they are trying to assist. Also, the school team—both teachers and pupil personnel—and the community-based team must be well acquainted and working toward common goals.

Other kinds of add-ons enhance the comprehensiveness of schools. Increasingly, Head Start programs are moving into school buildings and pre-kindergarten (Pre-K) classrooms are being added, raising the integration question. Head Start classrooms are sometimes located in a building that is disconnected from the rest of the school. To be more effective, Pre-K should be fully integrated with kindergarten and other classes, with close collaboration between the teachers and the parent advocates, ensuring coordination of educational plans and professional services.

Many programs can be "dropped" into a school building. Life-long learning is becoming an important theme throughout the nation, and thousands of school buildings are open for community and adult education. School facilities have hosted sports and cultural events for generations. While this greatly expands the use of school property for broader community purposes, fragmentation can also result. One inner city principal listed 200 programs community agencies held in his school, ranging from dance lessons to drug prevention discussion groups, but he did not feel the children benefited from these efforts. Only a few children attended each activity, and often they were not the children who really needed help. In this case, the principal finally opted for a school-based clinic, putting the clinic coordinator in charge of all extracurricular activities and continuing only those programs that met local needs, that could be integrated into the overall school efforts, and that fostered professional collaboration (Tiezzi, 1993).

Putting It All Together: Full-Service Community Schools

Full-service community schools began to emerge during the 1990s in response to the overwhelming difficulties that schools were encountering in coping with the social and economic problems of their communities. A description based on concepts supported by the Coalition for Community Schools (2002) follows:

A community school, operating in a public school building, is open to students, families and the community before, during, and after school, seven days a week, all year long. It is jointly operated through a partnership between the school system and one or more community agencies. Families, youth, principals, teachers, and neighborhood residents help design and implement activities that promote high educational achievement and positive youth development.

The school is oriented toward the community, encouraging student learning through community service and service learning. A before- and after-school learning component encourages students to build on their classroom experiences, expand their horizons, contribute to their communities, and have fun. A family support center helps families with child-rearing, employment, housing, immigration, and other issues and problems. Medical, dental, and mental health services are readily available. College faculty and students, business people, youth workers, neighbors, and family members come together to support and bolster what schools are working hard to accomplish—ensuring young people's academic, interpersonal, and career success.

Ideally, a full-time community school coordinator works in partnership with the principal. The coordinator is a member of the school's management team and is responsible for administering the services brought into the school by community agencies. Over time, most community schools consciously try to integrate activities in several areas to achieve the desired results: quality education; positive youth development; family support; family and community engagement in decision-making; and community development. In this process, the school emerges as a community hub, a one-stop center to meet diverse needs and to achieve the best possible outcomes for each child. (Community Schools, 2002, p. 1)

A fully developed community school puts together the most important add-ons to create a newly transformed one-stop educational institution. Such a community school would incorporate a primary health clinic, a family resource center, after-school care, and much more. None of those components would dominate; instead, they would be woven together with established school procedures to produce a new kind of child-centered environment in which an array of needs could be met. Several community agencies might be involved, including health and social services and community-based organizations. One community agency typically would take the lead and hire the coordinator, organize the activities, and assume responsibility for operating the community school functions.

Many different models that encompass some or all of these concepts have been promulgated. The Children's Aid Society (CAS) in New York City has designed and supported what some call "a settlement house in a school." CAS has worked closely with the local community school boards to bring social, health, and mental health services, family programs, after-school and weekend activities, and other community-specific services into school buildings. Community school staff have worked hard to integrate programs with school work and involve parents in their children's educational experience (see Quinn, this volume, chapter 8). The 10 CAS schools in New York City and the many adaptations around the country have full-time coordinators and professional and non-professional staff members and volunteers. In this model, the community-based organization plays a strong role in school administration.

In the University-Assisted Community Schools approach, university professors and students form collaborative partnerships with school teachers and administrators to devise educational interventions in the classroom and enrichment experiences and service in the community (McCroskey, this volume, chapter 6; Walsh et al., 2000). Faculty at the University of Pennsylvania developed this model through the West

Philadelphia Improvement Corps (WEPIC) at the Center for Community Partnerships (see Benson & Harkavy, this volume, chapter 5). University professors and school teachers design new curricula to challenge children and interest them in the world around them. University students help teachers implement the curricula and spend time working with the students in creative projects in the school and the community both during and after school hours.

Other approaches fall somewhere in the middle of the continuum between add-on and fully realized community schools. While these models all intend to change the school experience and enhance outcomes, the level of incorporation into the school environment differs significantly from one place to another. No matter what the model, no two schools are alike; each reflects a particular combination of needs, school administrator's attitudes, capabilities of community-based organizations, and resources. The United Way's Bridges to Success initiative is oriented toward encouraging the United Way's constituent community agencies to move into school spaces. A city-wide representative council oversees the program and places coordinators in schools to ensure that services are integrated. Located in public schools, Beacons are community centers that offer an array of youth development activities during extended hours. The program began in New York City and is now a national model for "lighting up" public schools through extended-day community programs. Communities In Schools creates local councils that raise funds to hire social workers and other youth workers in schools to handle case management and to provide adult mentors.

Perhaps the least documented model of full-service community schools is principal-initiated, without the help of an intermediary organization such as CAS or WEPIC. The principal invites partners into the school to extend the day and to provide essential child and family services and enrichment programs particular to that school. The Molly Stark Community School in Bennington, Vermont, is one example. Principal Sue Maguire established relationships with 40 different community partners to keep her school open most of the day and to address needs that could not be taken care of by the school system, such as child care and dentistry (Dryfoos & Maguire, 2002).

The Quitman Street Community School

Quitman Street School is located in the middle of Central Ward of Newark, New Jersey, an area that has been disadvantaged for many years (Dryfoos, 2002). Quitman is a plain three-story brick building with concrete steps that lead up to a security door. Everyday more than 400 Pre-K to fourth-grade students parade through this door. The principal and the director of the community school program stand ready to receive them. In only 3 years, Quitman transformed itself from a troubled traditional school into a well-functioning, full-service community school, open from 7:30 a.m. to 9:00 p.m. during the week; on Saturdays for special events; and during the summer. As the principal observed, "It seems that my building never closes" (Louis Mattina, personal communication, September 20, 2001).

Today, children and their families can access primary health care, counseling and family services, extended-day programs, early childhood enrichment, arts and cultural events, adult education, and whatever else the school/community partners team views as needed. The theme of the school—"Rallying Around the Whole Village, Serving the Whole Child"—is enacted in the classrooms and in all other aspects of the school, all day and all year long. This transformation began in 1997 with support from the Prudential Foundation in Newark. The Foundation, long interested in helping Quitman School, worked with a deputy superintendent of the Newark school system and the building principal to introduce the CAS model to the school community. Through the years, additional partnerships have been established between Quitman and the Community Agencies Corporation of New Jersey (CACNJ), Children's Hospital of New Jersey at Newark Beth Israel Medical Center, Bank Street College of Education, the Newark Board of Education, and CAS, which provides technical assistance. Many other art, literacy, and mentoring programs provided by community agencies have been integrated into the community school. CACNJ, a substantial and prestigious community-based organization that runs many settlement houses and other programs in Newark, acts as the lead agency, hiring the coordinator and other community school staff.

Quitman's Newark location has special significance. Many attempts have been made to reform the schools in Newark since the 1960s. In 1995, the State Department of Education took over the school system, abolishing the board of education and mandating an outside administrator. In 1997, the New Jersey Supreme Court ruled that the state must supply funds to implement the historic *Abbott v. Burke* decision (1990), which required dramatic improvement in urban schools in the state. The following year the court ordered a series of entitlements for disadvantaged children, including whole school reform and full-day, full-year kindergarten and preschool for 3- and 4-year-olds. Other requirements included health and social services, increased security, technology, alternative education, school-to-work programs, and after-school and summer school programs.

Each school in Abbott districts was required to select and implement a model for whole school reform. Quitman chose the School Development Program created by James Comer of the Yale Child Study Center. In this model the school is mobilized to help children succeed. The model assigns priority to an inclusive planning and management team made up of parents, teachers, administrators, support staff, and students; a strong parent participation program in which parents serve in the schools as both volunteers and paid workers; a prevention team to work on mental health issues; and a comprehensive school plan to accomplish all of this (School Development Program, 1998).

Although the *Abbott* decision includes language that suggests the state might provide the funds for the community school work at Quitman, this has not yet occurred, and foundations continue to provide financial support.

Lessons Learned

Observations at Quitman and other programs around the country (Walsh et al., 2000) suggest some lessons learned about successful implementation of community school concepts and the strengthening of interprofessional relationships.

Committed People

People's determination to reach a common goal, and the strengths they bring to carrying out their particular responsibilities, determine the degree of collaboration. Sharing a vision of change is also important. At Quitman, each partner is represented by individuals committed to the implementation of the community school model. The Prudential Foundation, which initiated this effort, has continued to support the project despite some preliminary leadership problems with the first lead agency. The Foundation moved ahead rapidly to identify an effective partner, CACNJ, an organization with strong roots in the community and solid skills in youth work, community organizing, and management.

The technical assistance team from CAS provided continuity during the planning and visioning process. In the first summer, the CAS team stepped in to run the summer program. When the CACNJ took over in the fall of 1998, CAS offered guidance, made many site visits to the program in Newark, and arranged for community school staff to visit the model schools in New York City. The CACNJ staff was invested from the beginning, allowing their top-level staff to spend the necessary time to get the program up and running. They hired a highly qualified coordinator, who recruited dedicated people to carry out the day-to-day work.

The school staff response was fundamental to the success of this program. In the initial transactions, many barriers had to be overcome. For example, a change of principals coincided with the change from K–8 to Pre-K–4. Teachers were having a hard time maintaining discipline and teaching the students. The mobility rate hovered at 50%, indicating that half the students moved out of the school system in a year. Many children had health and behavioral problems that interfered with their ability to learn, and parents were not involved with the school. At first, the teachers were distrustful of the CACNJ team and the new staff. Within 3 years, however, most of these problems had been overcome through constant communication and negotiation. The teachers appreciate the extended day, the parent program, the health clinic, and the special events and claim that all these helped to change the school climate and improve the behavior and well being of students and their families. Teachers also recognize the value of having parents in their classrooms as aides and tutors.

No community school can be implemented without the cooperation of the principal. In this case, two principals were involved. The first principal, Chiarina DiFazios, had the vision: "When you have people all on the same page, you can move mountains" (Dryfoos, 2002). The new principal, Louis Mattina, supported the community school vision and had the necessary skills to carry out the community school concepts. Staff and parents described him as very receptive and made comments like, "He's not a stuffed shirt," "His door is always open," "He respects you and treats everybody alike," "His attitude is do what you have to do . . . it's not about him." The principal included the CACNJ community school staff in the school management team and communicated clearly and frequently with that group. He showed his support for all aspects of the community school and for the work of the community staff, while maintaining strong leadership of the school and making it clear that nothing would happen without his approval.

Responsive to Needs

Almost every methodology for changing schools begins with a needs assessment (Dryfoos & Maguire, 2002). After an initiative has been implemented, the recommendations made in the needs assessment can be used to test the relative progress. CAS worked with the community to develop an assessment process that included focus groups with parents and school staff. The results indicated familiar inner city problems, including drug use, child abuse and neglect, high crime rates, lack of safety, inadequate housing, and children coming to school unprepared. There were many problems with acting-out behaviors in school, such as fighting, cutting class, and "disrespecting teachers." Too many teachers were unable to deal with students. The community lacked recreational opportunities; parks and school playgrounds were in disrepair; hard-to-reach parents were not involved; and there was little mental health support or counseling.

At Quitman, the full-service school was created to address these needs. When asked what was so special about the community school, one involved parent responded with eight components: (1) extended day assures that homework gets done; (2) art, dance, music, and cultural enrichment programs bring out children's hidden talents; (3) health services and information about human growth and development are offered; (4) the programs work together; (5) computers and GED classes are available; (6) the Community School Room provides parents with a place to hang out; (7) free field trips are offered; and (8) the whole school is involved (D. Denise Crawford, personal communication, October 20, 2001).

Vice-principal Jacquelynn Hartsfield believes that the community school is "real" (J. Hartsfield, personal communication, October 2001). She highlights four key components: providing health care through the clinic; offering the extended day as a safe haven; meeting parents' needs; and addressing issues such as violence in the home. School personnel are convinced that having these capabilities in the school has greatly enhanced the classroom learning process. Children come to school ready to learn, making it easier for teachers to teach. Also, teachers are supported by open and frequent contacts with parents and with professionals in health, mental health, and child development.

Integration of Services

Community schools bring together specific add-on components to create the desired transformation. Merely dropping service components into a school building without linking them to the whole environment can create fragmentation. Integration of school work and service programs is one of the greatest challenges facing this emerging field. When we review the chronology of events at Quitman, the integration

process becomes apparent. While the basic community school components offered by the CACNJ staff—extended day, parent involvement—
would be expected to fit together, the school clinic has also been well
integrated into the community school. The Children's Hospital of New
Jersey at Newark Beth Israel Medical Center operates the clinic, and
the clinic and CACNJ staffs work in close cooperation with each other.
The Bank Street early education program New Beginnings concen-
trates on restructuring kindergarten and first grade classes so that they
become developmentally appropriate centers of learning. The CACNJ
staff called on the Bank Street staff to train parent volunteers in child
development.

School personnel and personnel from collaborative agencies are
equally involved in implementing the Comer school reform effort at
the Quitman School. The CACNJ staff was instrumental in selecting
and implementing the Comer model. The community school coordinator, principal, and vice-principal went to the initial Comer training
at Yale. Both the Comer School Development and the CAS concepts of
community schools emphasize parent involvement and participation,
child-centered classrooms, and teacher training, and call for a great
deal of committee work. Though overlap can sometimes cause difficulties, the overlap in these two programs reinforces the positive changes
in school climate rather than creating further redundancy.

The "Prevention of Child Abuse Dinner" is a good example of
how collaboration works at Quitman. One of the Comer committees
proposed the idea. Bank Street's New Beginnings was responsible for
the training and book display, the CACNJ staff provided dinner and
took care of the children, and the school organized an art exhibit of
student works.

The school-wide Child Well-Being Committee is co-chaired by a
vice-principal and the clinic nurse practitioner. This group brings
together stakeholders in the community school to address critical issues
in the school. For example, a security guard was observed over-disci-
plining students by making them stand at attention in the hall for com-
mitting minor infractions. Committee representatives worked with the
guard to establish gentler and more effective procedures for dealing
with children. The vice-principal feels that the atmosphere has changed
as a result of the community school efforts and says, "No one closes
doors. The children are nicer and everyone shares responsibility"
(Jacqueline Hartsfield, personal communication, September 20, 2001).

Perhaps the key word in regard to integration of components is
"intentionality." Each of the parties involved in creating the Quitman

Street Community School intentionally works with the other parties. They all recognize that the strength of the school transformation lies in its comprehensiveness. The CACNJ staff has provided significant leadership, carefully defining its role as facilitator, and always working within the fabric of the school.

Overcoming Turf Barriers

One of the major challenges community schools around the country report is the struggle over turf. Outsiders come into schools and invade the insiders' territory. Existing staff wonder what role the new staff will play, and the new staff wonder why the school staff have such difficulty controlling students. At Quitman a number of additional barriers had to be overcome. Teachers were in the middle of the transition from K–8 to Pre-K–4 and under enormous pressure from the school system to improve standardized test scores. They did not want their classrooms "messed up" by after-school programs. The school nurse must have felt supplanted when a full-service clinic staffed by a nurse practitioner moved next door. And in this school, there already was a school system-supported Parent Liaison, who operated out of a fully equipped parent resource room.

Much work went into selling the community school concepts to this community. The former School Improvement Team (which had become the School Management Team) was concerned that they would be replaced by a community school advisory board, and school staff were concerned that the health clinic would be serving people off the street. Three years into the program, most of these barriers have been overcome. Teachers report great satisfaction with all aspects of the program. Parents, teachers, and other school staff agree that enrichment efforts and increased parent involvement have helped to improve grades, and that the changed school climate has encouraged better student behavior and increased attendance. The school nurse's role is clearly defined and includes working closely with the clinic staff. The parent liaison acts as the initial entry point for all parent work and arranges some discussion groups and parent educational workshops. The liaison also assigns volunteer work to parents, particularly those who need credit for volunteer hours as part of their welfare requirement. Many parents in the community have bought into and love the community school.

Consistent Use of Technical Assistance

Many of the models mentioned above (CAS, Beacons, University-Assisted Community Programs, Bridges to Success, Communities In

School) have developed technical assistance capacities to work with local school-community partnerships. These intermediary organizations can help groups establish a planning process, conduct needs assessments, design governance arrangements, seek funding, and implement and evaluate programs. The Quitman Street Community School received support from the CAS technical assistance team from the start. The experienced CAS staff interpreted and adapted their model for the Quitman community. With a foundation grant, CAS staff were able to spend many hours on-site, lending support and offering ideas in a nonthreatening way. The CACNJ staff was open to suggestions and willing to try out techniques offered by CAS. Also, the Quitman staff benefited from visiting established CAS schools.

Selection of a Strong Lead Agency

Not every agency has the capacity to lead a community school program. The work is labor intensive, and so the lead agency should have considerable resources. The CAS is one of the largest child welfare organizations in New York City, which has allowed it to work with 10 city schools and more than 70 schools around the country. Their experience has shown that other youth-serving agencies, such as the Boys and Girls Clubs and YMCAs and YWCAs, can play the lead agency role. In other community school models, the local United Way and indigenous community-based groups such as local chapters of Aspira (a national nonprofit devoted to education and leadership development among Latino youth) have successfully acted as lead. In some communities, the principal has opened the schoolhouse doors and brought in an array of services without the help of a lead agency (Dryfoos & Maguire, 2002).

At Quitman, the CACNJ proved to be an excellent lead agency, with considerable resources and top-level staff who were available to work with site staff. Agency people knew the neighborhood well and had experience in youth development programs. They were able to successfully adapt the CAS model and play a catalyst role. Even though they were not responsible for running the clinic, the Bank Street College of Education's New Beginnings program, or school-sponsored efforts, the CACNJ staff were able to coordinate all aspects of the community school.

Supportive Foundations

Foundations have been critically important in getting school-community partnerships off the ground. The Charles Stewart Mott Foundation has been a major player in this field for the past half-century through its support of the community education/lifelong learning model. More recently the Mott Foundation has partnered with the Department of Education to launch the CCLC program (see De Kanter et al., this volume, chapter 10). The Mott Foundation, with a commitment of more than $100 million for a multiyear period, has been able to do things the Department of Education could not, including widespread training, convening meetings, identifying promising practices, supplementing federal evaluation dollars, bringing other funders to the table, and working with media, advocacy, and policy planners.

Other foundations' projects include the Wallace-Reader's Digest Extended Services Schools Initiative, which supported adaptations of four community school models in 80 sites around the country. The Polk Brothers Fund in Chicago was instrumental in starting a full-service school program in three schools and providing follow-up in collaboration with the Chicago Board of Education to adapt the model for other schools. The Ewing Marion Kauffman, Carnegie Corporation, Wallace-Reader's Digest, and Charles Stewart Mott foundations have made grants to the Coalition of Community Schools and also support specific community school programs around the country. The Coalition brings together more than 170 local, state, and national organizations to promote the replication and sustainability of community school models.

More recently, the Eisenhower Foundation, with support from the Department of Education, selected three schools—in Tukwila, Washington, in Indian Head, Maryland, and in Boston, Massachusetts—to replicate and evaluate full-service community schools. And in 2001, the Public Education Network (PEN), as part of a large-scale school improvement project with the Annenberg Foundation, launched the School and Community Initiative. Planning grants were awarded to local PEN affiliates who came up with schemes for building seamless, coordinated and comprehensive programs and supports for high achievement. The five sites selected for awards are Buffalo, New York; Lancaster, Pennsylvania; Lincoln, Nebraska; Paterson, New Jersey; and Providence, Rhode Island.

Without the Prudential Foundation, the events at the Quitman School might not have occurred. The idea of transforming Quitman into a community school was generated by a Prudential executive's visit to the school. The Foundation quickly responded to the concept and funded a lead agency backed up with technical assistance from CAS. Through all of this, the Foundation has continued to fund other aspects of Quitman's transformation, including Bank Street's work, a new playground, various arts and cultural programs, mentoring and volunteer activities, and special events. Having one major financial support has greatly enhanced the development of the community school, by averting the agony of piecing together small grants from multiple foundations and other sources of funds.

Effective Program Components

My study of the Quitman School revealed certain special program components that enhance the overall success of community schools.

Working with parents. An increase in parental participation seems to be a hallmark of community schools. At Quitman, parents whose children attend the after-school program are required to sign a "contract" to give 6 hours per month of volunteer services to the community school. They have responded enthusiastically and welcome the opportunity to participate in their children's education as aides in the classroom, cafeteria, and after-school program as well as on the playground and on field trips. The school has hired some of these parents as classroom aides. Two dynamic parents are running for president and vice president of the PTA, helping to bring the organization back to life. Both are frequent volunteers and deeply committed to the success of the community school. The school gives the impression of being full of parents—in the classrooms, halls, playground, and cafeteria. The large community school room is a family resource center, with computers for family use, information on referrals and continuing education, and space to hang out and meet other parents.

Providing access to health and social services. Access to on-site health care is a very important component of community schooling. Having designated space right in the school building creates a very visible program that almost all families use and like. At Quitman, the clinic offers health, mental health, and dental services for all students. Medical problems such as asthma, allergies, ringworm, and pink eye are the most common ailments. A social worker supported by the clinic program has been on site since the beginning of the community school and knows the neighborhood, having grown up there. He believes that providing one-on-one attention is an important intervention in communities where children often lack attachments to significant adults. Many of the students deal with bereavement, having lost parental support because of substance abuse and jail terms.

When health and mental health services are offered in schools, clinic staff are sometimes overwhelmed by the demand for services. Many children in these schools have rarely visited a physician or dentist.

The demand at Quitman for mental health services cannot be met by the current mental health staff of one social worker and a part-time psychiatric consultant. Thirty to forty percent of the students at Quitman are estimated to have mental health problems related to stress and anxiety.

Hiring local people. Many community schools are committed to improving social capital in the neighborhood, which might involve stimulating entrepreneurial efforts or preparing people for the work force. Employing local parents and community people to work in the after-school program as group leaders is a unique aspect of the Quitman School. Many group leaders start as volunteers, then work in paid positions in the CACNJ after-school program and go on to become paid classroom aides. One group leader went back to school to become a teacher.

Currently 12 group leaders receive ongoing supervision and training. Workshops are held weekly with assistance from the Bank Street program and health clinic personnel. Topics covered include team building, child development issues, group work skills, bereavement, and child behavior problems. The philosophy of the after-school program is nonauthoritarian and child-centered. After 3 years of programming, some group leaders are emerging as leaders of a community betterment movement centered on cleaning up the streets bordering the school and pressing for better housing.

Providing transportation. Transportation is frequently cited as a major problem for community schools, especially during the after-school hours. The CACNJ provided Quitman with a van for transporting children and their parents. Although the van may seem like a minor perk and is not usually something mentioned in most of the emerging community school planning guides, it is a necessity for all staff. For example, thanks to the van, a child can get to a medical appointment off-site, or a group of students can go to another site for enrichment classes or swimming lessons.

Evaluation of Community Schools

School reform of any kind is not easy. As educators know well, few school reform models have produced solid evidence of success in enhancing student achievement (Northwest Regional Educational Laboratory, 1998). A review of research on the 24 whole-school, comprehensive, or schoolwide approaches currently being implemented found limited evidence of success (American Association of School Administrators, 2000). Only three models provided strong evidence through rigorous research of positive effects on student achievement.

However, preliminary findings on community schools are more encouraging (Dryfoos, 2000). Through the Coalition for Community Schools in 2000, we were able to find 49 school/community programs that had produced recent evaluation reports or data on results (Dryfoos, 2000). Of course, these reports ranged widely in quality and methodology; no two initiatives or research protocols were alike. All of the reports presented findings that focused on one or more of the following outcome measures: academic achievement, changes in student behavior, or increases in parental involvement. Forty-six reported positive outcomes, while only three studies found no positive outcomes.

Achievement

Academic gains were reported by 36 of the 49 programs. Reading and math test scores improved over a 2- to 3-year period. Many of these successful programs were in elementary schools. At least eight of the programs that reported achievement advances pointed out that the outcomes were not schoolwide but were limited to students receiving special services, such as case management or intensive mental health services, or they were experienced only by high-risk students, or only by students attending the extended-day sessions.

Attendance

Nineteen programs reported improvement in school attendance. Four programs reported lower dropout rates, one specifically among pregnant and parenting teens. Teacher attendance improved in several programs, suggesting higher rates of teacher satisfaction.

Suspensions and High-Risk Behaviors

Suspensions or referrals for disciplinary reasons were down in 11 programs, though this may reflect changes in suspension policies rather than changes in student behaviors leading to suspensions. As schools transform into more child-centered institutions, the administration is likely to change suspension and expulsion policies.

Eleven programs reported reductions in substance abuse, teen pregnancy, or disruptive behavior in the classroom, or reported improvement in behavior in general. These decreases in high-risk behaviors suggest changes in school climate and participants' quality of life.

Access to Services

One program cited better access to health care, lower hospitalization rates, higher immunization rates, and better access to dental care. Access to child care was a significant improvement for many.

Parent Involvement

At least 12 of the programs reported increases in parent involvement, while in other programs, parents said that they "felt better." Providers reported lower rates of child abuse and neglect, less out-of-home placement, better child development practices, less aggression, and generally improved social relationships among participants. Students reported a heightened sense of adult support from both parents and teachers.

Neighborhood

Six programs noted lower violence rates and safer streets in their communities. One program reported a reduction in student mobility, suggesting that adding services to the school encouraged families to stay in the neighborhood.

Multiple Outcomes

Most programs reported changes in more than one area, reflecting the design and comprehensiveness of both the research and program. Quitman showed some improvement in test scores, although the mobility rate and the changing structure of the school make it difficult to track students or draw firm conclusions. However, on school climate measures Quitman shows marked changes in many areas, such as student social and emotional wellness and growth, parental involvement, family support and engagement, staff development, and community involvement and engagement. Changes in academic achievement do not happen overnight. The impact of an improved school climate may not be evident for 3 to 5 years.

The National Center for Family and Community Connections with Schools (Jordan, Orozco, & Averett, 2002) conducted a review of the literature on community schools and found a promising but incomplete picture. They identified four critical areas for further research: understanding cultural diversity, employing developmental approaches and integrated service delivery, facilitating student transitions through school, and preparing educators and other personnel to foster connections among family, schools, and communities. The Coalition for

Community Schools is in the process of collecting recent evaluation data for a new publication that will focus primarily on the impact of community schools on educational achievement (Coalition for Community Schools, in press).

Conclusions

Accepting the idea that children and families need additional services that can be provided by community agencies in school buildings invites a myriad of potential people problems. Each additional component brings in new people from different professions and domains, at varying levels of competency and authority. One of the goals of community schools is to open the school to youth workers, parents, and volunteers. Some may have no professional training or identity, while others may be university professors, psychiatrists, nurses, social workers, or lawyers.

The principal and the community school coordinator facilitate relationships among this array of people. We now have enough experience implementing the various models around the country to give clear advice: The goal must be to create a climate that encourages diverse individuals to work together in a comprehensive mode over the long term. This calls for careful planning for each component, linking the appropriate school personnel with the outside agency workers who come into the school, and then linking the components together to create an integrated whole. Communication, listening, patience, respect for and trust in other people, and regularly scheduled committee meetings are all necessary components of successful collaborations. Anthony Amato (2002), superintendent of the Hartford Public Schools, put it succinctly, "Collaboration is the hardest work I could possibly think of in the world" (p. 14).

Continuous inservice training is essential to the success of these community school models, especially in light of the endemic turnover problem. The availability of technical assistance through intermediary agencies like CAS should encourage educators to pursue these community school concepts. The primary message to school teachers, principals, and superintendents must be: You don't have to do this alone. Tap the resources in your community that will help children and their families overcome social, economic, and health barriers to learning.

Although this chapter focused on an elementary school, community schools can work in middle and high schools as well. Full-service community schools are emerging at every level, although they may involve different service configurations. Parent involvement is less challenging in the earlier grades, and community involvement through service learning may be more suitable for students in upper grades. School-based clinics started out in high schools, and family resource centers began in elementary schools. However, the basic formula applies across grade levels: The impact of integrated activities on school outcomes is greater than the sum of the separate activities.

With the focus on high-stakes testing and severe budget cutting, what are the chances that comprehensive schools will be widely repli-cated? Although many barriers have to be overcome, the current expe-rience shows that full-service community schools are being developed all around the country, as principals and community leaders come together and learn about these models. Funds are, of course, essential, especially to support the coordinator, a new position in a school. But existing funding can be used more efficiently when services are inte-grated.

Some take issue with this approach to transforming schools into neighborhood hubs, arguing that this is not what schools are for. Some critics are concerned that having all these extra programs will distract the school from producing academic achievers. However, empirical evidence from 49 reports cited here shows that full-service community schools can affect academic outcomes as well as behav-ioral, family, and neighborhood outcomes. The goal is to reduce the burden placed on educators alone to produce cognitively, physically, and emotionally healthy children, and to share this work with the rest of the community.

WEBSITES OF PROGRAMS MENTIONED

Bank Street College of Education: http://www.bnkst.edu/html/continuing/programs.html
Beacons: http://www.fcny.org/html/home.htm
Bridges to Success initiative: http://national.unitedway.org/mobilization/
The Children's Aid Society: http://www.childrensaidsociety.org/
The Community Agencies Corporation of New Jersey: http://www.cacofnj.com/
Communities in Schools: http://www.cisnet.org/
West Philadelphia Improvement Corps: http://dolphin.upenn.edu/~wepic/

Joy G. Dryfoos can be reached at JDRYF65322@aol.com.

REFERENCES

American Association of School Administrators. (2000). *An educator's guide to schoolwide reform.* Retrieved August 21, 2002, http://www.aasa.org

Blank, M., & Melaville, A. (1999). Creating family supportive schools: Taking the first steps. *Family Support Journal, 18*(3), 37-38.

Coalition for Community Schools. (2002). *Community schools: Partnerships for excellence.* Retrieved August 21, 2002, from http://www.communityschools.org/partnerships.html

Coalition for Community Schools (in press, 2002). *Linkages to learning: Making the case for community schools.* Washington, DC: Coalition for Community Schools, Institute for Educational Leadership.

Collaborative for Integrated School Services. (2002). *Building strong full service and community schools: Leadership and collaboration.* Cambridge, MA: Harvard Graduate School of Education.

Department of Education. (2002). *21st Century Community Learning Centers.* Retrieved August 8, 2002 from http://www.ed.gov/21stccl

Dryfoos, J. (1994). *Full-service schools: A revolution in health and services for children and families.* San Francisco: Jossey-Bass.

Dryfoos, J. (2000). *Evaluation of community schools: An early look.* Retrieved August 8, 2002 from http://www.communityschools.com

Dryfoos, J. (2002). *Quitman Community School: Rallying around the whole village, saving the whole child.* Newark, NJ: Prudential Foundation.

Dryfoos, J., & Maguire, S. (2002). *Inside full-service community schools.* Thousand Oaks, CA: Corwin Press.

Family support in the schools. (2002). *America's Family Support Magazine, 21*(1), 1-2. Retrieved August 20, 2002, from http://www.frca.org/content/afsm/21_1/conn3.htm/

Jordan, C., Orozco, E., & Averett, A. (2002). *Emerging issues in school, family & community connections.* Austin, TX: National Center for Family & Community Connections with Schools, Southwest Educational Development Laboratory.

Kentucky Office of Family Resource and Youth Services Centers. (2002). Retrieved August 8, 2002 from http://cfc.state/ky/us/frysc/Abot%2-Us.htm

Kolbe, L., Kann, L., & Brenner, N. (2001). Overview and summary of findings: School Health Policies and Programs Study 2000. *Journal of School Health, 71*(7), 253-259.

Making the grade: Access to comprehensive school-based health services for children and youth. (2000, Winter). Newsletter, George Washington University, Washington, DC, 4.

Northwest Regional Educational Laboratory. (1998). *Catalog of school reform models* (1st ed.). Available from the Northwestern Regional Educational Laboratory website, http://www.nwrel.org/scpd/catalog/index.shtml

School Development Program. (1998, April). *Model of the SDP process* [Handout]. New Haven, CT: Yale Child Study Center.

Southwest Educational Development Laboratory. (1998). Pulling together broader views of schools. *SEDLetter, 10*(3), 1.

Tiezzi, L. Director of Community and Health Education, Columbia University School of Public Health, New York. Interview, May 15, 1993.

U.S. Census Bureau. (2000). *Statistical abstract of the United States: 2000* (120th ed.). Washington, DC. Tables 264, 491.

U.S. Department of Health and Human Services. (2000). Healthy people 2010, 2nd ed. Washington, DC, USGPO.

Walsh, M., Brabeck, M., Howard, K., Sherman, F., Montes, C., & Garvin, T. (2000). The Boston College-Allston/Brighton Partnership: Description and challenges. *Peabody Journal of Education, 75*(3), 6-32.

CHAPTER 8

An Interprofessional Model and Reflections on Best Collaborative Practice

JANE QUINN

The Children's Aid Society's community school model represents one approach to interprofessional collaboration within a public school setting and is based on more than ten years of experience at multiple sites in New York City. The chapter will describe the model and review the research on which it is based, outline evaluation findings to date, and discuss the mechanisms used to foster and maximize the benefits of multiple disciplines coming together to work with and on behalf of low-income children, their families, and their communities.

Interprofessional Collaboration—One Approach

In March 1992, The Children's Aid Society (CAS), New York City's oldest and largest youth-serving organization, launched a new kind of interprofessional partnership at Intermediate School 218 (I.S. 218) in Washington Heights, a low-income neighborhood in northern Manhattan. This partnership brought together the collective resources and expertise of the New York City Board of Education and its local Community School District 6 with those of CAS, a comprehensive child and family service agency. Over the past decade, this local partnership has grown to 10 schools in three New York City neighborhoods and, nationally and internationally, to more than 120 schools that have adapted the model to their own local needs and circumstances.

The CAS community schools, which fit squarely within Joy Dryfoos's definition of a full-service community school (Dryfoos, 1994; this volume, chapter 7), are educational institutions that combine the rigorous academics of a quality school with a wide range of vital in-house services, supports, and opportunities aimed at promoting children's learning and development. The community school unites the most

---

Jane Quinn is Assistant Executive Director for Community Schools at the Children's Aid Society in New York City.

important influences in children's lives—schools, families, and communities—to create a web of support that nurtures their development toward productive adulthood.

This web of support might best be conceptualized as a triangle that incorporates three interconnected support systems into one structure:

- *A strong core instructional program* designed to help all students meet high academic standards.
- *Enrichment activities* designed to expand students' learning opportunities and to support their cognitive, social, emotional, moral, and physical development.
- *A full range of social, health, and mental health services* designed to safeguard children's well being and remove barriers to learning.

The CAS model of community schools involves interprofessional collaboration at many levels. The primary collaborative relationship involves a long-term partnership between educators and social workers who work together regularly to integrate the various components of the school, especially the extended-day and regular school day programs. But many other partners contribute as well. As the lead agency in the partnership, CAS employs doctors, dentists, nurse practitioners, psychologists, clinical social workers, youth workers, teachers, artists, writers, parents, college students, high school students, and other community residents to deliver the enrichment activities and social, health, and mental health services described above. The model calls for a full-time community school director who plays the central role of planning and coordinating the multiple program components. These directors typically are experienced master's-level social workers who serve as partners with the schools' principals.

One of the hallmarks of the CAS model is its adaptability. Even within New York City, the 10 CAS schools offer different menus of supports, services, and opportunities for students, their families, and the surrounding communities. Decisions about what components to include at a given school are driven by local needs assessments as well as by funding and other resource constraints. However, all 10 schools and most of the national and international adaptations share a common philosophy, rooted in the notion of transforming traditional public schools into institutions primarily focused on educating children while also helping to strengthen their surrounding communities.

Three key ideas inform this philosophy: comprehensiveness, coherence, and commitment. *Comprehensiveness* means implementing a full-service approach to address the multiple needs of children and families.

Coherence means that planning and decision making are shared by the three major partners (the school, CAS, and parents) to provide an integrated network of supports, opportunities, and services and to promote a community vision and sense of shared responsibility. *Commitment* means that CAS and its partner schools intend to work together with and on behalf of students and their families over the long term.

From an institutional perspective, the community schools approach has allowed CAS to develop an alternative service delivery system. Historically, CAS has run a variety of community centers (similar to settlement houses) in low-income neighborhoods such as Harlem and East Harlem. These multiservice agencies serve as permanent resources for children, families, and communities by building social capital at the neighborhood level. For CAS, community schools are a natural extension of this work because they build on many of the same organizational skills and commitments. At the outset, CAS viewed community schools as a way to extend its reach into additional low-income neighborhoods and to demonstrate the viability of an innovative delivery system predicated on partnership with public schools. Because long-term commitment and sustainability were at the forefront of the organization's thinking from the beginning, going to scale in New York City was never considered. (With 1,100 schools, more than 1.1 million students, and 32 local districts, New York City is the nation's largest school system.) Instead, CAS began with one community school in 1992 and has added roughly one school per year over the past decade. The current schools include five elementary schools, four middle or intermediate schools, and one high school.

As the oldest site, I.S. 218 illustrates how the core concepts of community schools come together "on the ground." This large urban middle school serves approximately 1,700 students in grades six through eight. The school's structure and core instructional program have been greatly influenced by the "Turning Points" philosophy of middle grade reform promoted by the Carnegie Council on Adolescent Development (1989). This philosophy and its resulting framework revolve around young adolescents' developmental needs for meaningful interpersonal relationships, small learning groups, and rich academic content applied to real-life issues. In accord with this conceptual framework, I.S. 218 is organized around an academy structure. Each of its four floors constitutes a "school within a school" in which teams of teachers work with the same students during their 3 years in the school. All students are exposed to a core instructional program that meets the New York City and New York State standards. Also, students are allowed to elect specialized courses in a major of their own (and their parents') selection. These majors currently include math, science, and technology; business studies; expressive arts; and community service. Teachers and other faculty lead student advisory groups consistent with the middle school philosophy to ensure that students' social and emotional needs are addressed and that all students are well known by at least one caring, competent adult and by a supportive group of peers.

According to the New York City Public Schools 2000-2001 school report card, the students at I.S. 218 are primarily Hispanic (94.6%), with the largest percentage (96%) of Dominican background (R. Bautista, personal communication, 3/15/02). Approximately 88.3% of the students qualify for the federal school lunch program and nearly a third are English Language Learners (New York City Board of Education, 2001). A 1987 needs assessment conducted by CAS documented that Washington Heights suffered from severely overcrowded schools, high dropout rates, and a dangerous lack of health and social services. A concurrent neighborhood resource assessment indicated that despite these and other problems, including pervasive poverty, Washington Heights possessed many strengths, including neighborhood cohesion, an entrepreneurial spirit demonstrated by its many resident-owned businesses, and strong community attitudes about the value of education and family life (Garb, 1998). The needs and resource assessment served as the basis for the initial agreement among CAS, the New York City Board of Education, and the local Washington Heights school district (District 6) to begin working together. Both the central Board of Education and Community School District 6 passed formal resolutions endorsing the new partnership (see Appendix).

Prior to the formal launch of the community school, several recommendations from the needs assessment were addressed. These involved new school construction, planning, fundraising, program development, and hiring of staff. Although the full-service community school has taken several years to evolve, today I.S. 218 offers a comprehensive set of supports, opportunities, and services that include:

- A rigorous core instructional program that is consistent with the New York City and New York State standards.
- An extended-day program, open to all students, that offers before- and after-school classes and activities for academic support (e.g., homework help and tutoring) and enrichment (e.g., chess and computer clubs, poetry workshops); dance, theater, music, and

other cultural activities; physical fitness, sports, and other recreational programs; community service projects; and special programs, such as Recycle-a-Bicycle and Recycle-a-Computer, in which students gain hands-on experience building, repairing, and ultimately owning bicycles and computers.

- Summer programs, including camps that offer educational enrichment, recreation, and trips.

- Teen programs during evening hours and Saturdays—often attended by I.S. 218 graduates who live in the neighborhood.

- Formal and informal parent involvement programs, including workshops on nutrition, human sexuality, adolescent development, and personal fitness; English as a Second Language, GED, citizenship, entrepreneurship, and computer training classes; and drop-in activities to encourage socialization and community building.

- A full-service health clinic, which includes medical, dental, and optometry services for students as well as social and mental health services for students and their families.

- A Town Meeting program for students, held during the regular school day and co-led by Board of Education and CAS staff, which gives students an opportunity to learn about and discuss key issues, many of their own choosing.

- Community events, including an annual Dominican Heritage celebration as well as Thanksgiving, Christmas, and other holiday celebrations.

The Underlying Research Base

Research from multiple professional disciplines supports the community school model. Research on child and adolescent development indicates that young people need ongoing guidance and support in every developmental domain if they are to achieve productive adulthood. These domains include cognitive, social, emotional, physical, moral, and vocational development. Productive adulthood is defined as having competencies to participate in the labor economy, in responsible family life, and in active citizenship (Eccles, 1999). A 13-year study in 10 diverse communities found that child and adolescent outcomes were enhanced in communities where the key developmental influences, which include home, school, and community resources, combined to provide consistent messages, opportunities, and supports for young people (Ianni, 1990). Research also has shown that fragmentation characterizes much of the service delivery system for children and families in this country (Hodgkinson, 1989). As is suggested by the Ianni research, Hodgkinson found that such fragmentation limits effectiveness.

Resilience theory indicates that children who have consistent access to adult guidance and support experience better outcomes, due to higher education and career aspirations and a lower incidence of high-risk behaviors (Benard, 1991). Other researchers have shown that parental involvement in children's education is a key factor in promoting academic achievement. Specifically, children do better in school when their parents regularly support, monitor, and advocate for their children's education (Epstein, 1995; Henderson, 1995).

In addition to collaboration among services and adult involvement, after-school activities are important aspects of children's development. Benefits from after-school activities range from academic improvement to improved peer relations. Educational researcher Reginald Clark (1988) has documented the importance of children's participation in constructive learning activities during the nonschool hours. He found, for example, that economically disadvantaged children who spend 20–35 hours of out-of-school time each week in engaged learning (e.g., reading for pleasure and playing strategy games) got better grades in school than their more passive peers. In work spanning more than a decade, University of Wisconsin researcher Deborah Vandell and colleagues (1999) have documented a host of positive benefits from elementary-age children's participation in high-quality after-school programs, including better grades, work habits, emotional adjustment, and peer relations.

Benefits of after-school programs are not limited to elementary school children. Stanford education professor Milbrey McLaughlin (2000) found that adolescents who participate regularly in community-based youth development activities, such as arts programs, sports, and community service, have better academic and social outcomes and higher education and career aspirations than similar teens.

Much research has been done on the impact of fragmented service delivery, on resilience, on adult and parental involvement in children's lives, and on the benefits of after-school programs. Community schools encompass all of these elements of children's lives. How do all of these elements affect each other, and ultimately children's lives? Joy Dryfoos (1994) synthesized a complex body of research on reducing risk and promoting resilience among children and adolescents, and concluded that the single most effective intervention was the development and establishment of schools that integrate the delivery of quality education with needed health and social services.

Results to Date

What happens when you put all of the pieces together, as CAS has done at I.S. 218? An interprofessional team from the Schools of Education and Social Services at Fordham University conducted a multi-year evaluation at I.S. 218 and its sister elementary school, Primary School 5 (P.S. 5), also in Washington Heights. The evaluation documented improved academic performance; improved attendance; the creation of positive, safe learning environments for children; increased parent involvement; better student-teacher relations; and greater teacher attention to instruction. The Fordham team also documented more positive student attitudes about school; successful implementation of critical health and social services; and the achievement of a greater sense of community, both within the schools and within the neighborhood. A variety of data collection methods were used, including surveys of students, teachers, and parents; observations; interviews; and reviews of standardized test scores and other Board of Education records (for example, attendance records). During the 3 years of the impact study (1995–1998), the researchers identified two similar schools in District 6 as comparison schools. Specific results are outlined in the following sections.

Improved Academic Achievement

Preliminary evaluations at I.S. 218 and P.S. 5 showed that reading and math scores were higher than at comparable neighborhood schools, and sequentially higher for students who had attended these schools for 2 or more years. At I.S. 218, math performance rose from 37% at grade level in 1994 to 44% in 1995, to 51% in 1996. Of the third grade students who entered P.S. 5 in 1993, the first year of the community school, only 10.4% were reading at grade level. By the fourth grade, 16.2% of these students were reading at grade level, and the number rose to 35.4% by the fifth grade. Math achievement at P.S. 5 increased from 23.4% at grade level in the third grade class of 1993 to 32.1% in fourth grade and to 56% in fifth grade. Later evaluations showed that students at I.S. 218 and P.S. 5 continued to improve their math and reading scores. This was true for students who graduated in 1997 and for the group that followed between 1996 and 1999, although 1998–99 test scores were not examined. Some evidence suggested that participation in extended-day programs correlated with improved test scores, although this was not fully investigated during the evaluation period.

Higher Attendance Rates

Attendance rates, including teacher attendance, were higher at CAS community schools than at other local schools. Evaluators observed that, at 92%, I.S. 218 had the highest attendance rate in its school district and significantly surpassed the middle school attendance standard of 85% in New York City during this period. Furthermore, the evaluators noted that the attendance rate for both students and teachers had improved each year since the school opened.

Positive School Environments

Interviews and observations have consistently found that CAS community schools differ from traditional schools in overall climate. Parents and students feel welcome, and the pleasant physical environment contributes to a sense of harmony, order, and safety. In addition, students' perceptions of themselves and their conduct were more positive than those of the comparison group, and students at both I.S. 218 and P.S. 5 had more positive attitudes toward school than comparison students. According to the Fordham evaluators, the environment in community schools was more cheerful, busy, and welcoming than in the comparison schools. The community schools experienced little or no violence or graffiti.

Teachers, students, and parents considered the school "special" and reported that they were safe places for children to be. Teachers in the community schools spent more time on class preparation and working with students than their counterparts in the comparison schools.

Safer Schools

In a city where violent incidents on school grounds are an all too common occurrence, and where students are accustomed to metal detectors and security searches, it is remarkable that I.S. 218 has had almost no violent incidents since its opening in 1992. The Fordham team found that while the suspension rate for all New York City middle schools stood at 6.8 per 100 students, I.S. 218 averaged only 2.2 suspensions per 100 students.

Greater Parental Involvement

The Fordham team observed that the high levels of parent involvement in CAS community schools were among the most striking findings of their study. Parents were more involved, took more responsibility for their children's academic progress, felt more welcome in the schools, and had a greater presence in the community schools than in comparison schools. Parents also took advantage of the many services offered to them, including the social events and the adult education services. In particular, the researchers noted that parent involvement was significantly higher in the community schools—78% higher at P.S. 5 and 147% higher at I.S. 218—than in the comparison schools. Parents were involved in many ways throughout the school, not just in their child's academic work. They served as volunteers and paid employees during the regular school day and in the after-school and summer programs; participated in workshops and adult education courses; attended rallies and other advocacy events; and took part in community events. According to staff and evaluator observations, parents had a significant and notable presence in the community schools, and teachers rated this parent involvement as a primary asset of their schools (Brickman, Cancelli, Sanchez, & Rivera, 1998).

Improved Student-Teacher Relationships

Researchers noted that the relationships between teachers and students improved. This improvement could be linked to teachers' participation in the extended-day program, where the atmosphere is more relaxed and informal than in the regular classroom. A formative evaluation of P.S. 5 found that teachers in the community school tended to perceive their students more holistically than did teachers in other schools (Brickman, 1996). Teachers were more attentive to students' social, emotional, and physical needs, and so were more likely to refer them for student support services (such as medical care, social services, and after-school programs).

Teachers' Focus on Education

In an evaluation of P.S. 5, the most frequent comment made during the Fordham team's interviews with staff and families was that the wealth of services offered at the school freed teachers to do what they were hired to do: teach the children. Because children's extracurricular needs are met in community schools and teachers have the luxury of providing individualized attention to students during the extended-day program, teachers are able to focus exclusively on teaching during classroom time.

Promising findings from research studies conducted between 1993 and 1999 (Brickman, 1996; Brickman & Cancelli, 1997; Brickman, Cancelli, Sanchez, & Rivera, 1998; Cancelli, Brickman, Sanchez, &

Rivera, 1999; Clark & Engle, 2001; Robison, 1993) led CAS to expand its own community school efforts in New York City by developing a national training and technical assistance center. The objective is to share the CAS model, and the lessons learned, with colleagues from other cities and countries. CAS also developed a second-level evaluation approach, which was recently launched in collaboration with a research team from the City University of New York (CUNY). The new evaluation will continue to focus on I.S. 218 and P.S. 5, but will add a third school, Primary School 50 (a new CAS community school located in East Harlem). The CUNY evaluation will move from the quasi-experimental approach of the Fordham team to a "theory of change" approach based on a logic model developed collaboratively by the CUNY team and CAS. The theory of change approach focuses on expected outcomes and offers greater support for attributing results to the programs studied (Weiss, 1995). The evaluation designed by the CUNY team, with advice from an external advisory group, will focus on a variety of student outcomes and will seek to understand whether and how the multiple components of the community schools contribute to positive results for students (Clark & Engle, 2000). Based in part on the notion that "dosage makes a difference," the evaluation will emphasize tracking students' participation in extended-day enrichment programs and assessing whether or not intensive student participation leads to positive outcomes, including academic achievement.

Best Practices: Lessons Learned About Collaborative Planning

For community schools to be effective and sustain their effectiveness, they must be developed collaboratively from the very beginning. This means that the initial partners must come together out of mutual interest to develop a shared vision and common goals. A critical first decision involves determining who the initial partners should be. Although the specifics will vary from community to community, the core group might well include school representatives, the lead community agency, other social service and youth-serving agencies, parents and other community members, students, and funders. Members of the planning group should have the authority and resources to make decisions and commitments.

One of the major benefits of this kind of teamwork is the multiple perspectives that will come together at the earliest possible stage. For CAS, this meant learning about the reality of life within schools, such as how decisions are made about space allocation; custodial contracts and opening fees; protecting valuable equipment and materials in school libraries and computer rooms; and the priorities of schools in an increasingly high-pressure political environment that emphasizes achievement on high-stakes tests above all. In turn, early conversations with school partners helped them understand the core competencies that CAS could bring to the partnership. These included obvious strengths such as knowledge of how to engage families and how to provide youth development enrichment programs, but also less apparent skills such as fundraising and the capability of brokering needed services (e.g., legal consultation around immigration issues). Parents and other community residents provided important ideas and insights about the needs and strengths of their neighborhood.

CAS learned the importance of planning at multiple levels during the early stages of its partnership with schools in New York City. These levels include the city/central level of the Board of Education, the community school district level, and the individual school level. This planning, although time-consuming, resulted in time- and cost-savings over the long term. Of particular assistance were the written resolutions passed by the New York City Board of Education and Community School Board 6, which gave formal endorsement to the partnership with CAS.

The Fordham evaluations revealed that the commitment of CAS at the most senior level of the organization during the early stages (especially the commitment of the Chief Executive and the Chief Operating Officers) was one important key to success. This high-level leadership opened doors at the Board of Education and enabled CAS to commit organizational resources over the long term.

The evaluation provided information that can inform larger planning decisions about community schools and interprofessional collaboration. For example, some educational researchers and observers have worried about the potential of the community schools approach to distract educators from their core instructional mission. The Fordham evaluations clearly found that the schools' instructional mission was enhanced when educators had an institutional partner who could address barriers to students' learning and provide enrichment services that are explicitly linked to the daytime curriculum (Brickman & Cancelli, 1997; Brickman et al., 1998; Cancelli et al., 1999).

Best Practices: Lessons Learned About Collaborative Implementation

CAS and its partners have developed a variety of formal and informal mechanisms that contribute to success. On the formal side, the

CAS community school directors participate actively and regularly in each site's School Leadership Team, the formal governance structure that consists of school administration, faculty, and parents. Because the main responsibility of the School Leadership Team is to develop the school's comprehensive education plan, CAS has found it essential to be "at the table" for the monthly meetings of this key organizational structure to both give and receive information and to contribute to planning decisions.

The CAS community school director also participates actively and regularly in the Principals' Cabinet meetings, which are critical opportunities to engage in joint problem solving and to deepen the partnership between the principal and director. Another important formal mechanism is the Pupil Personnel Committee, attended by the community school director or a designee. These regular meetings bring school psychologists, social workers, and guidance counselors together with CAS staff to discuss the problems and progress of individual students. All of these meetings are collaborative, with professionals from multiple disciplines, and frequently parents, sharing their expertise and perspectives on behalf of students.

Community school directors also hold regular meetings with CAS staff in each building. These sessions bring together medical, mental health, extended-day, and other staff (for example, Early Head Start and Head Start staff are employed by CAS in two of our elementary-level community schools).

Collaborative practice is fostered and enhanced through joint staff development. While CAS has not yet maximized this opportunity, experiences to date have proven useful. For example, at I.S. 218, CAS staff members have conducted joint staff retreats at the start of the school year. These retreats have provided a vehicle for revisiting the community schools vision, orienting new staff to that vision, and building professional skills and team spirit. Issues covered during past planning retreats include child and adolescent development, mental health issues of early adolescence, and integrating the after-school and regular school day programs.

These formal mechanisms at the individual school level are mirrored at the district and city levels. CAS staff regularly attend and participate in both district school board meetings and formal advisory groups at the New York City Board of Education. For example, the Chief Executive Officer of CAS serves on the Chancellor's Advocacy Task Force; the CAS Director of Health Operations serves on the Chancellor's Health Advisory Committee; and two members of the community schools staff have served as faculty on the Board of Education's New Principals Institute. These collaborative activities serve the dual purpose of fostering more effective partnerships in the 10 current community schools and of providing forums for exchanging new ideas and leveraging larger systemic change.

On an informal basis, CAS staff have developed three mantras during the past 10 years that guide the collaborative interprofessional work in community schools: (1) everything has to be negotiated; (2) it's all about relationships; and (3) to make these partnerships work, you have to have the word "yes" written in your heart.

These mantras remind CAS staff of the nature of this work and its inherent challenges. In overcrowded schools, negotiations about space are a given. Remembering that these negotiations are part of the work, rather than an impediment to doing it, is enormously helpful. Similarly, tending to relationships takes time and constant attention, and CAS staff have learned that this too is part of the work—in fact, is central to it. The third mantra, borrowed from colleague Marty Blank, staff director of the Coalition for Community Schools, also provides an important guidepost in times of challenge or disagreement (M. Blank, personal communication, March 8, 2000). "Getting to yes" is the goal of all negotiations, large and small.

Conclusion

During the past decade, both CAS and its Board of Education partners have observed that working together has required all of the partners to change the way they do business and to modify and expand professional practice. For CAS staff, this has meant reading *Education Week* as well as *Youth Today*; acknowledging that cognitive development is indeed part of youth development; learning about the New York City and New York State academic standards and using these standards in the development of after-school enrichment programs; delineating the organizational competencies of the CAS; and agreeing to share responsibility for results, including young people's academic achievement on high-stakes tests. These changes are not trivial. Rather, they are as transformational at the practice level as the community school is at the institutional level. These changes at such a fundamental level offer dual benefits: they keep the work exciting, and they contribute to producing more effective results for children and families.

REFERENCES

Benard, B. (1991). *Fostering resiliency in kids: Protective factors in the family, school and community.* Portland, OR: Northwest Regional Educational Laboratories, Western Regional Center for Drug-Free Schools and Communities.

Brickman, E. (1996). *A formative evaluation of P.S. 5: A Children's Aid Society/Board of Education Community School.* New York: Fordham University Graduate School of Social Services.

Brickman, E., & Cancelli, A. (1997). *Washington Heights community schools evaluation: First year findings.* New York: Fordham University Graduate School of Education.

Brickman, E., Cancelli, A., Sanchez, A., & Rivera, G. (1998). *The Children's Aid Society/ Board of Education community schools: Second-year evaluation report.* New York: Fordham University Graduate Schools of Education and Social Services.

Cancelli, A., Brickman, E., Sanchez, A., & Rivera, G. (1999). *The Children's Aid Society/ Board of Education community schools: Third-year evaluation report.* New York: Fordham University Graduate School of Social Services.

Carnegie Council on Adolescent Development. (1989). *Turning points: Preparing American youth for the 21st century.* New York: Carnegie Corporation of New York.

Clark, H., & Engle, R. (2000). *Community schools evaluation plan: Adopting a theory of change approach.* New York: The Children's Aid Society and ActKnowledge/CUNY Graduate Center.

Clark, H., & Engle, R. (2001). *Summary of research findings, 1992-99.* New York: CUNY Center for Human Environments.

Clark, R.M. (1988). *Critical factors in why disadvantaged children succeed or fail in school.* New York: Academy for Educational Development.

Dryfoos, J.G. (1994). *Full-service schools: A revolution in health and social services for children, youth, and families.* San Francisco: Jossey-Bass.

Eccles, J. (1999). The development of children ages 6 to 14. *The Future of Children: When School Is Out, 9*(2), 30-44.

Epstein, J.L. (May 1995). School, family, community partnerships: Caring for the children we share. *Phi Delta Kappan, 77*(9), 701-712.

Garb, M. (1998, December 27). Washington Heights: New hopes in a patchwork neighborhood. *New York Times,* archives.

Henderson, A.T., & Berla, N. (1995). *A new generation of evidence: The family is critical to student achievement.* Washington, DC: Center for Law and Education.

Hodgkinson, H.L. (1989). *The same client: The demographics of education and service delivery systems.* Washington, DC: Institute for Educational Leadership.

Ianni, F.A.J. (1990). *The search for structure.* New York: The Free Press.

McLaughlin, M.W. (2000). *Community counts: How youth organizations matter for youth development.* Washington, DC: Public Education Network.

New York City Department of Education. (2001). Annual School Report, District 6, I.S. 218.

Robison, E. (1993). *An interim evaluative report concerning a collaboration between The Children's Aid Society, New York City Board of Education, Community School District 6 and the I.S. 218 Salome Ureña de Henriquez School.* New York: Fordham University Graduate School of Social Services.

Vandell, D.L., & Shumow, L. (1999). After-school child care programs. *The Future of Children: When School Is Out, 9*(2), 64-80.

Weiss, C.H. (1995). Nothing as practical as good theory: Exploring theory-based evaluation for comprehensive community initiatives for children and families. In J.P. Connell, A.C. Kubisch, L.B. Schorr, and C.H. Weiss (Eds.), *New approaches to evaluating community initiatives: Concepts, methods, and contexts* (pp. 65-92). Washington, DC: The Aspen Institute.

APPENDIX

The following resolution was passed by the New York City Board of Education on September 26, 1990 in support of the community schools partnership described in this chapter:

Statement of Support for The Children's Aid Society/Community School District 6 Community School Partnership Plan

WHEREAS, The Children's Aid Society wishes to provide community-based social services to the thousands of children and families in the Washington Heights/Inwood area who are in need and underserved; and

WHEREAS, The Children's Aid Society has a history of successfully providing social services, including health, dental, mental health, recreational, educational and camping services to children, teenagers and families; and

WHEREAS, The Children's Aid Society has had a long and distinguished history of working jointly with the New York City Public Schools in developing services for the city's children; and

WHEREAS, The New York City Schools invite and welcome collaborative partnerships with public and private agencies as a means of providing increased resources for children; and

WHEREAS, in partnership with Community School District 6 and in collaboration with other service providers and associations, The Children's Aid Society is willing to raise funds and provide coordination in establishing community-based services in one or more new schools currently being constructed in Washington Heights/Inwood, to be used as full-service demonstration community schools open fourteen hours per day, six or seven days per week; now be it therefore

RESOLVED, that the New York City Board of Education welcomes this opportunity for a community school partnership with The Children's Aid Society and supports the establishment of this program in Community School District 6.

The Board of Community School District 6 subsequently passed a similar resolution. This second resolution added that the local district "agrees to work in the spirit of cooperation in establishing such a program in the district and to so inform other appropriate officials with the district and the Central Board of Education."

CHAPTER 9

Focusing on Core Academic Outcomes:
A Key to Successful School-Community Partnerships

JACOB MURRAY AND RICHARD WEISSBOURD

Across the country, public schools increasingly are turning to out-side agencies to address a wide range of health, social, and emotional troubles afflicting both children and their families. Many schools also are developing community partnerships to directly improve academic achievement. A community partner such as a local business will, for example, provide books, tutors, or homework help. Universities rou-tinely organize their students to assist in classrooms in diverse ways.

These various initiatives clearly produce tangible benefits for some children. But they also are hindered by significant limitations and drawbacks. Some schools suffer from "projectitis," taking on many projects and interventions designed to address an array of troubles without devoting the attention or resources needed to solve any one of these problems effectively. Partnerships designed to improve academic outcomes often fall short of their goals. Frequently these partnerships underestimate the "dose" needed—what it takes to improve the aca-demic prospects of a significant number of children.

The point, emphatically, is not that schools should abandon these partnerships. The point is that there may be better ways of going about them.

In recent years, a few cities have moved away from school-commu-nity partnerships that generate services or provide marginal forms of academic help toward those that focus on improving one or two core academic outcomes, such as school readiness at kindergarten, profi-ciency in reading or math, or enrollment in postsecondary education. Cities such as Baltimore, Boston, Charlotte-Mecklenburg, and Hous-ton have collaborated with community partners to improve reading

Jacob Murray is a policy analyst at the Harvard Children's Initiative. Richard Weiss-bourd is a lecturer in Education at the Harvard Graduate School of Education and the Kennedy School of Government.

skills. In Boston, many schools work hand-in-hand with some combination of families, libraries, after-school programs, colleges and universities, and other community organizations to promote reading and provide children with the integrated in-school and out-of-school reading support needed to reach this goal.

In this chapter, we discuss these emerging outcomes-based school-community partnerships as one promising strategy, as we offer answers to the following questions: Why have traditional school-community partnerships—partnerships designed both to address health, social, and emotional needs and to meet academic needs—had limited success? Why might organizing at least some services toward achieving a single-outcome goal, such as reading, be more fruitful? What are the key elements of effective outcomes-based initiatives? Finally, how should communities go about selecting one or two outcomes?

In discussing outcomes-based initiatives, we focus on ReadBoston, a citywide initiative launched by Mayor Tom Menino in 1995 and designed to dramatically increase the number of children reading by third grade. We also briefly discuss WriteBoston, a similar initiative for older children. One of us (Weissbourd) is the primary founder of ReadBoston, and both authors are founders of WriteBoston. Both ReadBoston and WriteBoston shed light on the great promise, as well as the problems and challenges, of outcomes-based initiatives.

Traditional School-Community Partnerships

Service-based Partnerships

Integrating services and schools is an old idea widely supported by education practitioners and scholars. Dewey conceived of schools as the "social centre" of communities and encouraged a variety of social uses for school time and space (see Benson & Harkavy, 1997, and this volume, chapter 5). Over the past two decades the Comer schools, originating in New Haven, have reinvigorated interest in school-linked services and school-community partnerships (Comer, 1988, 2001). These schools, named after their founder, a Yale psychiatrist, are devoted to meeting the needs of the whole child and commonly enlist outside agencies to address children's and sometimes families' health, social, and emotional needs. Joy Dryfoos has promoted "full-service schools" that seamlessly integrate a range of social supports for neighborhood children and families (Dryfoos, 1994, 1995, and this volume, chapter 7). Services may be school-based and school-governed, or school-linked, or schools may provide space for services administered by other agencies.

While the scope and form of these partnerships differ, the underlying premise is the same: For schools to be successful in educating children, they must tend to the needs of the whole child, if not the whole family (Bronfenbrenner, 1979; Epstein, 1992; Gardner, 2000; Sylvester, 1990). At the very least, schools need to meet children's safety, nutritional, and physical health needs before children can engage fully in learning. Because children and parents are easily accessible through schools and often live close to schools, schools are considered the ideal delivery system for these services (Adler & Gardner, 1994; Tyack, 1992).

The origins of these partnerships are telling. Community institutions initiate many service partnerships. Local colleges and businesses, for instance, feel a responsibility to contribute to their host community while providing productive opportunities for their students or employees (Harkavy, 1999; Walsh et al., 2000). They partner with local schools to provide employment assistance for parents, health services for children and families, or professional development opportunities for teachers. Other service partnerships are formed to address an obvious, pressing need. A rash of violent episodes or sudden media coverage of a problem such as teen pregnancy, for instance, might prompt a school to enlist the help of outside agencies.

These partnerships can provide access to much needed services and supports for children and families. They can pair struggling schools with dynamic businesses, community agencies, and higher education institutions that bring new energy and valuable resources. They can alleviate problems that directly cripple children's ability to learn (Benson & Harkavy, 1997; Dryfoos, 2000; Levy & Shepardson, 1992; Schorr, 1988, 1997; Tyack, 1992).

Yet there are also significant problems with many of these school-community partnerships. Most urban schools simply are not teaching children well; focusing on services can unwittingly drain attention from improving instruction. High-quality teaching is perhaps the most effective known strategy for improving the academic prospects of poor children (Darling-Hammond, 2000; Ferguson, 1998; Haycock, 1998). Research shows that as much as half of the achievement gap between poor and better-off students can be reduced by improving instruction (Darling-Hammond). Good teaching can also increase student interest and reduce behavior troubles. Students who are performing well in school are less likely to suffer from feelings of inferiority and shame, common precursors of depression, aggression, and anxiety disorders (Gilligan, 1991; Weissbourd, 1996). In this sense, good teaching may be the most powerful way we know of boosting children's resilience.

Yet learning to teach well is no simple process—it requires the ongoing, intensive attention and support of schools and school districts. Harvard literacy professor Catherine Snow argues that teaching children how to read is as least as hard as "doing surgery" and that teachers need to be trained and supported in many of the same ways as surgeons (Snow, 2000). That means that new teachers need ongoing, intensive mentoring from skilled veterans, and all teachers need to work in instructional environments where they have opportunities for deep and carefully crafted professional development. To do these things well, however, parents, teachers, and administrators must engage in a focused, continuous effort to reshape the culture and daily practices of schools.

Devoting attention to developing and managing services often distracts schools from the crucial work of improving instruction and, in some cases, changes the school's core focus altogether. Schools can become preoccupied with implementing a comprehensive service integration plan or building a multifaceted school-community partnership, rather than zeroing in on how they can better help struggling children learn key academic skills. Furthermore, once service providers set foot in schools, the challenges of merging separate professional cultures—resolving turf issues; coordinating service delivery; delineating tasks and responsibilities; and establishing accountability measures, governance, and funding arrangements—can be time-consuming and depleting (Adelman & Taylor, 2001; Farrow & Joe, 1992; Gardner, 1992; Levy & Shepardson, 1992; Melaville & Blank, 1998).

Sometimes schools and their partners become so bogged down that they struggle to meet any of their goals effectively, academic or nonacademic. With several organizations and projects operating in schools at once, resources become fragmented and diffused. Frontline staff are pulled in multiple directions, attempting to adhere to separate program goals, theories of change, funding mandates, or professional standards and practices (Adelman & Taylor, 2001; Farrar & Hampel, 1987; Gardner, 2000; Kirst & McLaughlin, 1990; Levy & Shepardson, 1992). Not only do time, energy, and resources to do anything well evaporate, but important synergies between schools and partners that lead to new, cross-disciplinary strategies for improving student learning often fail to emerge (Adelman & Taylor; Dryfoos, 1994; Walsh, Brabeck, & Howard, 1999).

School-community partnerships driven by sudden crises or media attention face another set of problems. Crisis services are often hastily developed, lacking the scale and careful planning needed to ameliorate complex problems that arise from various sources (Kirst & McLaughlin, 1990; Melaville & Blank, 1991). Crisis services often disregard the most common and pressing troubles of children. A violent episode or a relatively small rise in the local teen pregnancy rate might, for example, draw attention and resources away from the more pervasive and persistent problem of school failure among local high school students (Weissbourd, 1996).

In sum, while service-based partnerships hold great promise—most notably the successfully implemented full-service school models (see Dryfoos, 2000, and this volume, chapter 7; Melaville & Blank, 1998; Quinn, this volume, chapter 8)—schools must not adopt them reflexively. The act of partnering does not itself produce benefits for children. Several schools in Boston, for example, simultaneously work with as many as 10 to 15 community partners. Yet our own preliminary analysis of Boston schools indicates that no association exists between the number of school partners and improvement in students' academic performance.

The key is to foster partnerships that both ensure quality services and promote academic achievement, but therein lies the challenge. Clearly, scaling up effective service-based partnerships presents one set of difficulties (Farrow & Joe, 1992; Melaville & Blank, 1998; Payzant & Durkin, 2001). While a district might successfully field one or two dynamic, service-based partnerships that offer students and families an array of health and human services, successfully implementing such partnerships across many schools—hundreds in large city districts—is much harder. Not every school can be paired with a responsive health agency (or vice versa) or is located close to a college or university. Most schools have little or no space to accommodate on-site services, and funding is a significant barrier. Creative solutions for maximizing and deploying available resources so more schools can benefit from strong service-based partnerships are sorely needed.

Finally, more knowledge is needed to help schools and service partners construct effective collaborations. How do schools and partners provide children and families with access to health and social services while also maintaining an unwavering, intensive focus on academic improvement? What roles should agency providers play in supporting student learning? How do teachers, families, and service providers best communicate about specific student needs? What are the conditions needed to facilitate effective services? And what types of services are likely to be effective for what types of students? Unfortunately, research on service-based partnerships does not yet provide clear answers to these questions. Most studies report standard process measures, such as the number of students receiving a certain health service, or an improvement in some aspect of organizational climate. Research on the effect of service partnerships on student achievement is rare and often described as being "in the early stages" (Chavkin, 1998; Dryfoos, 2000; Gomby & Larson, 1992).

Partnerships Focused on Broad Academic Goals

In the past few decades, school-community partnerships designed to improve academic achievement have proliferated (Ferguson, 2001; Mondschein, 2001; Peterson-del-Mar, 1993). These partnerships, too, have common origins and characteristics. Often the public release of troubling student performance data compels local community leaders, such as CEOs, politicians, and university presidents, to create some broad and highly visible community response. Ambitious agendas are formed, such as "reducing the achievement gap" or "giving children the opportunity to thrive." Other partnerships result from an extensive community assessment and planning process, in which different community institutions and interest groups collaborate to develop priorities for children and youth. Still other partnerships are prompted by outside institutions such as universities and businesses, that are concerned about student achievement and are seeking simple ways to provide learning and community service opportunities for their students or employees.

School-community partnerships formed around broad academic goals have helped children in several ways. If nothing else, they heighten public awareness about the scope of student failure in certain communities and marshal additional resources for distressed schools (Newman & Sconzert, 2000; Peterson-del-Mar, 1993; Schorr, 1988, 1997). But real and persistent student learning gains are atypical and limited for common reasons. For one, vague and ambitious goals such as "helping children thrive" make it difficult to set clear objectives, establish pathways of change, evaluate success, and hold partners accountable for results. Instead, they lend themselves to diffuse and fragmented strategies.

Second, the large number of players in many community-wide, academically focused partnerships can make them unwieldy. Uniting a broad and diverse constituency around the interests of children is a crucial first step. School-community partnerships tend to attract neither resources nor political backing without ample community support. Yet large collaborations are notoriously cumbersome, inefficient, and difficult to govern over the long term (Blank et al., 2001; Mondschein, 2001; Newman & Sconzert, 2000). In trying to satisfy the needs of multiple partners, these collaborations often generate long lists of goals, disintegrating the attention needed to reach any one core academic goal.

Furthermore, when school and community partners are not working within a tightly focused plan that unites them in achieving a specific mission, their work frequently becomes segmented along categorical lines. Each partner simply does what it knows best and what flows from its professional interests. Some universities, for instance, tend to focus primarily on developing rich learning experiences for their own students or conducting field research, work that may flow from a prior research agenda. After-school programs continue to focus on general enrichment and recreational activities. Businesses donate or fund new resources, such as technology. Parents limit their involvement to attending sporting events and parent-teacher conferences. What seldom materializes is the essential, reinforcing roles that families and key community organizations can play when they are "on the same page" with schools, working directly with schools and classroom teachers toward key academic goals (Epstein, 2001).

Finally, many school-community partnerships simply underestimate what it takes to attain an academic goal. Businesses will provide books, computers, or volunteer reading tutors, believing that these will improve academic performance. Yet evidence now suggests that these strategies, unconnected to sound instruction, do not make a significant difference in student learning (Patton & Holmes, 1998; Regalado, Goldenberg, & Appel, 2001; Snow, Burns, & Griffin, 1998). Book drives on their own, for example, tend to produce few benefits, because teachers and child care providers lack the knowledge to use them effectively and because books are not keyed to children's reading level and interests. Faced with a lack of progress on key academic indicators, outside partners often become discouraged and withdraw altogether (Newman & Sconzert, 2000).

Outcomes-Based School-Community Partnerships

Over the past several years both of us have been engaged in two different kinds of initiatives designed to meet a single academic goal. ReadBoston is designed to improve third-grade reading proficiency, while WriteBoston seeks to improve writing skills in Boston middle and high schools. These initiatives are based on the premise that changing core academic outcomes in schools with many students who are underperforming is a monumental task, a task that requires the intensive, concerted, sustained work of multiple partners both inside and outside of school. These initiatives seek to fundamentally change business as usual, to focus schools not on doing many things with marginal success but on doing one critical thing well. They seek to elevate reading and writing because of their critical importance to school and work success. Children who do not master reading and writing skills are substantially more likely to suffer school failure, require remedial support, be placed in special education, or drop out of school (Lloyd, 1978; Lyon, 1998). They seek to align an array of in-school and out-of-school services in pursuit of reading and writing goals. Further, they seek to establish forms of public and political accountability for results.

ReadBoston, WriteBoston, and similar outcomes-based initiatives are also based on the notion that core academic outcomes can become the impetus for effective collaboration. Improving reading and writing outcomes provides community partners with clear roles and with direction about what is valued. After-school programs and churches, for example, can integrate reading and writing into their activities. Pediatricians can emphasize reading, distribute books during routine visits, and provide important tips about creating language-rich home environments. Businesses can sponsor book drives or encourage employees to volunteer as pen-pals, reading tutors, or writing mentors in schools.

Furthermore, outcomes-based partnerships such as ReadBoston and WriteBoston are potentially much easier to replicate than other forms of partnership. Outcomes-based partnerships are structured around academic goals, not the service capacity or resources of partnering agencies. The success of ReadBoston, for example, is not contingent on whether an area health provider is accessible or whether a university is nearby. Instead, each ReadBoston school may have very different community partners that align their efforts in innovative, flexible ways to promote student reading success.

Finally, focusing on outcomes provides a clear and accessible way to hold school-community partnerships accountable for results. Outcomes represent a bottom line; partnership efforts either achieve or fail to achieve specific outcomes. This basic accountability allows funders, school leaders, policymakers, and partnering agencies to gauge whether the partnership is working, make needed adjustments, and effectively target investments. When specific roles are clearly mapped out, each partner can also be held accountable for fulfilling that role.

The narrow focus on core academic skills, however, clearly has political drawbacks. Many educators and parents worry that such an intense concentration shortchanges other important academic areas and social and emotional learning opportunities. Some fear that shallow pedagogy will result; that this narrow focus reflects the mounting pressure on schools for passing scores on required competency exams in literacy and math (Kohn, 1999; Meier, 1995). Others are concerned that the intense focus on academics will dislodge schools' efforts to provide critical health and human services.

Yet well-planned outcomes-based school-community partnerships need not detract from schools' efforts to reach children in broader and deeper ways. Schools can offer well-rounded, challenging curricula that effectively promote reading and math skills. Rather than supplanting other content areas, literacy and math can be integrated more prominently throughout the curriculum. Students can be asked, for example, to keep journals in science classes, reflecting on what they are learning and its relevance to current events.

Nor does the focus on a core academic area like literacy mean that schools must ignore children's health or emotional needs. However, rather than attempting to address the complex, multiple needs of all children and families—an impossible task, given urban schools' capacity—schools give priority to those specific health or emotional issues that directly interfere with children's literacy development. For example, schools ensure that previously undetected vision and hearing problems, which undermine reading proficiency for many poor children, are treated.

Elements of Successful School-Community Partnerships

Outcomes-based school-community partnerships hold the promise of focusing schools, families, policymakers, and community agencies on key academic milestones in children's lives. However, this focus alone does not usually translate into the substantive interventions needed to improve academic outcomes on a large scale. Our informal survey of broad-based city literacy campaigns indicates that these campaigns, while highlighting the importance of reading and rallying considerable civic support, usually do not engage community partners in well-defined, research-based practices.

What, then, do effective outcomes-based school-community partnerships look like? What makes some partnerships more effective and politically and financially more durable than others? Based on a review of several promising models and our experience with ReadBoston and WriteBoston, we have identified six key elements of sound and stable outcomes-based school-community partnerships. These elements include

188 FOCUSING ON CORE ACADEMIC OUTCOMES

establishing a single, vivid goal; focusing on high-impact strategies; correctly estimating the dose; engaging in purposeful collaboration; publicly promoting academic goals; and accurately monitoring progress and establishing public accountability. Each element is described in further detail below.

Establishing a Single, Vivid Goal

Both ReadBoston and WriteBoston have attracted considerable funding and myriad community partners because their goals resonate broadly. Effective school-community partnerships tend to focus on one or two simple, accessible goals that are meaningful to diverse constituents, including funders, political leaders, and ethnically and economically diverse families. If, on the other hand, a partnership's goals are numerous, broadly defined, and open to interpretation, partnership planners will have difficulty from the outset, both in securing support and in translating goals into clear action steps.

Focusing on High-Impact Strategies

Outcomes-based school-community partnerships must determine which interventions or strategies are central to achieving their mission. Like other school-community partnerships, outcomes-based partnerships can fall into the trap of engaging in a wide array of activities and interventions that have only marginal academic impact. Initially, ReadBoston expended considerable resources and energy on book drives, volunteer tutors, and a public awareness campaign, generating activities in multiple locations in the city. Numerous city literacy campaigns (and major initiatives, such as President Clinton's "America Reads" campaign) are comprised entirely of these kinds of interventions.

Appealing and sensible as these efforts are, we have been unable to find any evidence that they have a significant impact on children's reading progress.[1] Politics may demand that cities engage in one or more of these interventions, but these kinds of interventions should not consume an initiative's resources. Sometimes they need to be weeded out altogether.

It took ReadBoston leaders 3 years to realize that only some strategies have high impact and that high-quality literacy instruction and intensive work with families on promoting literacy are the only roads to improving reading on a large scale. Literacy experts estimate that high-quality instruction can ameliorate reading difficulties in as many as 85–95% of school-age children who are poor readers—including many categorized as special needs learners (Blachman, 1996; Felton, 1993; Fletcher & Lyon, 1998; Snow, Burns, & Griffin, 1998). Similarly, attributes of families and home environments—such as the amount and quality of verbal interaction between children and parents—powerfully predict reading development (DeTemple & Beals, 1991; Dickinson & Tabors, 1991).

Whatever the goal, those forging school-community partnerships need to address early on the difficult intellectual and political challenge of extracting one or two core strategies or interventions essential to achieving their mission and make a public case for them.

Correctly Estimating the Dose

Creating outcomes-based school-community partnerships requires diligently investigating the needed depth and intensity of interventions. For example, while ReadBoston chose to focus on improving instruction in its early years, these efforts were modest given the scale of the challenge. The Boston Public Schools then funded several more intensive school literacy models. While these models have been a significant improvement over early efforts, many children still lag far behind in reading. If teaching children to learn to read is as hard as doing surgery, then ReadBoston and the Boston Public Schools need to consider intensive professional development activity that reflects this reality.

ReadBoston's family literacy efforts, like kindred efforts across the country, have similarly led to necessary but insufficient changes in school-family collaborations. The family literacy initiative requires participating schools to hold two individual parent-teacher conferences a year focused on literacy—a significant improvement, given that Boston schools were typically not holding any individual parent-teacher conferences prior to this intervention. Parents are also required to read to their children at least 3 times a week for 30 minutes. Yet large numbers of families still have inadequate communication with school staff, and many children receive inadequate language and literacy support at home. Other school-based family literacy initiatives fail to engage a wide range of parents in their child's learning, engaging only motivated parents who are comfortable in school buildings. Reaching more parents and changing home environments to promote reading require school staff with the time and resources needed to work on these goals. The El Paso Collaborative for Academic Excellence, for example, supports a parent liaison in schools who provides families with strategies for promoting literacy development at home, communicating with teachers about their child's literacy, advocating for additional services from school and community programs, and improving their own English proficiency.

More intensive interventions tend to be more expensive, making them hard to implement on a large scale. But piloting expensive interventions and making a case for expanding them if they work at least stands a chance of improving children's prospects, surely a better approach than implementing large-scale interventions that are known to have little or no effect. In any case, leaders of school-community partnerships should manage expectations, clarifying what dose is likely to achieve what outcome. It is damaging for leaders to claim, based on modest or unproven interventions, that they are eradicating illiteracy or greatly boosting math proficiency. Such claims can harden the cynicism of a public already disenchanted by a long parade of initiatives and programs that have fallen short of their lofty goals.

Engaging in Purposeful Collaboration

In the end, greatly improving progress toward any important academic goal, whether literacy, math achievement, or college attendance, is likely to require multiple, concerted strategies and interventions from many community partners. Yet the somber reality is that while collaborations among community partners have become common, it is hard to find convincing evidence that these collaborations have produced significant benefits for children. Collaboration has become such a mantra that school and community leaders often find it hard to ask critical questions: What kinds of collaborations, at what level, are likely to be most effective for achieving the stated mission? What is the cost, in resources and time, of these collaborations? What are the obstacles to effective collaboration, and how might they be overcome?

The ReadBoston experience illustrates both the possibilities and problems of collaboration. ReadBoston has tried to integrate several school, family, and community interventions in five schools and their surrounding neighborhoods in Dorchester, an area of Boston. We call this area our "Reading Zone." Rather than fragmenting our efforts, staff have sought to develop and integrate strong school, family, and community interventions in this one geographic area and then create other "zones" over time. The work has focused on aligning school and after-school interventions and developing home-school partnerships that reinforce teachers' efforts. Schools and community organizations also have received a good number of high-quality, leveled books.

Furthermore, we have sought to develop for children a meaningful, building sequence of literacy interventions over time—a "ladder of literacy." While some children in this area were benefiting from a single, high-quality literacy experience at one point in time, such as a high-quality preschool experience, rarely did any individual child have a sequence of high-quality literacy experiences from birth to age 8. We also have tried to create a culture of literacy—an environment in which the great pleasures and power of reading are regularly celebrated and where adults consistently emphasize the importance of reading and actively engage children in reading and language-building activities.

This zone has been successful in important respects. Two schools, for example, have used books and tutors effectively and have developed successful family literacy activities that reinforce teachers' efforts. A few community organizations are engaging children in valuable literacy activities. Preschool-age children and those in daycare are receiving significant forms of literacy support.

But we have also run into several problems typical of these collaborations. A great deal of time and energy is required to align programs or shepherd children from one program to another, and high family mobility works against these efforts. Too often, collaboration becomes the goal and partnering agencies lose sight of the outcome. Schools and communities often have been engaged in so many concurrent collaborations that they lack time to develop the kind of deep, sustained partnerships needed to integrate services in pursuing any single goal effectively. Staff have not been given the time and resources—and may not have the skills—to develop complex collaborations.

Complex collaborations such as ours may be undone by a more fundamental problem. Program planners assume individual interventions are working well. They reason that what stands in the way of solving childhood troubles is the failure to integrate these well-functioning interventions effectively. But the reality is that individual interventions, including the most important ones, often are *not* working well. Cobbling together mediocre or poor programs will not lead to a whole that is greater than the sum of the parts. Getting teachers, tutors, after-school providers, and a neighborhood family service program to meet regularly to discuss improving literacy is not only difficult logistically; it is also unlikely to lead to any substantial increase in children's reading abilities if none of these providers has good assessment skills, strong knowledge of the reading process, or a clear understanding of how these different interventions might work in concert to address specific reading difficulties.

Rather than simply touting collaboration or embarking on highly complex collaborations that are difficult to implement, ReadBoston suggests that school-community partnerships start with high-impact interventions, such as improving instruction, and then carefully layer in additional interventions over time. ReadBoston thus identifies schools in which teachers are using sound instructional strategies before providing supplemental forms of literacy support. Focusing on a few high-yield interventions and continually assessing whether they are working keeps partnering agencies focused on the outcome. Sequentially layering in other interventions over time makes integrating interventions more manageable for agencies and allows agencies to assess the value of additional services.

Layering in interventions over time, so children have a building sequence of supports and interventions, allows agencies to examine closely the many obstacles to this kind of continuity and develop more serious, realistic strategies for overcoming them. While providers and policymakers recognize, for example, that geographic mobility undermines service continuity, many agencies have not thought carefully about how to help families make transitions to another program, or about how to help families deal with the conditions that force them to pull up stakes. Most families move to a nearby neighborhood or town, yet agencies also typically give scant attention to keeping children engaged in the same supports and services when they move locally.

Publicly Promoting Academic Goals

Outcomes-based school-community partnerships should consider media and other public awareness strategies to promote their goals in the larger community. Strong promotion efforts can help educate the public about the importance of key academic outcomes and suggest ways in which families and community organizations can meaningfully support these outcomes. These efforts also can create a broader constituency that can advocate for continued investment in partnership activities.

ReadBoston has benefited greatly from its partnership with the *Boston Globe* and from Mayor Menino's political leadership. The *Globe's* coverage of ReadBoston has helped both to establish name recognition across the city and to broadcast the importance of third-grade reading proficiency. Mayor Menino's continued promotion of ReadBoston has kept third-grade reading proficiency at the forefront of the city's school improvement efforts and helped the initiative recruit additional partners and funders. In these ways, ReadBoston has influenced many children outside the Dorchester area "Reading Zone."

Further, growing evidence suggests that public awareness campaigns can cause targeted populations to reduce certain negative behaviors or can spark specific activities toward positive outcomes (Centers for Disease Control and Prevention, 1999; Kotler & Roberto, 1989; Pechmann, 2001). ReadBoston's community-wide promotion of reading, together with recent national ad campaigns, have contributed to the adoption of reading goals and curricular interventions in every elementary school in Boston. This promotion also may have influenced local foundations, after-school programs, and other community organizations to provide additional support for reading.

Accurately Monitoring Progress and Establishing Public Accountability

Another key ingredient of effective outcomes-based school-community partnerships is a willingness to be held accountable publicly. Both ReadBoston and WriteBoston are willing to be judged on whether they improve reading and writing skills among Boston students. Accountability is a crucial means of assessing whether these initiatives are meeting their goals and ensuring that partners are performing their stated roles.

School-community partnerships also should track progress in ways that allow each partner to modify its role and improve its practices. Thus, schools should use data to tailor instructional practices and professional development. After-school programs and volunteer agencies should have data that allow them to assess and modify their various supporting activities. Families need data to better advocate for solutions to identified problems. Funders, politicians, and community interest groups need data not only to hold school-community partnerships accountable for results, but also to lobby for support. To assess its effectiveness and to guide improvements in practice, ReadBoston monitors standardized test results such as the Massachusetts Comprehensive Assessment System (or MCAS, the state's mandated graduation exam) and the Stanford 9, parent participation in and satisfaction with parent-teacher conferences, and the frequency of parent/child reading activity. ReadBoston also is a partner in a federally funded evaluation of the impact of Boston's literacy models across different literacy domains, allowing us to develop a more finely-tuned sense of students' progress and struggles.

At the same time, effective partnerships don't saddle partners with unreasonable forms of accountability. Perhaps most important, partnerships are not expected to produce dramatic changes overnight. Partnerships accurately estimate the time period needed to achieve change. Many school-community partnerships generate early excitement but quickly lose momentum or are abandoned altogether when they fail to improve student outcomes significantly within a few years. Concerned about this possibility, we have tried to underline for Read-Boston and WriteBoston stakeholders that progress is incremental, that significant gains are not likely before 3 years, and that improving instruction is a long-term proposition. Four years after the inception of ReadBoston, reading scores have improved modestly in Boston's schools—improvements are substantial on the fourth-grade MCAS, but only minimal on the Stanford 9.[2] The federally-funded literacy evaluation shows improvement in certain domains but not others.

To legitimately hold partners accountable, progress must be measured from where a school or a student starts, rather than in reference to performance levels in other schools, other districts with different student populations, or national percentile rankings on standardized tests. Finally, it is crucial to educate the public on how to interpret the data.

Selecting the Right Outcome

Schools and their partners do not have a map for selecting outcomes. Research offers little instruction on what specific outcomes cities should pursue. For example, should school-community partnerships try to reduce dropout rates, improve math or literacy skills, or increase college attendance? What areas can partnerships realistically affect? What academic goals are likely to sustain public attention and financial support? Should an outcome goal be selected only after a thorough assessment of student needs?

The experiences of ReadBoston and WriteBoston highlight several criteria that should guide cities in selecting outcomes. First, it is vital that goals can be easily communicated and stated in simple, accessible terms. The public may have a hard time understanding a partnership to improve phonemic awareness among third graders or to ensure that every child has a stable health care provider, however important these campaigns may be. Nor do such partnerships ignite great passions, rallying communities.

Another reason for ReadBoston's ongoing support and Write-Boston's initial appeal is that they respond to a pervasive and enduring community need. More than half of Boston's children struggle with reading, and writing is acknowledged as critical to success in school and on the MCAS, and later to success in college and the workplace.

Our partnerships were based not on the latest crisis or media fad but on identification of problems that are common, enduring, and detrimental to Boston children's academic success.

ReadBoston, and now WriteBoston, have also mobilized resources and support because they are preventive. Improving third-grade reading proficiency is vital to preventing school failure. Improving writing helps students develop the habits of mind—a range of study behaviors (e.g., efficient note-taking, multiple redrafting, and sustained focus on a task) and critical thinking skills (e.g., self-assessment, perspective-taking, and persuasive argument)—that are key to future success in all academic areas. To be sure, work on almost any important childhood outcome will help prevent other childhood problems: preventing low birth weights, curbing drug abuse, or improving school readiness can all help avert many types of trouble. But schools and their partners should assess which outcomes are most likely to prevent serious problems of widespread community concern, or to increase the odds that children will attain critical academic or career goals. School-community partnerships also should assess whether achieving a goal will have positive ripple effects, helping with other important outcomes. When children become more interested in reading and more literate, for example, it may spark their parents to improve their own literacy.

Both ReadBoston's and WriteBoston's goals are perceived as achievable, another feature of an effective city campaign. Some people consider teaching children to read a relatively easy task and are puzzled by children's reading difficulties, a sentiment based in part on how natural and easy learning was for their own children. Paradoxically, this misunderstanding of the reading challenges faced by urban children has been a boon to ReadBoston, fueling optimism that third-grade reading proficiency is achievable. We are not arguing that cities should be misleading or overly optimistic. ReadBoston has done a good deal to educate funders and city residents about what it takes to improve children's reading on a large scale. These perceptions have a huge bearing on a campaign's viability, and partners should assess these perceptions before undertaking a school-community partnership. Because these perceptions also can be unduly negative, partners need to determine whether they can be changed.

The bigger question that school-community partnerships must grapple with is whether a goal *is* achievable. That may seem obvious, yet many partnerships pursue outcome goals without rigorously analyzing whether the outcome can be reached. Both ReadBoston and WriteBoston had ample evidence at the outset that some schools around the country were improving the reading and writing abilities of many children, including poor children and children dealing with serious burdens (Slavin, 1997).

At the outset ReadBoston and WriteBoston planners constructed a reasonable "theory of change" (Weiss, 1972), strategies, and a logical plan for achieving our mission drawn from literacy research and the experience of other cities. Before selecting an outcome, partnerships should seek to: (1) articulate a plan that explains how certain interventions will lead to the desired outcome; (2) cite evidence demonstrating the past success of these interventions; and (3) create mechanisms for assessing and modifying these interventions at regular intervals.

Before launching ReadBoston and WriteBoston, we also determined that sufficient political will and financial resources existed to sustain a robust campaign. Schools and their partners should consider whether an outcome is attractive to funders and aligned with local, state, and national funding priorities.

Finally, that ReadBoston and WriteBoston have *measurable* outcomes—such as improvements in test scores and parent participation rates—has been critical in allowing us to better train and sustain public attention on these partnerships and to know whether our goals are being met.

Conclusion

The current interest in school-community partnerships is an enormous opportunity. These partnerships not only bring much-needed resources to struggling schools and foster new, diverse forms of civic participation, they also embody a vibrant, collective compassion for children's well being.

Yet, school-community partnerships are not inherently effective. Many partnerships, despite their good intentions and success in marshalling resources, have little or no impact on student academic performance. Without thoughtful planning, the legacy of recent school-community partnerships easily could become one of missed opportunities and squandered resources.

In this chapter, we have put forth one model for purposefully aligning schools and community partners to improve key academic outcomes. We do not mean to suggest that only this model holds promise. Continual evaluation of current models, piloting and evaluating new models, and disseminating key findings are critical. Collecting and sharing this wisdom will allow us to avoid reflexively embracing school-community partnerships and to channel wisely the enthusiasm and resources of a wide array of stakeholders committed to improving the educational prospects of children.

A portion of this chapter was published in the *Handbook of Applied Developmental Science: Promoting Positive Child, Adolescent, and Family Development* (Vol. 2), edited by Richard M. Lerner, Francine Jacobs, and Donald Wertlieb. Thousand Oaks, CA: Sage Publications.

NOTES

1. There is evidence that high quality, intensive (at least twice a week) tutoring programs can help some children (Invernizzi, Rosemary, Juel, & Richards, 1997; Slavin, 1997). But these programs are atypical.

2. Because ReadBoston works so closely with these other institutions, we have been unable to disentangle and evaluate its independent impact.

REFERENCES

Adelman H., & Taylor, L. (2001). *Impediments to enhancing availability of mental health in schools: Fragmentation, overspecialization, counterproductive competition, and marginalization.* Los Angles: Center for Mental Health in Schools, University of California, Los Angeles.

Adler, L., & Gardner, S. (Eds.). (1994). *The politics of linking schools and social services.* Washington, DC: Falmer Press.

Benson, L., & Harkavy, I. (1997). School and community in the global society. *Universities and Community, 5*(1-2), 16-71.

Benson, L., & Harkavy, I. (2003). The role of the American research university in advancing system-wide reform, democratic schooling, and democracy. In this volume—M.M. Brabeck, M.E. Walsh, & R. Latta (Eds.), *Meeting at the hyphen: Schools-universities-communities-professions in collaboration for student achievement and well being. The 102nd yearbook of the National Society for the Study of Education,* Part II. Chicago: National Society for the Study of Education.

Blachman, B. (1996). Preventing early reading failure. In S.C. Cramer & W. Ellis (Eds.), *Learning disability: Lifelong issues.* Baltimore: Paul C. Brooks.

Blank, M., Hale, E., Housman, N., Kaufman, B., Martinez, M., McCloud, B., Sunberg, L., & Walter, S. (2001). *School-community partnerships in support of student learning: Taking a second look at the governance of the 21st Century Community Learning Centers Program.* Washington, DC: Institute for Educational Leadership.

Bronfenbrenner, U. (1979). *The ecology of human development.* Cambridge, MA: Harvard University Press.

Centers for Disease Control and Prevention. (1999). *Compendium of HIV prevention interventions with evidence of effectiveness.* Atlanta, GA: Centers for Disease Control and Prevention.

Chavkin, N. (1998). Making the case for school, family, and community partnerships: Recommendations for research. *School Community Journal, 8*(1), 9-21.

Comer, J. (1988). Educating poor minority children. *Scientific American, 259*(5), 42-48.

Comer, J. (2001). Schools that develop children. *The American Prospect, 12*(7), 30-35.

Darling-Hammond, L. (2000). *Teacher quality and student achievement.* Seattle, WA: Center for the Study of Teaching and Policy, University of Washington.

DeTemple, J., & Beals, D. (1991). Family talk: Sources of support for the development of decontextualized language skills. *Journal of Research in Childhood Education, 6*(1), 11-19.

Dickinson, D., & Tabors, P. (1991). Early literacy: Linkages between home, school and literacy achievement at age five. *Journal of Research in Childhood Education, 6*(1), 5-10.

Dryfoos, J. (1994). *Full-service schools: A revolution in health and social services for children, youth and families.* San Francisco: Jossey-Bass.

Dryfoos, J. (1995). Full-service schools: Revolution or fad? *Journal of Research on Adolescence, 5*(2), 147-172.

Dryfoos, J. (2000). *Evaluation of community schools: Findings to date.* Report prepared for the Coalition for Community Schools. Washington, DC.

Dryfoos, J. (2003). Comprehensive schools. In this volume—M.M. Brabeck, M.E. Walsh, & R. Latta (Eds.), *Meeting at the hyphen: Schools-universities-communities-professions in collaboration for student achievement and well being. The 102nd yearbook of the National Society for the Study of Education,* Part II. Chicago: National Society for the Study of Education.

Epstein, J. (1992). School and family partnerships. *Encyclopedia of Educational Research* (pp. 1139-1151). New York: MacMillan.

Epstein, J. (2001). *School, family, and community partnerships: Preparing educators and improving schools.* Boulder, CO: Westview Press.

Farrar, E., & Hampel, R. (1987). Social services in American high schools. *Phi Delta Kappan, 96*(4), 297-303.

Farrow, F., & Joe, T. (1992, Spring). Financing school-linked, integrated services. *The Future of Children, 2*(1), 56-67.

Felton, R.H. (1993). Effects of instruction on the decoding skills of children with phonological-processing problems. *Journal of Learning Disabilities, 26,* 583-589.

Ferguson, M. (2001). *Partnerships 2000: A decade of growth and change.* Alexandria, VA: National Association of Partners in Education.

Ferguson, R. (1998). Can schools narrow the black-white test score gap? In C. Jencks & M. Phillips (Eds.), *The black-white test score gap* (pp. 318-374). Washington, DC: Brookings Institution.

Fletcher, J.M., & Lyon, G.R. (1998). Reading: A research-based approach. In W. Evers (Ed.), *What's gone wrong in America's classrooms?* Stanford University: Hoover Institution.

Gardner, S. (1992). Key issues in developing school-linked, integrated services. *The Future of Children, 2*(1), 85-94.

Gardner, S. (2000). *Outcomes, standards and accountability in School/Community Partnerships.* Paper prepared for the Council of Chief State School Officers Conference on School/Community Partnerships, Los Angeles.

Gilligan, J. (1991). Shame and humiliation: The emotions of individual and collective violence. Lecture sponsored by the Erik and Joan Erikson Center, Cambridge, MA.

Gomby, D., & Larson, C. (1992). Evaluation of school-linked services. *The Future of Children: School-Linked Services, 2*(1), 68-84.

Harkavy, I. (1999). School-community partnerships. *Universities and Community Schools, 6*(1-2), 7-24.

Haycock, K. (*1998*). *Good teaching matters: How well-qualified teachers can close the gap.* Washington, DC: Education Trust.

Invernizzi, M., Rosemary, C., Juel, C., & Richards, H.C. (1997). At-risk readers and community volunteers: A three-year perspective. *Scientific Studies of Reading, 1*(3), 1193-1200.

Kirst, M.W., & McLaughlin, M. (1990). Rethinking policy for children: Implications for educational administration. In L. Cunningham & B. Mitchell (Eds.), *Educational leadership and changing contexts in families, communities, and schools: The Eighty-ninth yearbook of the National Society for the Study of Education,* Part II (pp. 69-90). Chicago: National Society for the Study of Education.

Kohn, A. (1999). *The schools our children deserve: Moving beyond traditional classrooms and tougher standards.* New York: Houghton Mifflin.

Kotler, P., & Roberto, E. (1989). *Social marketing: Strategies for changing public behavior.* New York: Free Press.

Levy, J.E., & Shepardson, W. (1992). A look at current school-linked service efforts. *The Future of Children: School-Linked Services, 2*(1), 44-55.

Lloyd, D. (1978). Prediction of school failure from third-grade data. *Educational and Psychological Measurement, 38,* 1193-1200.

Lyon, R. (1998). *Overview of reading and literacy initiatives.* Washington, DC: Statement prepared for the U.S. Senate Committee on Labor and Human Resources.

Meier, D. (1995). *The power of their ideas: Lessons from a small school in Harlem.* New York: Beacon.

Melaville, A., & Blank, M. (1991). *What it takes: Structuring interagency partnerships to connect children and families with comprehensive services.* Washington, DC: Education and Human Services Consortium.

Melaville, A., & Blank, M. (1998). *Learning together: A look at 20 school-community initiatives.* Flint, MI: C.S. Mott Foundation.

Mondschein, E. (2001). *Community schools in Illinois: Partnerships promoting academic excellence and life-long development.* Chicago: Voices for Illinois Children.

Newman, F., & Sconzert, K. (2000). *Improving Chicago schools: School improvement with external partners.* Chicago: Chicago Annenberg Research Project.

Patton, S., & Holmes, M. (Eds.). (1998). *The keys to literacy*. Washington, DC: Council for Basic Education.

Payzant, T., & Durkin, P. (2001). *Districts on the move: Unified student services in Boston Public Schools: Building a continuum of services through standards-based reform*. Washington, DC: National Institute for Urban School Improvement.

Pechmann, C. (2001). Changing adolescent smoking prevalence: Impact of advertising interventions. In *Smoking and Tobacco Control Monograph No. 14* (pp. 171-182). Bethesda, MD: National Cancer Institute.

Peterson-del-Mar, D. (1993). *Building coalitions to restructure schools* [Bulletin]. Eugene, OR: Oregon School Study Council.

Quinn, J. (2003). An interprofessional model and reflections on best collaborative practices. In this volume—M.M. Brabeck, M.E. Walsh, & R. Latta (Eds.), *Meeting at the hyphen: Schools-universities-communities-professions in collaboration for student achievement and well being. The 102nd yearbook of the National Society for the Study of Education*, Part II. Chicago: National Society for the Study of Education.

Regalado, M., Goldenberg, C., & Appel, E. (2001). *Building community systems for young children: Reading and early literacy*. Los Angeles: UCLA Center for Healthier Children, Families and Communities.

Schorr, L. (1988). *Within our reach*. New York: Doubleday.

Schorr, L. (1997). *Common purpose: Strengthening families and neighborhoods to rebuild America*. New York: Anchor.

Slavin, R. (1997). *Reading by nine: A comprehensive strategy*. Washington, DC: Paper sponsored by the Office of Educational Research and Improvement.

Snow, C. (2000). Preventing reading difficulties: Some first steps. Lecture presented at *Putting the research to work: Building literacy skills in children* [Conference] sponsored by the Harvard Children's Initiative, Cambridge, MA.

Snow, C., Burns, M., & Griffin, P. (1998). *Preventing reading difficulties in young children*. Washington, DC: National Academy Press.

Sylvester, K. (1990). New strategies to save children. *Governing, 3*(8), 32-37.

Tyack, D. (1992). Health and social services in public schools: Historical perspectives. *The Future of Children: School-Linked Services, 2*(1), 19-31.

Walsh, M.E., Brabeck, M.M., & Howard, K.A. (1999). Interprofessional collaboration in children's services: Toward a theoretical perspective. *Children's Services: Social Policy, Research, and Practice, 2*(4), 183-208.

Walsh, M.E., Brabeck, M.M., Howard, K.A, Sherman, F.T., Montes, C., & Garvin, T.J. (2000). The Boston College-Allston/Brighton partnership: Description and challenges. *Peabody Journal of Education, 75*(3), 6-32.

Weiss, C. (1972). *Evaluation research: Methods of assessing program effectiveness*. Englewood Cliffs, NJ: Prentice-Hall.

Weissbourd, R. (1996). *The vulnerable child: What really hurts America's children and what we can do about it*. Reading, MA: Addison-Wesley Publishing Company.

CHAPTER 10

Ensuring Quality and Sustainability in After-School Programs: How Partnerships Play a Key Role

ADRIANA DE KANTER, JENNIFER K. ADAIR, AN-ME CHUNG, AND ROBERT M. STONEHILL

In recent years, after-school programs have become increasingly important in the lives of school-age children and their parents. These programs provide academic support and enrichment, learning opportunities that complement the school day, mentoring for young people by caring adults in their communities, life-long learning opportunities for community members, and a safe place to support these activities during the after-school hours.

Because of increased demand for programs that provide after-school enrichment opportunities, local communities must develop diversified financial resources to support and staff these programs. Diversified funds will ensure that programs can be sustained beyond the life of any particular funding cycle. Public-private partnerships have played a critical role in helping local school systems and youth agencies serve students in need. These partnerships increase the ability of after-school programs to enhance student learning and ensure higher levels of quality and sustainability. Community and school partnerships clearly demonstrate this at the local, city, state, and national levels. This chapter will discuss and give examples of after-school program partnerships and detail their increasingly important role in education.

Children and Their Families Need After-School Programs

Over the past two decades, with a greater percentage of adults in the workforce, the demand for before- and after-school programs for

Adriana de Kanter is Director, Policy and Technical Analysis Support, in the Office of the Under Secretary, U.S. Department of Education. Jennifer K. Adair is a Recruitment/Retention Specialist and a graduate student in Social and Philosophical Foundations of Education at Arizona State University. An-Me Chung, Ph.D., is a program officer at the C.S. Mott Foundation. Robert Stonehill, Ph.D., is Deputy Director of Academic Improvement and Demonstration Programs at the U.S. Department of Education, and is the Director of the 21st Century Community Learning Centers program.

school-age children has grown tremendously. In general, after-school programs provide a variety of enriching learning opportunities, including a focus on academic improvement, in a safe and fun environment.

Academics

School-age children need after-school programs that complement the school day. These programs should provide academically enriching opportunities, embedded in youth development principles, that are not traditionally part of the regular school day. As after-school programs align program standards with educational standards, they should focus on learning opportunities that are enjoyable and that address children's cognitive, social, emotional, and physical needs. While there is no single formula for success in after-school programs, both practitioners and researchers have found that effective programs combine academic, enrichment, cultural, and recreational activities (Grossman et al., 2002). A balanced approach that meets the needs of the whole child guides learning and engages children and youth in wholesome activities. The child and the after-school provider, through creative exploration, can embrace different learning styles while reinforcing and extending academic skills through activities that focus on a number of outcomes. Projects offering the opportunity to explore and master activities such as art, dance, music, and sports can contribute to children's overall well being and academic achievement (Clark, 1989).

After-school programs can be important avenues for skill development. According to a recent survey, elementary- and middle-school parents want after-school programs to teach their children to use computers and to provide arts, music, and drama enrichment, service learning opportunities, and reinforcement of basic skills, rather than merely providing a babysitting service (National Opinion Research Center, 1998). The public sees after-school programs as a way to provide youth with access to computers and technology, produce opportunities to learn and master new skills, prepare children for a productive future, create excitement about learning, and provide tutoring (Lake Snell Perry and Associates & The Tarrance Group, 2001).

Quality after-school programs can also reach students who are struggling academically. Many believe that without after-school programming, students can fall behind in their schoolwork and overall achievement. A 1994 Harris poll found that over 50% of teachers indicated that the primary reason for students' difficulties in class stemmed from their being left alone after school (National Commission on Time and Learning, 1994).

Supervision and Safety

Along with learning opportunities and academic support, quality after-school programs provide adult supervision for student participants. In a 2001 survey of U.S. voters, respondents said they are most worried about keeping their children safe, out of trouble, and off the streets under adult supervision. Only 4 out of 10 believed their communities offered programs that addressed this need (Lake Snell Perry and Associates & the Tarrance Group, 2001). Even 10 years ago, 84% of elementary school principals believed that children in their communities needed supervision before and after school, and two thirds believed schools should offer after-school activities (National Association of Elementary School Principals, 1999).

Despite the increase in after-school programs, many students are still left alone after school. Fox and Newman (1997) reported that about 35% of 12-year-olds are left by themselves while their parents are at work. Experts estimate that even with school-based and other community-sponsored after-school programs, an estimated 7 to 15 million "latchkey children and youth" go home alone after school (Capizzano, Tout, & Adams, 2000; National Institute on Out-of-School Time, 2001; School-Age Child Care Project, 1997; Seppanen et al., 1993). These children are at the greatest risk of being the victim of a violent crime between 2 p.m. and 6 p.m.; sexual assaults are most likely to be committed between 3 p.m. and 4 p.m. (Snyder & Sickmund, 1999).

After-School Programs Need Public-Private Partnerships

After-school programs need partners to assist in providing quality programming and ensuring program sustainability. Such partners can be found at all government levels and in all types of organizations.

Quality Programming

Partnerships can help offer diverse, high quality curriculum for student participants while working toward financial stability and sustainability. Approaches and activities related to quality programming vary from site to site depending on needs and available resources. Community partnerships can address programming needs by providing skilled volunteers who can tutor, instruct, and guide student participants. Also, community partners can offer presentations and activities that involve new and exciting methodologies. For instance, students can learn about their own or other cultures from groups within the community, or partners can offer art, exercise, and/or music experiences to the students. According to the Shell Education Survey, high school youth in after-school programs are at least 5 to 10 percent more likely to earn A's and B's; to have attended a cultural event or visited a museum in the past month; to say they love or like school a lot; to believe being a good student is important; to say their schools are preparing them very well for college; and to plan on continuing their education after graduation (Hart, 1999).

The Ohio Urban After-School Initiative is a partnership among the Children's Hunger Alliance, state departments of Human Services and Education, 17 school districts, various community-based service providers, and the University of Cincinnati. The percentage of fourth graders in this program who met proficiency standards in math, writing, reading, and science exceeded the statewide percentage of students meeting this standard (University of Cincinnati, 1999). Higher levels of participation in Los Angeles's Better Educated Students for Tomorrow (BEST) after-school program, which partners with more than 100 community and civic organizations, led to better school attendance and higher academic achievement on standardized tests of mathematics, reading, and language arts. Students with limited English proficiency who participated in the BEST program were more likely to become proficient in English than their nonparticipating peers (Huang, Gribbons, Kim, Lee, & Baker, 2000).

Community partners, especially schools and universities, can also collaborate in developing after-school curricula that create an enriched learning environment aligned with classroom learning goals. School, community college, technical school, and university partnerships are essential in these efforts.

Sustainability

After-school programs are increasingly in demand. The U.S. Department of Education reports a sharp rise in applications for 21st Century Community Learning Center (21st CCLC) grants, from 1,950 in 1998 to 2,780 in 2001. The focus of the 21st CCLC grant program, as re-authorized under Title IV, Part B, of the No Child Left Behind Act of 2001, is to provide expanded academic enrichment opportunities for children attending low-performing schools. 21st CCLC programs provide academic enrichment activities that are designed to help students meet local and state academic standards in subjects such as reading and math, as well as youth development activities, drug and violence prevention programs, technology education programs, art, music and recreation programs, counseling, and character education. A dramatic increase in 21st CCLC funding—from $1 million to $1 billion over a 4-year period—has translated into an increase in children served, from 1,000 in 1997 to 1.2 million in 2001; in the number of communities served, from 6 to 1,600; and in the number of schools established as community learning centers, from 20 to 6,800.

In fact, in 1994, only 30% (18,000) of all elementary and combined schools offered after-school programs (National Center for Education Statistics, 1996). A recent survey found that number has almost doubled (Le Menestrel, 2002). In the last 21st CCLC grant competition administered by the U.S. Department of Education, only 310 of the 2,780 applications could be funded. Given that the demand for after-school programs far exceeds the supply of federal dollars, and given that federal funding for 21st CCLC programs cannot exceed 3 years, communities must turn to other sources—including private partners—for support.

Public-private partnerships not only increase financial and in-kind resources, they also increase sustainability by creating diversified funding sources. Sustainable after-school programs require stakeholders who are stable, dedicated, and diverse. Policy Studies Associates recently published a study based on phone interviews with 60 after-school experts and program leaders, as well as in-depth interviews with 10 leaders of long-standing after-school programs. The study concluded, "no more than a quarter to a third of a program's funding should come from any one source" (Pechman & Fiester, 2002, p. 11). Furthermore, the study cited three ways in which a diverse funding strategy reinforces sustainability:

First, it protects the program from changes in the priorities or fiscal instability of any one funder. Second, integrating resources from several funders with a common agenda for youth can support high-quality staffing and advocacy. Blended funding streams also give the program greater budgetary flexibility because funds from corporate, nonprofit, and private sources generally carry fewer restrictions than do state and federal resources. Third, programs with diverse resources can address emerging needs quickly, making them more responsive to long-term constituents. (Pechman & Fiester, p. 11)

As partners fulfill these services for the after-school program—whether at the local, state, or national level—the program is more likely to secure and diversify financial resources and maintain community support.

Local Partnerships

Local examples of successful partnerships are numerous. Local partnerships focus on creating exciting activities for school-age children while increasing their ability to be academically successful. This challenge is more feasible when community partners are involved. Moreover, local after-school programs often face challenges specific to their particular community. Partners share and understand local issues, such as high populations of non-native English speakers, high gang activity, or low math achievement. After-school programs need to recruit and retain quality staff, including volunteers who understand these needs.

Community partners can be from a myriad of organizations. Supporters of community schools note that:

Today, several thousand community schools . . . are involving just about every sector of the community: school districts, teachers' unions, parks and recreation departments, child and family service agencies, Boys and Girls Clubs, local United Ways, YMCAs, Girl and Boy Scout chapters, small and large businesses, museums and zoos, hospitals and health clinics . . . the true hallmark of this movement is the diversity of the approaches. (Harkavy & Blank, 2002, p. 52)

Cultural groups, interprofessional organizations, nonprofit organizations, universities and community colleges, and community members can also make significant contributions to after-school programs. All can volunteer, provide lesson and curriculum ideas, participate in activities, and offer support. Some will be able to contribute financially through donations or in-kind resources. Others, such as universities and community colleges, can provide tutors, teacher aides, evaluation assistance, or professional development, and—perhaps most important—offer an opportunity for high-poverty children to understand that they too can attend college. Local media organizations are other potential partners. Over the past 3 years, hundreds of articles have appeared in local papers ranging from the *Los Angeles Times* and *Boston Globe* to the *Cleveland Plain Dealer* and *Omaha World Herald* spotlighting the benefits of individual centers across the nation.

The following examples document successful local after-school programs partnered with community organizations. A record of high student participation and academic success characterizes each example.

Community Collaboration for Education Enrichment

The Community Collaboration for Education Enrichment at Hawthorne Elementary School in San Antonio, Texas provides services to at-risk youth and their families through well-developed partnerships with the local YMCA of San Antonio and The Hill Country and other youth service agencies. With some federal funding, the YMCA, foundations, school districts, the city of San Antonio, and the Texas Education Agency support and maintain services in 17 school districts in San Antonio. Services are based on consultation with students, parents, school faculty, collaborative partners, and community leaders. Services include child care; arts, sports, and outdoor education; tutoring and mentoring; service learning and experiential education; youth government and employment readiness; academic enrichment and supports; and intergenerational activities and family/community involvement programs.

The collaboration between Hawthorne staff and YMCA staff has created a seamless system in which activities throughout the day adhere to a core knowledge curriculum designed by Trinity University. The Campus YMCA is one of several strategic school improvement initiatives underway at Hawthorne. Together, as a coordinated effort, these initiatives have significantly improved attendance, attitude, and academic achievement. Attendance has improved from 63rd among elementary schools in the San Antonio Independent School District to 12th, and student achievement and standardized test scores have increased significantly. The San Antonio Independent School District has reported a jump in the scores of students at four of its schools participating in its after-school program. This jump was recognized by the Texas Education Agency in its re-rating of schools' status from "low performing" to "recognized improvement" (U.S. Department of Education, *Safe and Smart*, 2000; 2001 Grantee's Annual Performance Report).

PROYECTO SANO Y SALVO

The Proyecto Sano y Salvo after-school program opened its doors in September 1998 at three middle schools in Tucson, Arizona. Each middle school has an advisory committee made up of teachers, school administrators, parents, and community members who collaborate to design after-school enrichment courses aligned with the school's core curriculum. The after-school programs are open 5 days a week from the end of school until 6:30 p.m., and at least one Saturday a month for family activities. Each program has an after-school coordinator. Courses are taught by teachers, by community members, and by students from the University of Arizona and Pima Community College. Proyecto Sano y Salvo has also begun implementing a program improvement and evaluation model. Program and evaluation staff have designed instruments and templates, scannable surveys, and a continuous feedback system for program-level data collection and input, analysis, and feedback based on the Tucson Unified School District's data collection system.

Kaleidoscope Community Learning Center

The Kaleidoscope Community Learning Center (CLC) in Morgantown, West Virginia, has 600 school-age children at nine different sites. The Kaleidoscope CLC provides a wide variety of opportunities through its varied partnerships with the United Way, Shack Neighborhood House, Mountaineer Boys and Girls Club, West Virginia University, Visiting Homemaker Services, and the Board of Parks and Recreation. These partners support and provide homework help, computer classes, art activities, and academic assistance tailored to current classroom instruction for participants. Parents, teachers, community members, and university students serve as instructors and bring important community insight to the centers. One parent was so thrilled with her autistic son's academic improvement after participating in the program that she petitioned the local school board for more sustainable funding. Students also have the opportunity to provide service through Meals on Wheels and the "Make a Difference Day" with the United Way. One student said of the program, "I think it helps me to help someone else. I don't have as much time to think about my problems" (2001 Annual Performance Report, Monongalia County, WV, Schools).

The Kaleidoscope CLC program is also academically successful. Seventy-five percent of student participants maintained their math grade and 21% increased their math grade by at least half a letter grade. Also, 24% of the participants increased their reading scores by at least half a letter grade. Standardized tests show that students were more likely to score at the 50th percentile or higher than they were to fall below the 50th percentile mark when participating in the after-school program (Kaleidoscope Annual Report, 2001).

Kids Learning in Community Klubhouses

Kids Learning in Community Klubhouses (KLICK) focuses on providing a safe and engaging after-school environment for at-risk youth through modern technology. Seventeen urban and rural Michigan school districts developed 20 middle school computer clubhouses through partnerships with Michigan State University and several technology vendors and community organizations. Apple Computer Corporation provides technology resources and trainers for several KLICK events. Michigan State University's Virtual University provides technical support and training for kids and school coordinators in advanced web design and digital animation techniques. A partnership with a Boston-based software firm has produced an entire robotics curriculum and has supported regional competitions. The 4-H Club runs an extension program for community activities in three clubhouses. KLICKers designed and maintain websites for Armada Ace Hardware, Old Kent Bank, Michigan Business Consultants, and the Institute for Healing Racism. KLICKers also designed a tourist brochure for the DeTour Village Chamber of Commerce. The Cass City American Association of University Women sponsors several "girls only" and "mother-daughter" technology events. Closing The Gap is a Lansing, Michigan community-based organization that trains welfare parents to use technology. Lawrence Technological University sponsors a statewide robotics tournament and offers free enrollment for KLICKers. PTC Software and Think Detroit both provide technology training and certification. SMART Technologies provides discounts and scholarships for Smart-Boards in clubhouses.

One student found computer-based instruction helped him improve his target grade in spelling and his overall academic performance. Another student who came into the KLICK program as a C student in the fall left in the spring as a B+/A- student. Even more dramatic was the progress by a student who began the program in the fall with a 1.2 average (on a 4.0 scale) in language arts and a 2.2 in math. By the end of the school year, his average in language arts was 3.4 and his math average was 3.8. Overall, students are responding well to the technology-based program. The most recent annual progress report states that 39% of students improved their math grades by at least half a letter and 47% improved their reading grade (Project KLICK Annual Report, 2001).

Citywide Partnerships

Providing universal access to services is a greater challenge for citywide after-school programs than for neighborhood-based programs. City planners must ensure that the services are sufficient and reach the students most in need. They work with government and community organizations to expand services and involve the city in after-school efforts. Despite these challenges, some cities have experienced early success in creating webs of support for their children.

San Diego, California

The San Diego After School Regional Consortium developed the "6 to 6" program, an extended-day program serving all public elementary and middle schools and some private schools in San Diego. The program serves approximately 25,000 children at 202 school sites.

The program is administered by the city's office of Economic Development and Community Services, and direct services are provided by community-based organizations at each program site. Contractors such as the YMCA, Harmonium, and SAY Inc. provide activities that support program goals. These goals include improving student academic outcomes and creating enrichment and recreation programs that foster student resiliency and improve neighborhood and student safety. The city acts as the fiscal agent and is responsible for program management, monitoring, and assessment. The contractors are responsible for program facilities and staff, school security, and participant documentation.

The consortium provides technical assistance, training, coordination, and dissemination of program outcome data. In 2001, an independent evaluator conducted an analysis of the 1999–2000 school year with a random sample of 187 students who participated in the city-sponsored after-school program. The study found that within one year, 57% of the students sampled increased their reading scores and 44% increased their math scores. Individual SAT-9 scores showed statistically significant increases in reading, from 64.3% in 1999 to 66.1% in 2000 (San Diego Unified School District 6 to 6 Program Annual Report, 2001).

Boston, Massachusetts

In 1998, the mayor of Boston launched the Boston 2:00-to-6:00 After-School Initiative to support the expansion of high-quality after-school programming across the city, providing new learning and development opportunities for children. To achieve its mission, the initiative has supported partnerships between youth-serving organizations and public schools and contributed to 44 new full-time after-school programs opening in school buildings. As of September 2001, a total of 69 schools—more than two thirds of Boston's elementary and middle schools—operate full-time after-school programs.

The Boston 2:00-to-6:00 After-School Initiative leads Expanding Youth Horizons, which began as a partnership with The Children's Museum and now involves Citizen Schools, Boys and Girls Clubs, the Disability Law Center, Parents United for Child Care, and the YMCAs of Greater Boston. The primary focus of Expanding Youth Horizons is to help after-school staff support children's learning in literacy, mathematics, and science. The Children's Museum and the other partners have been invaluable in two main ways. The partners worked together in planning two conferences, bringing more than 300 members of

Boston's after-school community together to participate in workshops that presented activities and materials that staff could use to support local and state educational standards in their programming. Also, the Boston 2:00-to-6:00 After-School Initiative's involvement in Expanding Youth Horizons has produced a catalog of technical assistance, training, and resources for Boston's after-school programs.

In 2001, the Boston 2:00-to-6:00 After-School Initiative was also instrumental in creating Boston's After-School for All Partnership, the largest public-private partnership dedicated to serving children in Boston's history. The public-private venture brings the City of Boston and the Mayor's office together with many of the largest Boston-based philanthropic institutions, including foundations, corporations, civic organizations, and Harvard University. Each partner has made a commitment to invest substantial funds in after-school programs in Boston. The partnership will provide $24 million in new resources over the next 5 years for advocacy projects, infrastructure support, and before- and after-school programs.

New York City, New York

The After-School Corporation (TASC) began in 1998 and has developed into a comprehensive and model program for citywide after-school collaboration. TASC is dedicated to enhancing the quality, availability, and sustainability of after-school programs in New York City (NYC) and New York State. Currently, TASC oversees 162 programs in NYC, with student participation of more than 42,000, and another 7,000 students in 50 more programs statewide. TASC began through a challenge grant from the Open Society Institute, contingent on matching funds on a three-to-one basis. TASC collaborates with state and city government agencies, including the city's Board of Education, Department of Employment, Office of Children and Family Services and NYC Department of Youth and Community Development, and the New York State Education Department and Division of Criminal Justice.

Other community-based not-for-profit organizations operate after-school programs, working closely with TASC. These include the East Side House Settlement, Chinatown YMCA, Children's Aid Society, Episcopal Social Services, Mosholu Montefiore Community Center, and various Boys and Girls Clubs throughout the city. Universities such as Columbia University, New York University, and the City University of New York and cultural institutions like the American Museum of Natural History also operate programs. TASC provides professional development and training to after-school staff through collaboration with the Partnership for After-School Education.

The TASC partnerships have been successful both in numbers of students served and in participants' academic improvement. Student enrollment in participating programs has nearly tripled since 1998. In an independent evaluation of data collected during 1998–2001, Policy Studies Associates, Inc. (2001) found that students who had low school attendance before enrolling in TASC were significantly more likely to improve their attendance than students who did not participate. Student participants who scored at the lowest level of math proficiency ("below basic") were more likely to raise their math achievement to "basic" or "proficient" than students who did not participate.

Los Angeles, California

LA's BEST After School Enrichment Program began in 1988 at the request of then-Los Angeles mayor Tom Bradley. The program was developed to address the alarming rise in drug activity, street crime, and gang activity involving younger children. The Mayor named 55 appointees from education, child care, local businesses, and community organizations to serve on an Education Council. The Council helped to shape and launch the program in 10 elementary schools within the Los Angeles Unified School District. Over the past 14 years, the program has expanded to 104 sites throughout Los Angeles, serving more than 18,000 students each day after school.

Child care consultants, small business owners, community volunteers, foundation executives, local industry professionals, and university faculty comprise the LA's BEST board of directors and advisory board, who foster and raise funds for the program. LA's BEST also collaborates with more than 100 community-based organizations to ensure quality programming and diverse after-school activities. For example, Girls Incorporated organizes curricula to help girls and boys build skills and interest in science, math, and technology. The Amateur Athletic Foundation sponsors a citywide seasonal sports program. BEST participants record their community through a variety of experiences, including walking field trips and photo journals, through a collaboration with the Thomas Brothers Education Foundation. Action Learning Systems is piloting a project called "The Literacy Loop," a cross-age tutoring program. High school student participants in LA's BEST program offer tutoring and training to local elementary school students and assist them with the regular school day reading curriculum.

In June 2000, UCLA completed a longitudinal study of LA's BEST. The report stated:

Our results show that higher levels of participation in LA's BEST led to better subsequent school attendance, which in turn related to higher academic achievement on standardized tests of mathematics, reading, and language arts. (Huang, Gribbons, Kim, Lee, & Baker, 2000, p. 9)

State Partnerships

States face many of the same administrative challenges as citywide programs. However, states must ensure that local programs are fulfilling the unique needs of their communities and families, a challenge inherent in working with diverse communities. States must also sustain relationships with different stakeholders, balance efforts to ensure universal access, and collect and evaluate data on the financial and academic effectiveness of after-school programs. Some states, such as California, Nebraska, Missouri, and Ohio, have formed advisory councils to bring together expertise and funding sources. California and Indiana are working toward regional centers that maintain state connections to local needs.

Missouri

The Missouri Department of Elementary and Secondary Education (DESE) has recently formed a statewide network, the 21st Century Community Learning Center Steering Committee, to bring schools, community organizations, and foundations together to enlarge and improve after-school programs throughout the state. Among the network participants are Educare, St. Louis for Kids, YouthNet, a group of public school districts, Southeast Missouri State University faculty, two representatives from the Missouri state legislature, and LINC (the Local INvestment Commission, a coalition of schools, businesses and foundations that pool resources for Kansas City). DESE also works with other initiatives and child care agencies to collaborate and provide technical assistance and training. The Missouri School-Age Care Coalition conducts an annual state conference on child care and after-school issues.

As Missouri works toward a streamlined process for after-school programming, it will continue to build on existing partnerships. DESE also has been working closely with the state legislature, which recently passed a resolution calling for an after-school task force to look at statewide after-school efforts and to conduct a comprehensive analysis of the quality and equality of Missouri after-school programs. The task force intends to develop a plan that ensures quality after-school programming for every Missouri child who needs it.

Missouri is already seeing the effects of quality programming. A locally based evaluation of Missouri after-school programs found improvement in both math and language arts. The majority of students who participated in the Home Alone after-school program for at least 90 hours during the 1999–2000 school year improved both their reading and math scores on the Terra Nova, a national standardized test measuring student progress in math, English language arts, and reading. Teachers also reported that more than 75% of the Home Alone participants improved their attendance, academic performance, and classroom behavior, while 78% improved their homework performance and timeliness (Home Alone Program Annual Report, 2001). Project PASS (Partners Assisting Student Success) in Camdenton, Missouri works directly with regular school day programs and has seen immense improvement throughout the district. One school now boasts that all PASS students have raised their reading scores on the state's standardized test above state standards (Project PASS Annual Report, 2001).

California

In 1999 a group of after-school stakeholders formed the Foundation Consortium/California Department of Education Public-Private Partnership. These groups were concerned about students' activities and whereabouts during the after-school hours. Currently the consortium is organized into three main bodies of responsibility: the Advisory Committee, an intermediary organization, and regional leads. The statewide Advisory Committee discusses the needs of local programs and determines how various groups can collaborate to meet these needs. The intermediary builds local and regional capacity to help programs succeed by offering technical assistance and assessment and mentoring new programs throughout the state, and also by acting as liaison between districts, regions, and the state. Regional leads oversee regional learning centers, where meetings are held every 6 weeks for training and collaboration with program representatives, intermediary mentors, and consultants.

While the consortium incorporates many different stakeholders in decisions and direct services, consortium members disseminate information about the after-school effort by submitting articles for publication,

serving on advisory committees, developing helpful resources and curriculum, and providing workshops and professional development training to after-school program staff throughout the state. The consortium
works nationally to develop funding agents that will expand the program's reach while increasing sustainability. The intermediary in California has worked with sites throughout the state, as well as sites in
other states, to help develop statewide after-school support networks.

California's efforts to increase the breadth and sustainability of
after-school programming across the state are proving effective, as evidenced by the academic improvement of program participants. The
consortium reported significant academic gains between 1999 and
2001 in their most recent executive summary, noting improvement of
SAT-9 reading and math test scores, with the greatest change in reading levels. They also pointed out improvement in regular school attendance, in direct proportion to the level of participation in an after-
school program (An evaluation of California's after-school learning and
safe neighborhoods partnership program: 1999-2001, 2002).

A National Partnership: The U.S. Department of Education and the C.S. Mott Foundation

In 1997, U.S. Department of Education (the Department) officials
approached a private philanthropy, the Charles Stewart Mott Foundation (Mott), for assistance in making high-quality after-school enrichment opportunities widely available to communities and families in
need. The first conversation between the Department and Mott took
place during the 1997 White House Conference on Child Care and
quickly evolved into a new relationship focused on their mutual interest in the 21st Century Community Learning Centers program, the
Clinton Administration's cornerstone in addressing after-school issues.
The main thrust of the partnership is to help communities provide
after-school programming that complements the school day and
enhances student learning. Both Mott and the Department maintain
that after-school programs may be an opportunity for public schools
to rethink the structure of the school day as well as offering learning
experiences not available in a traditional classroom. Both Mott and the
Department believe that, in time, after-school programs and community education may lead to new ideas about time and learning with
respect to the school day and school year, making significant differences in how schools and communities work together in support of
student learning and life-long learning opportunities for adults.

Another key focus of the Mott-Department partnership is to bring child care, education, and youth development into a meaningful conversation about after-school programming (Miller, 2001). The Mott-Department partnership incorporates the best practices from each of these perspectives to reach a vision of quality and balance in after-school programming. The Department encourages 21st Century Community Learning Centers to develop partnerships with child care providers and youth development advocates to provide a holistic and balanced program of math, reading, arts, nutrition, recreation, technology, and cultural enrichment.

Using Resources

The Department and Mott each bring unique contributions to the partnership. The Department's substantial federal resources pay for the direct costs of school-based after-school programs, including personnel, supplies, and equipment. Department staff members assist with outreach and provide technical assistance to potential grantees nationwide.

Mott resources, totaling $100 million over 7 years, support policy, public awareness campaigns, evaluation, training and technical assistance, identification of promising practices, and an access and equity task force that guides grantmaking decisions. Mott provides grants directly to the nonprofit organizations engaged in these activities, and does not fund local 21st Century Community Learning Centers programs per se. Mott funds workshops for potential grantees, who now number almost 18,000 parents, educators, and community members. Department staff members conduct the workshops and provide technical assistance supported by the Mott funding. The training emphasizes and encourages quality programming, especially in reading, and demystifies the application requirements for a federal grant. This outreach has stimulated so much interest in the program that 1 out of every 7 schools nationwide (12,500 schools out of 89,000) participated in the 2001 grant competition. One in 3 inner city or rural schools (58,000 total) were involved in the initiative this past year, either as a grantee or as an applicant, as noted in U.S. Department of Education records.

The Department and Mott also worked together to found a coalition, originally a media partnership, known as the Afterschool Alliance. This coalition is an independent umbrella organization expanding many of the original policy and public outreach activities of the Mott-Department partnership. The Afterschool Alliance collaborated with the Ad Council to produce a national public service campaign funded by Mott called *What Is a Hero?* This campaign includes billboards, web banners, television, bus advertising, and radio and print ads. *The New York Times* adopted the ad campaign as one of its public service messages for the year and has been running a full-page copy of the print ad weekly. Across the country, networks have provided almost $80 million worth of free advertising through web banners; television, radio, and print ads; and billboards and other outdoor media. About 250 phone inquiries are generated by these public service announcements each week. The 21st Century Community Learning Centers program and the partnership also have been featured separately by two major PBS stations, WGBH in Boston and WNET in New York. Both stations have accompanying websites focused on after-school issues.

Students are better served as a result of the Mott-Department partnership. Because Mott assumes financial responsibility for many outreach and technical assistance activities, federal money can provide more direct services for school-age children. As noted earlier, the 21st Century Community Learning Centers program rapidly expanded from a $1 million demonstration project serving 1,000 youth to a $1 billion per year federal program serving a projected 1.4 million children in 1,600 communities and 6,800 schools in every state and almost every territory in 2002. This federally funded program has now surpassed the YMCA in number of children served, and the Boys and Girls Clubs in number of sites, to become the largest provider of comprehensive after-school services in the nation. Also, grantees serve more minority students and high-poverty students than the average school, and more than two thirds of the participating schools have greater than 50% poverty rates, according to an analysis of the grant applications submitted to the U.S. Department of Education. These statistics indicate that funds are reaching students, families, and communities with the greatest need, a key goal of the partnership.

The unique contributions of this public-private partnership have been widely recognized. In 2001, the 21st Century Community Learning Centers partnership between the Department and Mott was named a semifinalist for the prestigious Harvard University/Kennedy School of Government *Innovations in American Government Awards*. In 2002, the 21st Century program won the *Public Service Excellence Award*, administered by the Public Service Roundtable, in the public-private partnership category.

Future Direction of the Department-Mott Partnership

In December 2001 Congress reauthorized the 21st CCLC program in the No Child Left Behind Act and transferred the management responsibility to the States. Congress also focused services more explicitly on academically based interventions for poor children and their families, especially children in failing schools, and opened up eligibility of funding to include public schools, community-based organizations, and other public and private entities. In response to these new mandates, the Mott-Department partnership is moving in new directions while continuing to provide leadership in the national after-school movement. This leadership remains grounded in understanding the contributions that local school-community partnerships can make in improving student achievement through enrichment activities that are embedded in youth development principles.

In providing continued national leadership, the Department and Mott will initiate and promote activities directed at program quality and sustainability. Both partners will work to promote quality in after-school programming by infusing school-day content into after-school programming. They will also disseminate research, best practices, and training materials to parents, teachers, after-school staff, and community and business organizations. Mott and the Department will also assist with sustainability plans at the state and city levels.

Conclusion

Partnerships at both local and national levels are the key to after-school success. At the local level, community organizations can lend their talents, resources, knowledge, and experience to the after-school program. In the process, both the organization and the after-school program contribute to the success of children in their own community. City and state collaborations provide strategic expansion and guidance to local programs. Their role will become even more important, as recent legislative changes have mandated state efforts to expand after-school services. On a national level, partnerships between private and public institutions can work to provide more quality instruction that enhances school-day learning, as well as offer assistance with developing sustainable resources for after-school programs. Most importantly, public-private partnerships increase the likelihood that school-age children will continue to benefit from after-school programs, and that the number of children served will continue to rise.

REFERENCES

An evaluation of California's after-school learning and safe neighborhoods partnership program: 1999-2001. (2002). University of California at Irvine: Department of Education.

Capizzano, J., Tout, K., & Adams, G. (2000). *Childcare patterns of school-age children with employed mothers.* Washington, DC: The Urban Institute.

Charles Stewart Mott Foundation. (1999). Afterschool makes the grade. *In Focus, 2*(3). Flint, MI: Charles Stewart Mott Foundation.

Clark, R. (1989). *The role of parents in ensuring educational success in school restructuring efforts.* Washington, DC: Council of Chief State School Officers.

Fox, J., & Newman, S. (1997). *Crime or programs: Tuning into the prime time for violent juvenile crime and implications for national policy.* Washington, DC: Fight Crime: Invest in Kids.

Grossman, J.B., Price, M.L., Fellerath, V., Juvocy, L.Z., Kotloff, L.J., Raley, R., & Walker, K.E. (2002). *Multiple choices after school: Findings from the extended-service schools initiative.* New York: Public/Private Ventures.

Harkavy, I., & Blank, M. (2002). Community schools: A vision of learning that goes beyond testing. *Education Week, 21*(31), 52.

Hart, P.D. (1999). *The Shell education survey.* Houston, TX: The Shell Oil Company and Peter D. Hart Research Associates.

Home Alone Program, Bloomfield, Missouri. (2001). Annual Performance Report. Submitted to the U.S. Department of Education.

Huang D., Gribbons, B., Kim, K.S., Lee, C., & Baker, L. (2000). *The impact of the LA's BEST after school program on subsequent student achievement and performance.* Los Angeles: University of California, Los Angeles, Center for the Study of Evaluation.

Kaleidoscope Community Learning Center, Monongalia, West Virginia. (2001). Annual performance report. Submitted to the U.S. Department of Education.

Kids Learning in Community Klubhouses (Project KLICK), Armada, Michigan. (2001). Annual Performance Report. Submitted to the U.S. Department of Education.

Lake Snell Perry and Associates & The Tarrance Group. (2001). *Mott Foundation/JC Penney nationwide survey on afterschool programs.* Flint, MI: Afterschool Alliance.

Le Menestrel, S. (2002). *A view from the field: What do afterschool staff need and how do they get it?* Washington, DC: Academy for Educational Development, Center for Youth Development and Policy Studies.

Miller, B.M. (2001). The promise of after-school programs. *Educational Leadership, 58*(7), 6-12.

National Association of Elementary School Principals. (1998). *Child care survey: Survey of 1,175 elementary and middle school principals.* Alexandria, VA: Author.

National Association of Elementary School Principals. (1999). *Programs and the K-8 principal: Standards for quality school-age childcare* (Rev. ed.). Alexandria, VA: Author.

National Center for Education Statistics. (1996). *Schools serving family needs: Extended-day programs in public and private schools.* Washington, DC: Government Printing Office.

National Center for Education Statistics. (1999). *National household education survey (NHES).* Washington, DC: Government Printing Office.

National Commission on Time and Learning. (1994). *Prisoners of time.* Washington, DC: Government Printing Office.

National Institute on Out-of-School Time. (2001). *Fact sheet on school-age children's out of school time.* Wellesley, MA: Author.

National Opinion Research Center at the University of Chicago. (1998). *Family involvement in education: A snapshot of out-of-school time.* Washington, DC: Government Printing Office.

Newman, S., Fox, J.A., Flynn, E.A., & Christianson, W. (2000). *America's choice: The prime time for juvenile crime, or youth enrichment and achievement.* Washington, DC: Fight Crime: Invest in Kids.

Ohio Hunger Task Force. (1999). *Urban school initiative school-age care project: 1998–1999 school year evaluation report*. Columbus, OH: Author.

Pechman, E., & Fiester, L. (2002). *Leadership and sustainability in school-linked after-school programs*. Washington, DC: Policy Studies Associates.

Project PASS, Camdenton, Missouri. (2001). Annual Performance Report. Submitted to the U.S. Department of Education.

School-Age Child Care Project. (1997). *School-age care out-of-school time resource notebook*. Washington, DC: U.S. Department of Health and Human Services.

San Diego Unified School District 6 to 6 Program, San Diego, California. (2001). Annual Performance Report. Submitted to the U.S. Department of Education.

Seppanen, P.S., Love, J.M., deVries, D.K., Bernstein, L., Seligson, M., Marx, F., & Kisker, E.E. (1993). *National study of before and after school programs* (Final report). Portsmouth, NH: RMC Research Corporation.

Snyder, H., & Sickmund, M. (1999). *Juvenile offenders and victims: 1999 national report*. Washington, DC: U.S. Department of Justice, Office of Juvenile Justice and Delinquency Prevention.

U.S. Department of Education. (1999). *Promising results, continuing challenges: The final report of the national assessment of Title I*. Washington, DC: Author.

U.S. Department of Education. (2000). *Safe and smart: Making afterschool programs work for kids*. Washington, DC: Author.

Name Index

Note: This index includes names associated with a theory, concept, program, experiment or other work with a substantive description. It does not include names given in examples or passing references.

Subject Index

223

RECENT PUBLICATIONS OF THE SOCIETY

1. The Yearbooks

102:1 (2003) *American Educational Governance on Trial: Change and Challenges.* William Lowe Boyd and Debra Miretzky, editors. Cloth.

102:2 (2003) *Meeting at the Hyphen: Schools-Universities-Communities-Professions in Collaboration for Student Achievement and Well Being.* Mary M. Brabeck, Mary E. Walsh, and Rachel E. Latta, editors. Cloth.

101:1 (2002) *The Educational Leadership Challenge: Redefining Leadership for the 21st Century.* Joseph Murphy, editor. Cloth.

101:2 (2002) *Educating At-Risk Students.* Sam Stringfield and Deborah Land, editors. Cloth.

100:1 (2001) *Education Across a Century: The Centennial Volume.* Lyn Corno, editor. Cloth.

100:2 (2001) *From Capitol to the Cloakroom: Standards-based Reform in the States.* Susan H. Fuhrman, editor. Cloth.

99:1 (2000) *Constructivism in Education.* D. C. Phillips, editor. Cloth.

99:2 (2000) *American Education: Yesterday, Today, and Tomorrow.* Thomas L. Good, editor. Cloth.

98:1 (1999) *The Education of Teachers,* Gary A. Griffin, editor. Paper.

98:2 (1999) *Issues in Curriculum,* Margaret J. Early and Kenneth J. Rehage, editors. Cloth.

97:1 (1998) *The Adolescent Years: Social Influences and Educational Challenges.* Kathryn Borman and Barbara Schneider, editors. Cloth.

96:1 (1997) *Service Learning.* Joan Schine, editor. Cloth.

96:2 (1997) *The Construction of Children's Character.* Alex Molnar, editor. Cloth.

95:1 (1996) *Performance-Based Student Assessment: Challenges and Possibilities.* Joan B. Baron and Dennie P. Wolf, editors. Cloth.

94:1 (1995) *Creating New Educational Communities.* Jeannie Oakes and Karen Hunter Quartz, editors. Cloth.

94:2 (1995) *Changing Populations/Changing Schools.* Erwin Flaxman and A. Harry Passow, editors. Cloth.

93:1 (1994) *Teacher Research and Educational Reform.* Sandra Hollingsworth and Hugh Sockett, editors. Cloth.

93:2 (1994) *Bloom's Taxonomy: A Forty-year Retrospective.* Lorin W. Anderson and Lauren A. Sosniak, editors. Cloth.

92:1 (1993) *Gender and Education.* Sari Knopp Biklen and Diane Pollard, editors. Cloth.

92:2 (1993) *Bilingual Education: Politics, Practice, and Research.* M. Beatriz Arias and Ursula Casanova, editors. Cloth.

91:1 (1992) *The Changing Contexts of Teaching.* Ann Lieberman, editor. Cloth.

91:2 (1992) *The Arts, Education, and Aesthetic Knowing.* Bennett Reimer and Ralph A. Smith, editors. Cloth.

Order the above titles from the University of Chicago Press, 11030 S. Langley Ave., Chicago, IL 60628. For a list of earlier Yearbooks still available, consult the University of Chicago Press website: www.press.uchicago.edu

2. The Series on Contemporary Educational Issues

This series has been discontinued.

The following volumes in the series may be ordered from the McCutchan Publishing Corporation, 3220 Blume Drive, Suite 197, Richmond, CA 94806. Local phone: (510)758-5510, Toll free: 1-800-227-1540, Fax: (510)758-6078, e-mail: mccutchanpublish@aol

Academic Work and Educational Excellence: Raising Student Productivity (1986). Edited by Tommy M. Tomlinson and Herbert J. Walberg.
Adapting Instruction to Student Differences (1985). Edited by Margaret C. Wang and Herbert J. Walberg.
Choice in Education (1990). Edited by William Lowe Boyd and Herbert J. Walberg.
Colleges of Education: Perspectives on Their Future (1985). Edited by Charles W. Case and William A. Matthes.
Contributing to Educational Change: Perspectives on Research and Practice (1988). Edited by Philip W. Jackson.
Effective Teaching: Current Research (1991). Edited by Hersholt C. Waxman and Herbert J. Walberg.
Moral Development and Character Education (1989). Edited by Larry P. Nucci.
Motivating Students to Learn: Overcoming Barriers to High Achievement (1993). Edited by Tommy M. Tomlinson.
Radical Proposals for Educational Change (1994). Edited by Chester E. Finn, Jr. and Herbert J. Walberg.
Reaching Marginal Students: A Prime Concern for School Renewal (1987). Edited by Robert L. Sinclair and Ward Ghory.
Restructuring the Schools: Problems and Prospects (1992). Edited by John J. Lane and Edgar G. Epps.
Rethinking Policy for At-risk Students (1994). Edited by Kenneth K. Wong and Margaret C. Wang.
School Boards: Changing Local Control (1992). Edited by Patricia F. First and Herbert J. Walberg.

The two final volumes in this series were:

Improving Science Education (1995). Edited by Barry J. Fraser and Herbert J. Walberg.
Ferment in Education: A Look Abroad (1995). Edited by John J. Lane.

These two volumes may be ordered from the Book Order Department, University of Chicago Press, 11030 S. Langley Ave., Chicago, IL 60628. Phone: 1-800-621-2736; Fax: 1-800-621-8476.